Praise for Marie Hoffm
Toward Mutual Recogniti..

"*Toward Mutual Recognition* is a remarkable work of cross-fertilization. Drawing on her intimate knowledge of both traditions, Marie Hoffman interprets contemporary psychoanalytic theory to her Christian colleagues and conveys the core tenets of Christian theology to the psychoanalytic community. In the process, she explores conceptual and historical links between the two discourses that may surprise readers in both groups. The writing is both scholarly and accessible as Hoffman moves back and forth between explicating broad intellectual issues and illustrating their applicability via a frank, detailed account of her devoted work with a severely traumatized woman. The author's contagious passion, compassion, and erudition make this a must-have text for anyone interested in the history of psychoanalytic thought or in the timeless concerns of the major religious traditions. And it will inspire and console ordinary therapists, who inevitably bear witness, hour after hour, to both the fragility and the resilience of the human soul."

—Nancy McWilliams, PhD, Rutgers University Graduate School of Applied and Professional Psychology

"This moving and challenging book, filled with rich material both scholarly and clinical, will inspire many to rethink the relationship between religious faith and psychoanalysis. Hoffman has created a fascinating, innovative dialogue, using the idea of recognition to build a bridge between two dissonant traditions—relational psychoanalysis and Christian theology. Focusing on intersubjectivity, she finds a conjunction between these two transformational practices while squarely facing their differences. She traces a path that is at once redemptive and unflinchingly honest about the complexities of psychodynamic work, both personal and theoretical. Illustrated by the case of Mandy, a courageous young woman who has suffered scarcely imaginable horrors, Hoffman powerfully supports her case for a relational psychoanalytic approach to trauma inspired by faith."

—Jessica Benjamin, PhD, Clinical Associate Professor, NYU Postdoctoral Program in Psychotherapy and Psychoanalysis

"Not since the late Randall Sorenson's *Minding Spirituality* have we seen a book with such combined theological and clinical depth, theoretical and practical acumen, scholarly and historical analysis. With incredible psychoanalytic, spiritual, and postmodern sensitivity, Hoffman narrates her work with Mandy, navigating between holding and idolatry, mothering and fathering, transparency and reserve. Building on the relational psychoanalytic insights of Benjamin and Aron, and the philosophical/theological contributions of Hegel and Ricoeur, Hoffman pairs three phases in psychoanalytic treatment (identification, surrender, and gratitude) with three classic theological themes (incarnation, crucifixion, and resurrection). In each of the three sections of the book she avoids any simplistic identification of theology with psychoanalysis but prefers to let them speak to each other; each member in the pair is an analogue for the other. However, as she incorporates the different cadences, no longer are theology and clinical practice simply correlative, but a creative, symphonic synthesis has taken place. In the future, those who do not ponder this book risk the danger of facile integration of faith and clinical practice."

—Alvin Dueck, PhD, Evelyn and Frank Freed Professor of the Integration of Psychology and Theology, Fuller Theological Seminary

"Hoffman enlightens the proposals of great European thinkers, such as Kierkegaard, as well as those of British and American psychoanalysts, such as Ian Suttie, Izette de Forest, and Clara Thompson. She shows newly discovered connections between these people, who paved the way for a possible renewal of psychoanalytic thinking and practice, stressing the importance of relationship, intersubjectivity, love, and dedication. In addition, a thrilling chapter on Sándor Ferenczi, based on thorough research, opens a new pathway of innovative vistas for present and future work."

—André Haynal, MD, University of Geneva

"Marie Hoffman draws impressively on philosophical and theological resources in the tradition of Hegel as she develops an interdisciplinary theory of mutual recognition. By applying the theory to her clinical work, and to one case in particular, she demonstrates through careful analysis that recognition is a profound resource for human social existence and mental health in general."

—Peter C. Hodgson, PhD, Charles G. Finney Professor of Theology, Emeritus, Vanderbilt University Divinity School

"Marie Hoffman's attention to the Hungarian context of Sándor Ferenczi's psychoanalytic theory and practice sheds important new light on their religious sources and appeal."

—Lee Congdon, PhD, James Madison University

"Hoffman builds a psychoanalytic model for applied patient treatment on the formulation of Hegel's brilliant notion of incarnation, crucifixion, and resurrection as it is mediated into a psychoanalytic world view, especially by Pfister, Fairbairn, Winnicott, Klein, and Ferenczi. She translates this world view through case presentations into an applied treatment model. This is a rigorously crafted scientific work on the interface of psychology and spirituality. It moves with great clarity and enticement across the frontiers of research and breaks fertile new ground for our field. It is an urgently necessary work for religious and secular scholars alike."

—J. Harold Ellens, PhD, Executive Director, Emeritus, CAPS, and Founding Editor, ***Journal of Psychology and Christianity***

"With this profoundly integrative book, Marie Hoffman has emerged on the analytic scene in a groundbreaking way. Her deep passion for and thorough culling and intertwining of historical, theoretical, and clinical analytic concepts with a broad array of philosophical and theological ideas is remarkable. For those hoping to better understand the development of analytic perspectives as they have been influenced by theorists' spiritual genealogies, Hoffman offers a more thorough text than has ever been written thus far. For those wishing for complex yet personal clinical training in how a relational psychoanalytic approach might sensitively and masterfully combine an understanding of both spiritual and psychological dynamics, she ventures to unfold an in-depth case study of her own. For those wishing to understand the march of psychoanalytic theory toward a more relational perspective, between patient and analyst as well as with God, Hoffman leads us on that path, uncovering gems of wisdom from various theorists and offering powerful new metaphors of her own. This is a book I highly recommend to any serious student of psychology, psychoanalysis, theology, and philosophy; I hope it will become a primary text in graduate schools within each of these disciplines, helping to encourage dialogue between them for years to come."

—Beth Fletcher Brokaw, PhD, Rosemead School of Psychology

"When faith meets scholarship, creativity and insight follow in *Toward Mutual Recognition*. Marie Hoffman brings depth and richness to her perspectives from the fields of relational psychoanalysis and Christian faith, thereby creating a rare and profound work of integration. It is a far-reaching contribution that traces the historical influence of Judeo-Christian thought in the relational stance of Ferenczi, the impact of Christian tradition in Winnicott's revelation of incarnational processes in both development and treatment, as well as a stunning and serious examination of the philosophical resonance between Hegel's phenomenology and the analytic work of Benjamin and others in the relational school, as illuminated through Ricoeur's hermeneutic of faith. She uncovers a weave between disciplines that has largely gone unrecognized, and that illuminates the process of healing in both disciplines. Threaded throughout the academic story is a case of searing pain and clinical tenderness in which the analytic work of identification, surrender, and gratitude echoes in themes of incarnation, crucifixion, and resurrection. This is a formidable work of a passionate and articulate woman which will impact the field for years to come."

—John D. Carter, PhD, Lecturer, California Baptist University

"For too long, psychoanalytic writers have mostly excluded religious and spiritual concerns from their field of study. Marie Hoffman has done much to correct that oversight in this deeply felt, eloquent, and scholarly work describing the parallels between the Christian narrative and the intersubjective aspects of relational psychoanalysis."

—Peter Shabad, PhD, Associate Professor of Clinical Psychology,
Northwestern University Medical School,
and author, *Despair and the Return of Hope*

Toward Mutual Recognition

Relational Perspectives Book Series
Volume 48

RELATIONAL PERSPECTIVES BOOK SERIES

LEWIS ARON & ADRIENNE HARRIS
Series Editors

The Relational Perspectives Book Series (RPBS) publishes books that grow out of or contribute to the relational tradition in contemporary psychoanalysis. The term "relational psychoanalysis" was first used by Greenberg and Mitchell (1983) to bridge the traditions of interpersonal relations, as developed within interpersonal psychoanalysis and object relations, as developed within contemporary British theory. But, under the seminal work of the late Stephen Mitchell, the term "relational psychoanalysis" grew and began to accrue to itself many other influences and developments. Various tributaries—interpersonal psychoanalysis, object relations theory, self psychology, empirical infancy research, and elements of contemporary Freudian and Kleinian thought—flow into this tradition, which understands relational configurations between self and others, both real and fantasied, as the primary subject of psychoanalytic investigation.

We refer to the relational tradition, rather than to a relational school, to highlight that we are identifying a trend, a tendency within contemporary psychoanalysis, not a more formally organized or coherent school or system of beliefs. Our use of the term 'relational' signifies a dimension of theory and practice that has become salient across the wide spectrum of contemporary psychoanalysis. Now under the editorial supervision of Lewis Aron and Adrienne Harris, the Relational Perspectives Book Series originated in 1990 under the editorial eye of the late Stephen A. Mitchell. Mitchell was the most prolific and influential of the originators of the relational tradition. He was committed to dialogue among psychoanalysts and he abhorred the authoritarianism that dictated adherence to a rigid set of beliefs or technical restrictions. He championed open discussion, comparative and integrative approaches, and he promoted new voices across the generations.

Included in the Relational Perspectives Book Series are authors and works that come from within the relational tradition, extend and develop the tradition, as well as works that critique relational approaches or compare and contrast it with alternative points of view. The series includes our most distinguished senior psychoanalysts along with younger contributors who bring fresh vision.

RELATIONAL PERSPECTIVES BOOK SERIES

LEWIS ARON & ADRIENNE HARRIS
Series Editors

Vol. 48
Toward Mutual Recognition: Relational Psychoanalysis and the Christian Narrative
Marie T. Hoffman

Vol. 47
Uprooted Minds: Surviving the Politics of Terror in the Americas
Nancy Caro Hollander

Vol. 46
A Disturbance in the Field: Essays in Transference-Countertransference Engagement
Steven H. Cooper

Vol. 45
First Do No Harm: The Paradoxical Encounters of Psychoanalysis, Warmaking, and Resistance
Adrienne Harris & Steven Botticelli (eds.)

Vol. 44
Good Enough Endings: Breaks, Interruptions, and Terminations from Contemporary Relational Perspectives
Jill Salberg (ed.)

Vol. 43
Invasive Objects: Minds Under Siege
Paul Williams

Vol. 42
Sabert Basescu: Selected Papers on Human Nature and Psychoanalysis
George Goldstein & Helen Golden (eds.)

Vol. 41
The Hero in the Mirror: From Fear to Fortitude
Sue Grand

Vol. 40
The Analyst in the Inner City, Second Edition: Race, Class, and Culture Through a Psychoanalytic Lens
Neil Altman

Vol. 39
Dare to be Human: A Contemporary Psychoanalytic Journey
Michael Shoshani Rosenbaum

Vol. 38
Repair of the Soul: Metaphors of Transformation in Jewish Mysticism and Psychoanalysis
Karen E. Starr

Vol. 37
Adolescent Identities: A Collection of Readings
Deborah Browning (ed.)

Vol. 36
Bodies in Treatment: The Unspoken Dimension
Frances Sommer Anderson (ed.)

Vol. 35
Comparative-Integrative Psychoanalysis: A Relational Perspective for the Discipline's Second Century
Brent Willock

Vol. 34
Relational Psychoanalysis, V. III: New Voices
Melanie Suchet, Adrienne Harris, & Lewis Aron (eds.)

Vol. 33
Creating Bodies: Eating Disorders as Self-Destructive Survival
Katie Gentile

Vol. 32
Getting From Here to There: Analytic Love, Analytic Process
Sheldon Bach

Vol. 31
Unconscious Fantasies and the Relational World
Danielle Knafo & Kenneth Feiner

Vol. 30
The Healer's Bent: Solitude and Dialogue in the Clinical Encounter
James T. McLaughlin

Vol. 29
Child Therapy in the Great Outdoors: A Relational View
Sebastiano Santostefano

Vol. 28
Relational Psychoanalysis, V. II: Innovation and Expansion
Lewis Aron & Adrienne Harris (eds.)

Vol. 27
The Designed Self: Psychoanalysis and Contemporary Identities
Carlo Strenger

Vol. 26
Impossible Training: A Relational View of Psychoanalytic Education
Emanuel Berman

RELATIONAL PERSPECTIVES BOOK SERIES

LEWIS ARON & ADRIENNE HARRIS
Series Editors

Vol. 25
Gender as Soft Assembly
Adrienne Harris

Vol. 24
Minding Spirituality
Randall Lehman Sorenson

Vol. 23
September 11: Trauma and Human Bonds
Susan W. Coates, Jane L. Rosenthal, & Daniel S. Schechter (eds.)

Vol. 22
Sexuality, Intimacy, Power
Muriel Dimen

Vol. 21
Looking for Ground: Countertransference and the Problem of Value in Psychoanalysis
Peter G. M. Carnochan

Vol. 20
Relationality: From Attachment to Intersubjectivity
Stephen A. Mitchell

Vol. 19
Who is the Dreamer, Who Dreams the Dream? A Study of Psychic Presences
James S. Grotstein

Vol. 18
Objects of Hope: Exploring Possibility and Limit in Psychoanalysis
Steven H. Cooper

Vol. 17
The Reproduction of Evil: A Clinical and Cultural Perspective
Sue Grand

Vol. 16
Psychoanalytic Participation: Action, Interaction, and Integration
Kenneth A. Frank

Vol. 15
The Collapse of the Self and Its Therapeutic Restoration
Rochelle G. K. Kainer

Vol. 14
Relational Psychoanalysis: The Emergence of a Tradition
Stephen A. Mitchell & Lewis Aron (eds.)

Vol. 13
Seduction, Surrender, and Transformation: Emotional Engagement in the Analytic Process
Karen Maroda

Vol. 12
Relational Perspectives on the Body
Lewis Aron & Frances Sommer Anderson (eds.)

Vol. 11
Building Bridges: Negotiation of Paradox in Psychoanalysis
Stuart A. Pizer

Vol. 10
Fairbairn, Then and Now
Neil J. Skolnick and David E. Scharff (eds.)

Vol. 9
Influence and Autonomy in Psychoanalysis
Stephen A. Mitchell

Vol. 8
Unformulated Experience: From Dissociation to Imagination in Psychoanalysis
Donnel B. Stern

Vol. 7
Soul on the Couch: Spirituality, Religion, and Morality in Contemporary Psychoanalysis
Charles Spezzano & Gerald J. Gargiulo (eds.)

Vol. 6
The Therapist as a Person: Life Crises, Life Choices, Life Experiences, and Their Effects on Treatment
Barbara Gerson (ed.)

Vol. 5
Holding and Psychoanalysis: A Relational Perspective
Joyce A. Slochower

Vol. 4
A Meeting of Minds: Mutuality in Psychoanalysis
Lewis Aron

Vol. 3
The Analyst in the Inner City: Race, Class, and Culture through a Psychoanalytic Lens
Neil Altman

Vol. 2
Affect in Psychoanalysis: A Clinical Synthesis
Charles Spezzano

Vol. 1
Conversing with Uncertainty: Practicing Psychotherapy in a Hospital Setting
Rita Wiley McCleary

Toward Mutual Recognition

Relational Psychoanalysis and the Christian Narrative

Marie T. Hoffman

Routledge
Taylor & Francis Group
New York London

Routledge
Taylor & Francis Group
270 Madison Avenue
New York, NY 10016

Routledge
Taylor & Francis Group
27 Church Road
Hove, East Sussex BN3 2FA

Printed in the United States of America on acid-free paper
10 9 8 7 6 5 4 3 2 1

International Standard Book Number: 978-0-415-99913-7 (Hardback) 978-0-415-99914-4 (Paperback)

Library of Congress Cataloging-in-Publication Data

Hoffman, Marie T.
Toward mutual recognition : relational psychoanalysis and the Christian narrative / Marie T. Hoffman.
p. cm. -- (The relational perspectives book series ; vol. 48)
Includes bibliographical references and index.
ISBN 978-0-415-99913-7 (hardcover) -- ISBN 978-0-415-99914-4 (pbk.) --
ISBN 978-0-203-88127-9 (e-book)
1. Psychoanalysis and religion. 2. Christianity--Psychology. I. Title.

BF175.4.R44H64 2011
150.19'5--dc22 2010022012

Visit the Taylor & Francis Web site at
http://www.taylorandfrancis.com

and the Routledge Web site at
http://www.routledgementalhealth.com

To
My husband and soul mate, Lowell
and
My parents

Contents

About the Author

Marie T. Hoffman, PhD, clinical psychologist and psychoanalyst, is a graduate of New York University's Postdoctoral Program in Psychotherapy and Psychoanalysis. The 2006 Stephen Mitchell Scholar, she has been a visiting professor at Rosemead School of Psychology and Fuller Theological Seminary and a visiting lecturer at Wheaton Graduate School. In addition, she is codirector (with her husband) of the Brookhaven Center for Counseling and Development in Allentown, PA, and is founder and codirector of the Society for Exploration of Psychoanalytic Therapies and Theology (SEPTT).

Acknowledgments

The generosity extended to me throughout the writing of this book has deeply moved me. Lewis Aron placed faith in my ability to write an interdisciplinary book that advanced dialogue between psychoanalysis and the Christian narrative, and he has supported me through every chapter of writing. I am deeply indebted to Lew and to Adrienne Harris, co-editors of the Relational Perspectives Book Series, who accorded me the privilege of being one of their authors. Kristopher Spring and Tara Nieuwesteeg of Routledge have been a joy to work with, responding promptly and with care to my many requests for guidance. For this opportunity both with the Relational Perspectives Book Series and with Routledge, I am grateful.

The idea for this book evolved from a paper I wrote on psychoanalysis and Christianity—one initiated and encouraged by Neil Altman and facilitated by Charles Spezzano. That initial inspiration has blossomed into ideas that extend far beyond the first paper. Nancy McWilliams prodded me to write my ideas several years ago, unfailingly encouraging me to that end over the years. Beth Brokaw, a friend and brilliant colleague, has been a primary source of inspiration to work in an interdisciplinary fashion. To these friends and mentors I say, "Thank you."

Each segment of the book has been reviewed and revised by scholars with particular expertise. Of these, my first words of appreciation must be to Jessica Benjamin, whose theoretical work birthed the ideas I developed. Dr. Benjamin graciously agreed to review the manuscript, offering detailed suggestions to render aspects of the book that touched on her theory more accurate and cohesive. I cannot express sufficiently my gratitude for her contribution.

The theoretical segments dealing with Hegel were carefully examined and thoughtfully commented on by Peter Hodgson, who confirmed and supported my early trajectory on this project. John Wall's contributions on the sections involving Ricoeur were invaluable, his astute assessment of my early drafts leading to efficient revisions. Jack Marsh offered incisive, initial guidance in philosophy. I am so appreciative for the critique and encouragement they each provided.

The chapter on Ferenczi brought me in contact with an array of benevolent scholars. Lee Congdon generously dialogued about Hungarian history and then provided supportive and clarifying commentary on my manuscript. André Haynal graciously opened the Balint Archives in Geneva, met personally with me to discuss Sándor Ferenczi and the cultural climate of Hungary, and offered many helpful edits to my manuscript. Viktor Karády responded quickly to my request for information on Ferenczi's education, providing Ferenczi's actual report card. Botund Gaal introduced me to Ference Eros, who guided me to excellent contacts in Hungary. Tamás Demeter pointed me to sources that would elucidate the philosophical climate of Hungary. Krisztián Kapusi sent me papers he had written in Hungarian, which Rita DiFiore efficiently and carefully translated. To all of these people I am deeply grateful.

This journey has been profoundly nurtured by the training and experience of community I enjoyed in the Postdoctoral Program in Psychotherapy and Psychoanalysis at New York University, an experience that has been unparalleled in my educational career. As a result of that training, I was introduced to Randy Sorenson, who urged me to keep writing. After Randy's untimely death, I taught courses on psychoanalysis at Rosemead School of Psychology, where doctoral candidates enthusiastically received my ideas, encouraging me to continue my exploration of the interface of psychoanalysis and theology. To these groups of people, I wish to express my appreciation, as well as posthumously to Randy.

There are other specific people whom I wish to thank. My colleagues at SEPTT (Society for the Exploration of Psychoanalytic Therapies and Theology) provided support through the many months that I have been writing. I wish to recognize Jack Hartke, who first turned my attention to relational psychoanalytic writing in the early 1990s. Lewis Aron, Linda Barnhurst and John Carter, Beth Brokaw, Nancy McWilliams, and J. Harold Ellens have graciously and thoroughly read and responded to my final draft. Their labors have made all the difference. Justine Myers, our efficient and ever-pleasant office administrator, was responsible for proofing and correcting the final manuscript.

This book would not be what it is without the permission of "Mandy" to tell her story. She is an amazing woman whose life of resilience and faith has already touched many. I wish to express my deepest appreciation to her and to the many other patients whose lives have inspired me to write this book and who have been patient with me as I sometimes labored to be present to them during my writing.

I wish to acknowledge my family. My husband and brilliant colleague, Lowell Hoffman, has been the consummate editor of this book, travailing with text weekend upon weekend as he supported my writing. He has also been my greatest inspiration. My ultimate thanks must be to him. Finally, my children—Bob, Karissa, and her husband Chris—have cheered me on and been patient with my time of intense focus, providing me with delightful stories of their own achievements in their individual life journeys.

A personal note to my readers

I have written this book with several audiences in mind, and I would like to offer some suggestions as to its reading. If you are interested in a comprehensive exposure to theory that explores the analogue between psychoanalytic and theological constructs, along with clinical perspectives and historical material, then reading through the entire text is the most appropriate method. If you wish to benefit primarily from the theoretical and clinical material, it is possible to skip over the historical sections located in Chapters 4, 7, and 10 and return to them later. For professors utilizing this book, you may find it helpful to segment the text into portions appropriate for personality theory, history and systems, and specific psychoanalytic psychotherapy courses.

Most importantly, I want to welcome all to this dialogue. To my fellow psychoanalysts who are secular, I trust that this book will both aid you in understanding the religious narratives that are vital to some of your patients and also help you examine the religious narratives that are embedded in your preferred theory and practice. To colleagues who are from other religious traditions, I hope that this book will inspire you to reflect on your own tradition's resonance with psychoanalysis. To students, welcome to this field! Don't worry if you don't understand everything; it has taken me many years to form these ideas. Read and think. As a result of the ingestion and transformation of these and other ideas, I delight in knowing that I will be reading your works someday too. To therapists who are just starting to develop interest in psychoanalysis, I do desire to attract you to something about which I am passionate. I encourage you to interrogate these ideas and incorporate what you are able into your own perspectives. Finally, to those of you who revel in philosophy and theology, I hope you will feel challenged and satisfied with the depth of this study. I trust as well that you will be stimulated to carry these ideas forward in many more directions than I can possibly imagine.

Marie T. Hoffman, PhD

Chapter 1

Introduction

Charting a path toward mutual recognition

Mandy first came to see me late in the summer of 1994. I was not at all prepared for her story—a gruesome saga of abuse, murder, and mutilation that made national headlines—though from my present vantage point in her 15-year treatment, I recognize that I was being readied to help her for quite some time.

For me, my husband, Lowell, our 2-year-old son, Bob, and our soon-to-be-born daughter, Karissa, life together in 1978 was holding great promise. Raised in fundamentalist Christian churches and meeting at a conservative Christian college, Lowell and I had moved to eastern Pennsylvania in order for him to pursue seminary training. Little by little, a deep hunger arose for a more relational and authentic experience of Christianity. In an act of faith, we journeyed to Switzerland to study with a theologian/philosopher whose books had given us hope that such an experience was possible. Our fall of 1978 was spent preparing for a sojourn in Switzerland that would be life-altering and culminate in our decision to become psychologists.

Only a few miles from our residence and totally unknown to us, a little girl suffered a very different sort of fall in 1978. In the spring, 6-year-old Mandy watched her mother and almost full-term brother die at the hands of her father. That was the last scene that her right eye would ever document, for her crazed father would attack her face with a screwdriver, leaving lacerations that would necessitate over 150 stitches. Her father would be committed for life to a state mental hospital. Humiliated by her injuries and almost unrecognizable to herself, Mandy returned to school that fall as an orphaned and handicapped survivor of a domestic violence so gruesome that it reverberated across the national media. She would become a custodial minor in her maternal grandparents' chaotic household. As my husband and I were wrestling with the impact of our fundamentalist upbringing in a distant Swiss alpine village, Mandy would be settling into a fundamentalist church and school that would come to serve as her extended family.

That summer of 1979, the Hoffman family grew to four and returned to Pennsylvania. We embarked on our psychology training, inspired by a revitalized Christian faith, but cognizant of its dangers when it devolves from the faith of Christianity to the dogma of "Christianism."[1] We started our psychology practice in 1988, and in 1994 my heart and mind were ready to embrace Mandy.

In our attempt to reflect an authentic Christianity in our vocation, we have come to believe that relational psychoanalytic psychotherapy closely parallels the Judaic and Christian covenantal call to truth and love. I utilize the nomenclature "relational psychoanalytic psychotherapy" in its broadest sense, encompassing a number of contemporary psychoanalytic approaches that hold to a view of relationship as the epicenter of change. We see the relational emphasis as marked by humility. From initial interactions with a patient to final parting, the relational analyst attunes to the mystery and wonder of each person and each journey. Discovery proceeds through an incarnational or lived interaction with the patient, made possible through the development of a safe and authentic alliance. This is facilitated by a psychoanalytic psychotherapist's extensive training, supervision, and self-understanding through requisite personal psychotherapy, an echo of the sacred call to self-examination and surrender. Ongoing treatment attends not simply to words, but to relational interactions between therapist and patient that yield meaning and context to the words, and carry the treatment through disruptions, or crucifixions, to an experience of a new beginning, a resurrection. In a relational psychoanalytic psychotherapy,[2] patients and therapists come to deeply know one another, mutual recognition lying at the heart of this orientation. From a Christian perspective, patients are not only recognized in their complexities and struggles, but they are also recognized as bearing God's indelible image within them (Carter & Narramore, 1979; Jones, 1991; Olthuis, 2001; Sorenson, 2004) and having a meaningful destiny before them, a destiny in which the therapist has a role to play.

As I studied relational psychoanalysis, the concept of *mutual recognition* captured my attention. Jessica Benjamin had introduced G. W. F. Hegel's writings into her work, and through study of his theological and philosophical contributions on incarnation, crucifixion, and resurrection, a confluence soon emerged for me between Christianity and psychoanalysis. In this book I will share my study of Hegel's Christian narrative of *incarnation*, *crucifixion*, and *resurrection*, and present it as an analogue to themes in relational psychoanalytic theory. Utilizing Hegel's paradigm as the framework, I will build the central project of this book: to explore the influence of the Christian narrative on the theories, clinical practices, and history of psychoanalysis.

I believe the force that propels movement from incarnation to resurrection facilitated the weaving of the threads of Mandy's life into a tapestry of redemption. For Mandy, this book is a monument of remembrance, bearing testimony to a resurrection in her life. Thus she offers her story in support of my endeavor to recognize the spiritual force described in the sacred narratives that have become assimilated into psychoanalytic theory and practice, and which, I believe, has operated in the very development of psychoanalysis itself.

PSYCHOANALYSIS AND RELIGION

> God's defenders are not necessarily closer to God than God's accusers. ... In the Psalms, protest and jubilation ring out in the same voice. Wherever in history the combination ceased to work, the theologians would learn as much about God from atheists as the atheists could perhaps learn from the theologians.
>
> —Moltmann (Bloch, 1971, p. 28)

Many Christians sadly accede to a popular notion that psychoanalysis is as atheistic as its progenitor Sigmund Freud claimed to be. My initial task is to transform this perspective by offering a historical context for the antipathy of psychoanalysis toward religion. I posit that a prophetic and relationally oriented, redemptive Jewish tradition—cloaked in secular garb, and muted by logical positivism—forms an indelible subtext to psychoanalysis, a subtext that drew Christians to the discipline.

In spite of Freud's directives to the contrary, one cannot think of psychoanalysis apart from its Jewish heritage. By extension one cannot understand the repudiation of religion in psychoanalysis unless it is contextualized in Jewish history. By locating Freud's repudiation of religion within the broader struggles of European Jewry, I hope to deconstruct the tragic reasons that the Judaic subtext of psychoanalysis became cloaked.

To Dr. Freud, with deep regret

Dear Dr. Freud,

It is with a degree of justifiable temerity that we write you: Our correspondence has been far too long delayed. Permit us to explain.

Far too easy. Yes, it has been far too easy to denounce you for the repudiation of religion that your psychoanalysis at times has blatantly espoused: religion as "universal obsession," religion as primitive relic, and, in agreement with Feuerbach, religion as projection of the human psyche. For these profane pronouncements, we have facilely declared your guilt, neglecting to recognize our utterly despicable culpability.

Forgive us for forgetting the long history that preceded your choice to hide the intrinsic Judaic character of your craft. It has been advantageous for us to ignore the centuries in which Christianity as empire decimated your Jewish brothers and sisters. We failed to acknowledge the history texts that attested to the pogroms, the prohibitions, and the ridicule that power structures bearing the convenient imprimatur of religion wielded against the children of Israel.

We, in your terms, projected our own guilt onto you and failed to see the wounds we caused, the shame that was ours to bear, the denial of God in ourselves that we located in you. We have handily dissociated ourselves from those imposters who bore the name of *Christian* and tormented you and your family. Thus, we read your texts through eyes of arrogance, rather than through mists of tears.

We want to revisit psychoanalysis, approaching it with the veil of atheism lifted, with your Judaic subtext in high relief. We wish to contemplate that perhaps, in the mystery of a Jewish and Christian Providence, your works were yet another prophetic clarion call to truth, yet another redemptive outworking of God's irrevocable covenant with Jew and Gentile.

With deep regret,
A contrite Christian Church

The Judaic narrative

Prior to a pervasive colonization of Jewish culture by a secular narrative, Jews had maintained, to greater or lesser extents, an ethnic differentiation or transcendence that included a faith in the covenantal God of Abraham, Isaac, and Jacob. Being ethnically Jewish meant, *de rigueur*, that one was observant of Jewish faith. Radiating through the haze of Freud's atheism are the twin beacons of his ancestral Jewish faith: an emphasis on truth[3]—that is, the focused interpretation and reinterpretation of sacred texts (*mitzvoth/halakhah*) that revealed God's desires for His people, interpretations that presupposed hidden and obscured meanings—and an emphasis on loving relationship. The underlying covenantal relationship with God and therefore with one's neighbor was the loving reason the divine gift of mitzvah/*halakhah* was transmitted. "Judaism was not concerned only with obedience to the authority of the *halakhah*. It above all strove to make the *halakhah* expressive of the covenantal relationship with God" (Hartman, 1997, p. 200). The extension of the emphasis on loving relationship was the covenantal promise that Israel would influence the world for good through its roles as teacher, model, and co-worker for redemption (Greenberg, 2004; Samuels, 2001).

This emphasis on truth for the purpose of undergirding covenantal relationship with God and neighbor birthed the centuries of prophets who addressed deficiencies either in the understanding or application of God's laws. Truth and its covenantal application were never to be severed, and when they were, the prophets would rise up. Greed, violence, oppression of the poor, injustice, idolatry, lack of mercy, and immorality were cried against, a cry that became echoed in Jesus' later prophetic invectives against hypocrisy and his promoting of loving relationship.

With the secularization of Jewish culture, ethnicity and faith became separated. I wish to chronicle some factors that contributed to this divide, and consider some ways in which an imperial Christianity was complicit in this colonization.

Anti-Semitism: The Jewish experience in Europe

Anti-Semitism was pervasive in Europe for centuries prior to Freud's birth. From at least the fourth century on when Christianity became coupled with the state, the Christian church as empire (LaMothe, 2008) would impinge upon the freedoms of Jews. The list of restrictions against Jews ranged from refusal of employment to sequestering in their homes during Passion Week; from confinement to particular areas of a city or ghettoes that served to segregate Jewish people from the larger culture, to mandated dress or wearing of badges.

Jewish populations were targeted for violence as well. The Jewish Talmud and other Jewish writings were burned; expulsions *en masse* occurred repeatedly from countries (England in 1291, France in 1394, Spain in 1492) (Brustein, 2003); and pogroms, or incited riots, would murder thousands of Jews over the course of centuries.

Assimilation

Fortuitously, the more humanistic Enlightenment brought about the enactment of laws that emancipated Jews from previous discriminatory treatment. This welcome development led, for some in the Jewish population, to a modification or elimination of participation in Jewish customs such as dress, kosher dietary rules, and even the speaking of Hebrew. In response to a more humanistic cultural shift, leaders of European Jewry such as Moses Mendelssohn would support a movement called *Haskalah*, which intentionally aided Jews in integrating into Gentile society. However, according to Susannah Heschel (1998), Jews not only assimilated but effectively became "colonized" by the prevailing Christian culture of Europe. Thus Jews became divested of the recognition both of their ethnicity and their faith.

The allure of secularism

Charles Taylor (2007) poignantly depicts the post-Enlightenment shift to secularism that progressively influenced Jew and Christian alike:

> I have been drawing a portrait of a world we have lost, one in which spiritual forces impinged on porous agents, in which the social was

> grounded in the sacred and secular time in higher times, a society moreover in which the play of structure and anti-structure was held in equilibrium; and this human drama unfolded within a cosmos. All this has been dismantled and replaced by something quite different in the transformation we often roughly call disenchantment. (p. 61)

The rise of secularism was a disenchantment of Western civilization, a shift from a belief in the mysterious goodness of the transcendent to an immanent, humanistically based frame that empowered the human subject. This shift was ironically abetted by the Protestant Reformation (Taylor, 2007) that challenged the mysticism of a medieval Catholic Church. But the humanism of the Enlightenment, particularly the Continental Enlightenment, marched forward to sweep away any vestiges of the transcendent that remained, placing the human subject at the center of the universe. In these centering movements toward the human subject, that subject's rights and privileges became a matter of construction, not religion.

For Jews, the Enlightenment provided more security against religious prejudice than had ever been enjoyed. An imperial Christianity had first driven Jews toward secularism by their "othering" of Judaism, and this perverse Christianity then condemned Jews for being secular. Thus, the "enemy of my enemy," secularism, became a friend to many Jews.

Secularism not only protected Jews but in time evolved into a humanistic belief system that translated some Jewish religious ideals into a nonreligious creed. The vital, relationally based narratives of Jewish faith were first colonized through Jewish assimilation into the Christian European culture. But imperial Christianity, being bankrupt of true faith, augmented the colonization of the Judaic narrative through its own colonization by secularism, ultimately profoundly obscuring all original ties to Abrahamic faith.

Freud's experiences

Many scholarly volumes have been written about Freud's rejection of religion (Gay, 1987, 1988; Meissner, 1984; Rizzuto, 1998; Vitz, 1988; Yerushalmi, 1993) and provide a more comprehensive exploration of that rejection. I will simply focus on the effects of the anti-Semitism supported by a state Christianity that may have served to ensure Freud's utter dismissal of religion.

Freud had experienced the effects of virulent anti-Semitism in his native Vienna, which at the turn of that century was ruled by the Hapsburgs, a Catholic Church/State marriage. Etched in his memory was this story of an interaction with his deeply religious father, Jakob. He writes:

> I may have been ten or twelve years old, when my father began to take me with him on his walks ... on one such occasion he told me a story

> to show me how much better things are now than they had been in his days. "When I was a young man," he said, "I went for a walk one Saturday in the streets of your birthplace; I was well-dressed, and had a new fur cap on my head. A Christian came up to me and with a single blow knocked off my cap into the mud and shouted: 'Jew! Get off the pavement!'" "And what did you do?" I asked. "I went into the roadway and picked up my cap," was his quiet reply. This struck me as unheroic on the part of the big, strong man who was holding the little boy by the hand. (Vitz, 1988, p. 36)

When Freud attended the University of Vienna, he was expected by his Gentile peers to "feel inferior" (Gay, 1988, p. 27) because he was Jewish. Throughout the university, anti-Semitism was encouraged even among faculty. The one exception was the medical faculty, and that was where Freud found a haven in the midst of the scourge of Church-sponsored anti-Semitism.

Beyond the academy, Freud encountered prejudice as well and "reserved a special fury for anti-Semites" (Gay, 1988, p. 28). Gay recounts two further personal instances of anti-Semitic attack against Freud or his family:

> In 1883, on a train journey, he encountered several of them [anti-Semites]. Angered by his opening the window for some fresh air, they called him "miserable Jew," commented scathingly on his un-Christian egotism, and offered to "show" him. Apparently unperturbed, Freud invited his opponents to step up, yelled at them, and triumphed over the "rabble." (p. 28)

Freud's son, Martin, recalled that once in the Bavarian resort of Thumsee, his father "routed a gang of about ten men, and some female supporters, who had been shouting anti-Semitic abuse at Martin and his brother Oliver, by charging furiously at them with his walking stick" (Gay, 1988, p. 28). Gay adds, "Freud must have found these moments gratifying contrasts to his father's passive submission to being bullied" (Gay, 1988, p. 28).

A corollary prong of anti-Semitic attack focused on Jewish males, who were stereotyped as feminine. Jill Salberg (2007), sourcing Daniel Boyarin (1997), links this additional component of prejudice to Freud's religious father's unheroic conduct when he was a child. Salberg notes:

> The type of man Boyarin was referring to was the "Yeshiva-Bokhur," a young unmarried man devoting himself to the study of Torah and Talmud. This man was seen as softer, gentler, perhaps even passive, but was very much a cultural ideal. Jakob Freud certainly fit this description. We are told by a few of Jakob's grandchildren (Anna Freud, Judith Heller, and Martin Freud) that he spent much of his time studying the Talmud in the original (Aramaic) at home. This suggests that Jakob

> had an advanced degree of Talmudic knowledge, as Jews rarely studied Talmud without a partner. Clearly Jakob was not out in the world aggressively earning a living. (p. 202)

Freud eschewed his father's passivity. Instead, he nurtured a version of Jewish manhood that was described by Nordau (1903) as a "Jewry of Muscle." Freud would not pattern himself after his devout father's unheroic conduct, but would fight back.

The role of supersessionism

The centuries-old doctrine of *supersessionism* has historically been held by many Christians and has in certain cases lent itself to the perpetuation of anti-Semitism. This perspective views God's covenant with Israel as having been annulled and replaced by a new covenant with the Christian Church, effectively engendering a most destructive dichotomy between Jews and Christians.

Many first-century Christians were also Jewish, the differentiated relationship between them having been the product of centuries of evolution. Susannah Heschel (2006) observes:

> This is not just interfaith boilerplate; it is responsible history. Rather than a "parting of the ways" between Judaism and Christianity with Jesus' emergence, scholars now call the first three centuries the era in which both faiths came to take on shapes we would recognize—they were, in these years, "the ways that never parted," as scholar Annette Yoshiko Reed describes it. (p. 59)

According to Boyarin (2004), in order to establish its own identity, Christianity needed to differentiate itself from Judaism. Boyarin goes so far as to say that "Christianity in its constitution as a religion ... needed Judaism to be its other—the religion that is false" (p. 11). Though many Christians would not go so far as to view Judaism as "false," nonetheless I concur with Boyarin that an ultimately destructive binary was instituted. This binary first served to differentiate Judaism from Christianity, but later rendered Christianity prone to anti-Semitism. In turn, Judaism was rendered susceptible to colonization by secularism. In years to come, in fact, Jewish identity for many Christians became undifferentiated from secularism.

From supersessionism to shared vision

Supersessionism has in recent years received considerable critical rebuttal from Christian theologians (Hauwerwas, 2001; Moltmann, 1990; Yoder, 2008) who recognize that this doctrine contradicts the immutable nature of

God's covenants. Seen through this transcendent, covenantal perspective, it was God's *design* to develop Christianity as a complementary redemptive vehicle for Gentiles (Greenberg, 2004; Moltmann, 1977, 1990). Moltmann observes: "The mission of Christianity is to be seen as the way in which Israel pervades the world of the Gentile nations with a messianic hope for the coming God. Christianity loses nothing by recognizing that its hope springs from this enduring Jewish root" (p. 2–3). Martin Buber, philosopher and Hassidic theologian, concurred that Christianity provided for the "'mysterious' spread of the name, commandments and kingdom of its [Judaism's] God" (Moltmann, 1990, p. 3). Thus, through the lens of eschatology and a shared hope of redemption, Rabbi Irving Greenberg (2004) can say:

> Both Judaism and Christianity share the totality of their dreams and the flawed finiteness of their methods. ... From the perspective of a divine strategy of redemption rather than from within the communities embedded in historical experience and needs—both religions have more in common than they have been able to admit to themselves. Both Jews and Christians have a revolutionary dream of total transformation. ... For what often seems an eternity, both have hoped and waited, and both have transmitted the message and worked for the final redemption. Both need each other's work (and that of others) to realize their deepest hopes. (p. 233)

Sharing this eschatological vision, Christian theologian Jurgen Moltmann (1985) echoes Greenberg's hope that:

> The great theological dualities will be free from their position as mere antitheses. They will be revitalized. ... They will no longer be defined over against one another, by way of mutual negation; they will be determined in all their complex interconnections in relation to a third, common to them both. (p. 8)

The Christian narrative

Christians, like Oskar Pfister, seeking truth and human love in their quest to heal the broken-hearted and be transformative agents in this world, found themselves drawn to psychoanalysis, in spite of Freud's decided rejection of religion (Browning 1987; Rieff, 1979). Pfister recognized the prophetic subtext underlying Freud's militant stand against religion, though he felt Freud's universal disparaging of religion was misguided. He writes:

> And he who through the creation of psychoanalysis has provided the instrument which freed suffering souls from their chains and opened

> the gates of their prisons, so that they could hasten into the sunny land of a life-giving faith, is not far from the kingdom of God. ... Will you be angry with me if I see you, who have intercepted such glorious rays of the eternal light and exhausted yourself in the struggle for truth and human love, as closer, figuratively, to the throne of God, despite your alleged lack of belief, than many a churchman, mumbling prayers and carrying out ceremonies, but whose heart has never burned with knowledge and good will? (Roazen, 1993, p. 557)

Freud, though heavily influenced by the Enlightenment with its optimistic posture toward humanity, retained even more than the Christian church a hermeneutic of suspicion, one that apprehended the remarkable capacity for human self-deception. Many Christians who were drawn to psychoanalysis had become disappointed with the hypocrisy of the church and yearned for understandings that recognized the complexities of the human heart. For them, Freud's call to the pursuit of truth in the therapeutic enterprise was a necessary return to honesty and humility.

Psychoanalysts influenced by the Christian narrative not only held in common a zeal for honesty that decried hypocrisy, but also tilted toward a relational perspective. For Christians this relational tilt originates in the Judaic belief in a multifaceted, personal God in whose image humans were created and by whom life is sustained. That Judaic narrative speaks of human failure and God's design to ultimately redeem creation (Starr, 2008). This redemptive hope was reconstituted in the New Testament through a particular extension of Judaism—one that renders it uniquely Christian—the doctrine of the Trinity. God exists as one, but also, specifically, as three in one: Father, Son, and Holy Spirit, Christianity's model for the negotiation of God's "otherness" and "oneness" with creation—that is, His[4] transcendence and immanence, which are held in tension. It is this doctrine of the Trinity that gives a berth in Christianity for its redemptive narrative of incarnation, crucifixion, and resurrection.

INCARNATION, CRUCIFIXION, AND RESURRECTION: THE CHRISTIAN NARRATIVE AND PSYCHOANALYTIC THEORY

> The asymmetry of divine-human relations is similar in certain respects to the asymmetry that is present in interhuman relations. In the latter relationship, asymmetry is an essential aspect of reciprocal recognition for Hegel: Asymmetry and reciprocity do not cancel each other out. ... Divine love that divests itself for the sake of reconciliation with its other—a reconciliation that has an element of the tragic because of the

> necessity of sacrifice—is at the core of Hegel's theology and his account of the ethical life ... The divine sacrifice is primary; the human follows from and images it.
>
> —Hodgson (2005, p. 255)

The Christian narrative of incarnation, crucifixion, and resurrection, from which Hegel's intersubjectivity theory emerges, forms the framework on which this book takes shape. As psychoanalysis developed, the mutual influence of Judaic and Christian narratives subliminally became registered in the emergent dynamic theories. Relationality, a corrective to Freud's valid but Enlightenment-hobbled emphasis on truth, was propounded by many analysts influenced by the Christian narrative and became the dominant theme in evolving psychoanalytic thinking (Aron & Mitchell, 1999). With this augmented focus on human relationship, intersubjectivity and "mutual recognition" as defining constructs of human community became centerpieces of what came to be known as relational psychoanalysis. Mutual recognition validates the subjectivity of each individual, yet also validates the intersubjective relational matrix that bonds one person to another. This seminal philosophical and psychoanalytic concept becomes a basis for individual rights, for ethics, and ultimately for love.

Through Jessica Benjamin[5] and her writings on mutual recognition, Hegel becomes woven into the fabric of relational psychoanalytic thought. Benjamin lifts an integral part of Hegel's thinking, his chapter on lordship and bondage, master and slave, and makes it central to understanding the problem of recognition. This chapter has often been used as a self-contained trope, separated from many of his other premises. Indeed this chapter could be seen as the midpoint of Hegel's thinking.

Benjamin also opens the door to my present study of what precedes and what follows Hegel's midpoint, which I believe can extend the present understanding of recognition and its application to the treatment process. For Hegel, the midpoint of destruction—crucifixion—was preceded by the first movement toward recognition, that of incarnation. The midpoint was followed by yet another important movement in the process of recognition, which is resurrection. Hegel's mutual recognition can be traced along the path described in sacred Christian narrative as *incarnation, crucifixion, resurrection.* I will offer a juxtaposition of these three movements of Hegel's system with Benjamin's intersubjectivity theory and augment my focus with the work of the philosopher Paul Ricoeur.

In my decision to utilize Hegel, I am aware of submitting my ideas to the fascinating debates that surround his work. My choice naturally emerged from psychoanalytic theory that had already been developed by Jessica Benjamin. In my further research of Hegel's system, I found sufficient basis for the development of my ideas in the works of Peter Hodgson, Hans Kung, Laura Werner, and Robert Williams, who do not view Hegel as presenting "a panlogism in which God or Absolute Spirit has no real relations outside itself ... a pantheism that can easily convert into an atheism or a humanism, and reason [that] is reduced to a bloodless abstraction" (Peter Hodgson, personal communication). Through consultation with Hegel scholars such as Peter Hodgson, I have borrowed major themes from Hegel for the purpose of demonstrating generative correlations between psychoanalysis and the Christian narrative. Thus, I present my study with the caveat that it is not principally a philosophical or theological treatise. I approach Hegel not with a modernist search for the objective truth of his ideas, but with a postmodern sensibility that studies his works for resonance, for a renewed understanding of the narrative symbols they depict—the incarnate infant, the cross, the empty tomb—that have given rise to the thoughts relational psychoanalysts are thinking (Ricoeur, 1967).

I will now briefly summarize Benjamin's contributions on mutual recognition that will be crucial to an understanding of this book. Following that, I will present biographical material about Hegel. To extend our understanding of recognition, I will introduce the readers to the work of Paul Ricoeur, whose phenomenological, hermeneutic method will be deployed at both the beginning and the end of the study.

Jessica Benjamin and intersubjectivity theory

Drawing primarily on Winnicott and infancy research in psychoanalysis and on Hegel in philosophy, Benjamin (1988, 1990, 1995) developed a nuanced, relational rendering of intersubjectivity theory and one of its core components, mutual recognition. Benjamin depicts mutual recognition as the capacity to see others as equal subjects with needs, desires, and perspectives that can differ from one's own, and the reciprocating experience of the other's acknowledgment of oneself. This capacity allows each person to give and receive that kind of acknowledging response. It is the developmental achievement of this capacity that is Benjamin's initial focus and which then forms the basis for her elaboration of intersubjectivity theory.

Benjamin traces a developmental trajectory of recognition beginning with early face-to-face interaction and shared affect but followed by a phase of conflict between the aspiration for autonomy and control of the other and the realization of dependency on an other who has her own will and different desires. The infant's *omnipotence* as Winnicott called it (1959) clashes with the perceived reality of the other's separate subjectivity. Benjamin, following Winnicott, shows how the infant's denial of the other's separate subjectivity through "ruthless" attacks on the object in fantasy or reality

(Winnicott 1968) is transformed into acceptance of the outside other as less controllable but safer, more real and enjoyable.

Winnicott proposed, and Benjamin affirmed, that if the mother survives the destructive attack without retaliation, the infant (having destroyed the projected mother in fantasy) regains her in reality, though beyond its narcissistic, omnipotent control. Thus, the infant acquires the formative experience of that parent as a separate subject (Benjamin, 1990; Winnicott, 1968), as a (transcendent) "other" with needs, wishes, and will of her own. Benjamin (1990) concludes: "The denial of the mother's subjectivity, in theory and in practice, profoundly impedes our ability to see the world as inhabited by equal subjects" (p. 186). Principally constructing her theory from Hegel's idea of the master/slave relationship and the struggle for recognition, and bringing this idea into conjunction with Winnicott, Benjamin views recognition of separate subjectivity as both the necessary predisposition for ethical behavior and "love, the sense of discovering the other [Eigen, 1981; Ghent, 1990]" (p. 192). However, Benjamin does not simply accept Hegel's views. Rather, mediated by feminist thought, Benjamin challenges what she interprets as Hegel's position, that struggle ends in domination. For Benjamin, struggle ends in mutuality, an achievement of holding the tensions of difference rather than ever reaching a zero-tension equilibrium.

G. W. F. Hegel: From Christian theology to intersubjectivity

"These days it is hardly possible for a theoretical idea of any scope to do justice to the experience of consciousness, and in fact not only the experience of consciousness but the embodied experience of human beings, without having incorporated something of Hegel's philosophy," mused Theodor Adorno (1993, p. 2), social philosopher and member of the Frankfurt School. Hegel's significance for Western thought remains unparalleled.

Most of the well-known expositions of Hegel have approached his work from an atheistic perspective, the so-called Left Hegelians, led by French philosopher Alexander Kojève. Kojève's highly secularized interpretation of Hegel's works radically colonized the sacred aspects of Hegel's writings. In Chapter 5 I will comment in a footnote on Kojève's perspective, but here, I will attempt to recontextualize Hegel's work both with respect to his personal life and his cultural surround.

Georg W. F. Hegel was born in 1770 into a thoroughly Protestant German family. The firstborn of a civil servant father whose clergy kin had baptized Schiller, he excelled in his studies and seemed destined to be a theologian. Yet in spite of Hegel's interest in the study of religion and his subsequent degree from the seminary at Tubingen, for most of Hegel's earlier works, we see the icy gloss of the Enlightenment encasing the substance about which he is writing.

Christianity following the Enlightenment took on a cast of arid intellectualism, reflecting even in its Reformation break with religious scholasticism a tilt toward reason. That tilt would shift in time, the ultimate merits of the Enlightenment becoming questioned, as skepticism and materialism became the *heirs apparent* of "our God reason." Kant's *Critique of Pure Reason* (1781) stands at the forefront of major German works that attempted to address these cultural dilemmas that arose from an Enlightenment privileging of reason.

In addition to the revolt against Enlightenment thinking ignited by Kant, a sociopolitical revolution was afoot in France. France, whose Enlightenment proceeded with an excision of all things religious, was beginning to experience the ramifications of this Enlightenment in its social structure. Louis XVI had been put to death, and mass executions under Robespierre had occurred; nonetheless, the fundamental principles of the French Revolution continued to be deeply held by Hegel and his colleagues Schelling, Hölderlin, Herder, Schiller, and others.

These colleagues, whose passions continued to be theology and philosophy, hoped for a full revolution of spirit. It was their hope that not only politics but art, philosophy, and especially religion would be revitalized. So much was this their passion, that as Hegel and his colleagues would take leave of each other, it was their practice to say, "Kingdom of God" (Kung, 1987, p. 43). The coming of the kingdom of God was the hope that infused all that they did, and was the lens through which they interpreted historical events. For Hegel, this movement toward the climax of history was mediated by the manifestation and diffusion of the Holy Spirit in the world. Nothing restorative happens in the world without this mediation: Mediation by the Spirit, *Geist*, becomes the central idea for Hegel.

The Trinitarian God who vitalizes human progress was for Hegel the *dunamos*, or empowering dynamic of his philosophical system and the template for his work on intersubjectivity. The God of the past had been a God of the celestial; the Enlightenment God was concerned with things terrestrial; thus the point of contact between theology and philosophy was becoming humankind. This shift from transcendence to immanence focused Hegel on the relevance of the incarnation of God—God as human—not only for theology but for philosophy and for anthropology. Hegel's organizing principle became "in worldly thought, the world does not become godless, and that, in religious thought, God does not become unworldly" (Kung, 1987, p. 2). Hegel did not merely want an intellectual understanding of God; he wanted to combine a "positive religion of revelation with a natural religion of reason" quickened by *Geist* or the Holy Spirit, that included both heart and mind (p. 58).

This conviction worked on the soul of Hegel over the course of his life, moving his thinking from an earlier arid exposition of academic theology and philosophy to a proclamation that begins the *Lectures on the Philosophy of Religion* (Hegel, 2006) with the passion of a prophet:

> God is the beginning of all things and the end of all things; [everything] starts from God and returns to God. God is the one and only object of philosophy. [Its concern is] to occupy itself with God, to apprehend everything in God, to lead everything back to God, as well as to derive everything particular from God and to justify everything only in so far as it stems from God, is sustained through its relationship with God, lives by God's radiance and has [within itself] the mind of God. Thus philosophy *is* theology, and [one's] occupation with philosophy—or rather *in* philosophy—is of itself the service of God [*Gottessdienst*, "worship"] [1:84]. (Hodgson, 2005, p. 14)

The world continued to be jolted by revolutions spreading into Belgium and Poland, and Hegel would have his own world shaken by the cholera epidemic in Germany of 1831. He and his family fled to the countryside, where he celebrated his 61st birthday. He delivered the first of his new semester lectures, but on the 13th of November, 1831, he took ill with a virulent case of cholera. At five in the afternoon he died in his sleep. "In the words of his wife, he died like a 'saint': 'it was the slumber crossing of a transfigured person.' The last work on his desk, which was intended for publication, remained a torso: it was the *Proofs for the Existence of God*" (Kung, 1987, p. 412).

Paul Ricoeur: Hermeneutics and the movements of recognition

In similar fashion to Benjamin, whose interpolation of Winnicott with Hegel addressed the absolutizing[6] elements of Hegel, I have chosen for the same reason to incorporate the work of Paul Ricoeur. In that I am approaching Hegel with a postmodern sensibility, I will formulate my movements of recognition first through Ricoeur's phenomenological/hermeneutic method, and then correlate the movements with Hegel's incarnation, crucifixion, and resurrection. In this fashion, a dialogue of present and past narratives may provide creative material. By utilizing Ricoeur I can explore resurrection and, as Benjamin, seek to present an alternative to the popular reading of Hegel which consummates in domination.

Unlike Benjamin, who focuses on one aspect of Hegel's work (i.e., recognition and survival of the "other"), the work of Paul Ricoeur (*The Course of Recognition*, 2005) provides a basis for elaborating on the moments or movements of recognition that precede and follow Benjamin's focus on survival of destruction. In *The Course of Recognition*, Ricoeur proposes that the progressive development of variations in meaning in the lexicon anticipates the actual trajectory of the experience of recognition. Ricoeur lends amplification to "recognition" through his study of the lexicographic development and usage of the word in a manner that augments Jessica Benjamin's theory of "recognition." The achievement of intersubjectivity parsed by Benjamin substantially follows the path of development charted by the lexicon. These evolving lexicographic definitions form a "course," according to Ricoeur, and reflect the progressive movement of the process of mutual recognition. With regard to psychological development, we can outline the trajectory of recognition according to the course of the lexicon.[7,8]

The first movement in the lexicon (*Merriam-Webster's Dictionary of English Usage*, 1994) implies an awareness of reality (i.e., "to recognize"). This awareness is based on prior knowledge because it is *re*known (from Latin *recognescere*); i.e., what is being recognized had previously been identified. This movement toward mutual recognition declares, "I feel like you, you feel like me—we feel alike," i.e., "I *identify* with you."

The second movement in the lexicon reveals an awareness of the differentiated status of the other, that is, the "particular" or "independent" status. This second movement declares, "You are separate from me; you have a center from which you see things differently from me—I can't control you," i.e., "I *surrender* to your rights."

The third movement in the lexicon signifies acknowledgment of a differentiated status by a show of appreciation. This third movement toward mutual recognition declares, "You and I perceive things differently, we struggle to offer our views of what is significant to each other—We appreciate each other's views in our dialogue," i.e., "I have *gratitude* for you."

Extrapolating from Ricoeur and Benjamin, I suggest three movements of recognition that course along the following trajectory:

1. acknowledging the existence of someone, i.e., *identification*, leading to
2. acknowledging the differentiated, independent status of that someone who has rights, i.e., *surrender*, culminating in
3. acknowledging the differentiated, independent status of that someone who has rights and whom I appreciate, i.e., *gratitude*.

Embedded within the word *recognition* is a commentary on the theme of recurrence in the experience of recognition. The trajectory repeats itself in a cyclical pattern: *re*-cognition, a return to something that was already known and yet became unrecognized. Recognition is repeatedly lost and rediscovered. In this distinction Hegel is differentiated from Benjamin and Ricoeur, who understand that mutual recognition is never fully and finally achieved but is striven for, gained, lost, and recaptured, as domination of other gives way to the ongoing pursuit of dialogue.

IDENTIFICATION, SURRENDER, AND GRATITUDE: PSYCHOANALYTIC PROCESS AND THE CHRISTIAN NARRATIVE

In this book I hope to show how the process of psychotherapeutic transformation is an analogue to ancient redemptive narratives. Psychoanalysis has already benefitted from interdisciplinary studies with Buddhist thought (Cantor, 2008; Epstein, 1995; Magid, 2000; Rubin, 1996; Young-Eisendrath & Muramoto, 2002), those studies having generatively opened the door to explorations of other spiritual narratives. In this study, I will suggest that relational psychoanalysis has been influenced by numerous theorists who were shaped by an embedded Christian narrative. As a result, the redemptive Christian narrative of incarnation, crucifixion, and resurrection may be traced in its theories, emerging as an analogue of a relational psychoanalytic transformational process of identification, surrender, and gratitude. The transcendent God of the Christian narrative chooses to identify with humans in the incarnate form of Jesus, chooses to surrender to crucifixion though he is not guilty, and chooses in His resurrection to offer the gift of renewed life, which can be transmitted redemptively to others in a spirit of gratitude. This transcendent God was not coerced to love; He did so freely. His move to redeem humans and instantiate the model of incarnation, crucifixion, and resurrection as the means of transformation was a function of His grace. Religion scholar Martin Marty poignantly describes *grace*, an attribute of God's love:

> God had the freedom to remain unrelated; instead God was moved to create a universe, to situate humans in it, and to move towards them. ... God is love ... this reality suggests that God is moved by nothing other than that love to visit humans, bring them back to God, and restore them. This love, unmotivated and spontaneous—which means that it does not need to find redeeming qualities in its object—finds expression in grace. Grace ... exemplifies the revelation of the divine character in action and the relation of the divine to human beings. Consequently, grace is conceived as personal, a movement from the being of God to the drama of human existence. (Marty, 1992, p. 210)

In similar fashion, the relational therapist/analyst, not out of coercion but out of love, allows him- or herself to deeply know, *identify with* and be transformed, or *incarnate*, into characters in the patient's enacted life drama, even as the patient begins to mutually identify with the therapist/analyst (Terrell, 2007). The analyst *surrenders* to this process, which will lead to his/her enduring repetitive destructive assaults or *crucifixion* during the therapeutic process—assaults endured as the analyst either partly becomes or is misperceived as a harmful character from the patient's past. Through a nascent faith in a new relationship, the patient also surrenders to a process muddled with the mist of the past in the realities of the present. In the course of the therapeutic relationship, the projections recede as both patient and analyst survive mutual destruction and *resurrect* into a new experience of intersubjectivity, one marked by the experience of mutual *gratitude*.

ORGANIZATION OF THIS BOOK

The book is divided into three parts: Part I: "Identification/Incarnation"; Part II: "Surrender/Crucifixion"; Part III: "Gratitude/Resurrection." Each of Hegel's movements is located in psychoanalytic theory, practice, and history, aided by the hermeneutic investigatory process employed in the work of Paul Ricoeur. Hegel's *incarnation* is linked with the psychoanalytic concept of *identification*, his *crucifixion* is linked to psychoanalytic *surrender*, his *resurrection* is linked to psychoanalytic *gratitude*. In an effort to transcend what some feel are the absolutizing aspects of Hegel's narrative, I will resource Paul Ricoeur's hermeneutic method, and seek to offer a new perspective on "gratitude" and its analogue in *resurrection*.

Part I

Chapter 2 will offer theoretical perspectives on psychoanalysis and the Christian narrative. The chapter will be devoted to establishing parallels between the first movement of mutual recognition—identification—and its analogue in Christian incarnation: the voluntary taking on by God of human finiteness and pain. This will be accomplished through exploration of *identification* in infancy, in the therapeutic relationship, and as it is extrapolated in Hegel's writings on incarnation.

Chapter 3 will begin with a description of the distinctives of a clinical practice that is both psychoanalytic and acknowledging of a Christian worldview. I will then begin to present a clinical case in which identification and incarnation are demonstrated in the case notes, narrative, and clinical theory in the long-term treatment of my patient, "Mandy."

Chapter 4 will introduce the first of three segments appearing in Parts I–III, which traces the process of recognition in the development of psychoanalysis. In this chapter I will introduce the reader to early-20th-century psychoanalysts who were identified both with the Christian narrative and with psychoanalysis. In their adaptations and reactions to

Christianity, they introduced an incarnation of the Christian narrative to psychoanalytic thought.

Part II

Chapter 5 returns to theoretical perspectives, exploring the correspondences between the psychoanalytic concept of *surrender* and Hegel's portrayal of crucifixion—the surrender of God to his own negation in his death. I will examine the psychoanalytic concept of *surrender* as it appears in infancy, in the therapeutic relationship, and in Hegel's system informed by the Christian narrative.

Chapter 6 rejoins my ongoing clinical case in which surrender and crucifixion are both experienced by Mandy and me, and I offer my clinical perspectives informed by the Christian narrative.

Chapter 7 revisits the work of Ronald Fairbairn and D. W. Winnicott in greater depth than in Chapter 4, using them as exemplars of "destruction and survival" of both the Christian and psychoanalytic narratives in their work. Their theories, significantly influenced by their Christian narratives, led the way to the mutual influence of psychoanalysis and Christianity which contributed to a paradigmatic transformation in psychoanalytic thought.

Part III

Chapter 8 shifts my theoretical focus away from exclusive reliance on Hegel's system. After sharing biographical material about Paul Ricoeur, I resource his perspectives on resurrection, gratitude, and gift. Resurrection heralds the point in Hegel's narrative in which new creation begins, when the third movement of recognition—a validation of separate subjectivity that can be appreciated, or gratitude—consummates the path to mutual recognition. The gift can now be received, used, and appreciated. With Hegel's system as background, I defer to the mystery and complexity of Ricoeur's post-Hegelian, Kantian orientation. There is hope of resurrection, of a fulfilled eschatology, but the continued presence of evil modulates any impulse toward triumphalism and reorients a love based in integrity to the reality of suffering and the necessity of mourning, even as we wait in hope.

Chapter 9 chronicles a final aspect of my work with Mandy insofar as this book is concerned. Our continuing encounters with evil and mourning lace the wonder of resurrection and gratitude, which permeates our relationship.

Chapter 10 focuses attention on the resurrection of Sándor Ferenczi as the final theorist that I will examine in the historical development of psychoanalysis. Ferenczi is an exemplar of a theorist whose ideas were in part influenced by the Christian narrative and who suffered destruction. I investigate evidence pointing to the influence of Jewish and Christian relational narratives in the work of Ferenczi, linking his *resurrection* to the process of recognition in which gratitude for the gift of his work became possible.

Chapter 11 is the conclusion. In this chapter I extend the findings of Chapter 10 as I review the pervasive utopian hopes of early-20th-century European culture and the messianic strivings that these hopes represented. I suggest that the resonance of Ferenczi's thinking with Jewish and Christian narratives appealed to theorists who had been influenced by those narratives. These 20th-century theorists transformed Ferenczi's resurrected perspectives into their particular, divergent psychoanalytic streams, which reunited in the confluence we know as relational psychoanalysis. Thus, the path of recognition reaches its high watermark in the emergence of relational psychoanalysis whose spirit embodies a resurrected Jewish and Christian emphasis on truth, loving relationship, and redemption.

ENDNOTES

1. I wish to distinguish *Christianity*, that narrative which reflects the teachings of Jesus of the Gospels, from *Christianism*. Andrew Sullivan (2006) elaborates, "Christianity, in this view, is simply a faith. 'Christianism' is an ideology, politics, an 'ism'" (p. 2).
2. For more on relational psychoanalysis, please consult writings by Aron, Benjamin, Davies, Ghent, Mitchell, Shabad, and Sorenson. A good starting place is Aron and Mitchell's *Relational Psychoanalysis: The Emergence of a Tradition* (1999).

   Nancy McWilliams represents the best of contemporary psychoanalysis and, though not specifically identified with the "school" of relational psychoanalysis, subscribes to a deeply relational theory and methodology. Her books *Psychoanalytic Diagnosis: Understanding Personality Structure in the Clinical Process* (1994); *Psychoanalytic Case Formulation* (1999); *Psychoanalytic Psychotherapy: A Practitioner's Guide* (2004); and *Psychoanalytic Diagnostic Manual* (2006) are some of the most clearly written texts on psychoanalytic psychotherapy.

   This book wishes to support an ethic of relationality that is practiced by psychoanalysts of divergent technique and theory, whether or not they belong to a distinct *relational school*. The danger is that though relationality is a valid and powerful lens through which to understand human nature, by dint of accretion to political forces it risks becoming *relationalism*.
3. "The Jewish method of interpretation of multiple meaning, which worked by means of association, [and] by which the objects of interpretation, the holy texts, were seen as given once and for all and time to a large extent as circular, that is to say, the realities of the soul were relatively unchangeable, was pushed back by the victorious progressive, Greco-Christian, Aristotelian theology demanding one-dimensionality, and eventually ghettoized. However, the main principles of the Jewish method of interpretation—the theses about the relative unchangeableness of the fundamental psychic structures

and the endless variability of meaning adjacent to the multitude of relevant interpretations—survived in the so strongly Jewish-influenced [discipline of] psychoanalysis" (Enckell, 2001, p. 168).

4. For purposes of uniformity, God will be referred to in the masculine gender, though it is immediately acknowledged that such categories are entirely arbitrary in referring to deity.
5. Jessica Benjamin is a faculty member and supervisor at the NYU postdoctoral psychology program in psychotherapy and psychoanalysis. She is the author of three books: *Bonds of Love*, *Like Subjects Love Objects*, and *Shadow of the Other*, which have been translated into many languages. She has written about intersubjectivity and recognition as well as gender and sexuality. More recently, she has directed a project on acknowledgment in the Middle East for Palestinian and Israeli mental health professionals and written about collective trauma and witnessing. She is co-founder of the IARPP and the Mitchell Center for Relational Studies in New York City.
6. By the term *absolutizing*, philosophers allege that Hegel's system ultimately reduces everything to one (i.e., domination).
7. Since Benjamin derives her constructs through a study of *Phenomenology of Spirit*, originally written in German, a lexicographical study of the German word yields this information: The word for *recognition* in German is *Anerkennung*, first used by Hegel as a philosophical concept in his early Jena writings (Werner, 2007). In German, recognition or *Anerkennung* carries three meanings: to recognize something *as* something (e.g., an approaching figure as a friend); giving recognition *to* something or acknowledging that it *is* something (the performative act of, e.g., recognizing the new government of some country or waving a greeting to an approaching friend); and *positive* recognition, or the confirmation of something's value (p. 99).
8. *Merriam-Webster* identifies these current usages: 2a: to recall knowledge of: make out as or perceive to be something previously known; b: to perceive clearly: be fully aware of: realize; 3: to acknowledge formally: as (a) to admit as being of a particular status; (b) to admit as being one entitled to be heard (as in a meeting): give the floor to; (c) (1): to acknowledge the de facto existence of (as a government in a state); (2): to acknowledge the independence of (as a community or body that has thrown off the sovereignty of a state to which it was subject) and treat as independent or as otherwise effective; 4: to acknowledge in some definite way: take notice of; (a) to acknowledge with a show of approval or appreciation; (b) to acknowledge acquaintance with; (c) to admit the fact or existence of.

Part I

Identification/Incarnation

In Part I, I am working with identification in psychoanalysis (the first movement toward mutual recognition) as an analogue to incarnation (the first movement of Hegel's system).

In Chapter 2, I create a parallel between identification in the mother–infant relationship, identification in the treatment process, and incarnation in Hegel's system. In each of these sections, the sense of immanence or oneness dominates. The infant and mother start by seeking connection with one another, the patient and therapist seek to identify and connect with one another, and in Hegel's view, God sought to identify with and connect to humanity in the incarnation of Jesus. From a theoretical standpoint, the narrative of God's incarnation appears to resonate with the first movement of the treatment process, identification—the initial movement in the journey to mutual recognition.

In Chapter 3, I first present the framework for a psychoanalytic treatment that is practiced from a Christian perspective. I then trace the development of mutual identification in the treatment of Mandy, keeping in mind the treatment as analogue to incarnation. I describe the process as it unfolds, the means by which identification developed, and the love and need which animated it. I consider aspects of Mandy's faith that appeared to undergird her resilience. I discuss key dialectics to be held in tension during treatment, which are derived from Hegel, Ricoeur, and relational psychoanalysis, and which inform an optimally balanced Christian worldview. I discuss relational psychoanalytic ideas regarding multiplicity of self states, linking them to the Christian narrative of Trinity. I place considerable emphasis on the topic of *enactment*, describing its historical development, its meaning, its linkages with neuroscience, and its function in therapy. I link enactment with the concept of Christian incarnation and explain how enactment functions to incarnate both a good and a bad object for the patient. I also consider enactment in Christian incarnation as a lived, affective experience of God. All of the above is demonstrated in my narration of the treatment and use of verbatim session dialogue.

In Chapter 4, I begin with a review of Freud's exposure to Christian theism and his ultimate disidentification with religion. Due to Freud's antipathy for religion, which became reified in psychoanalytic theory and practice, the faith background of many analysts went unrecognized. Thus, my first step in bringing recognition to the Christian narrative in psychoanalysis is to identify early psychoanalysts who bore the Christian narrative in their life histories. I then chronicle how analysts who retained (adapters) and those who renounced (reactors) Christian faith were drawn to aspects of psychoanalysis that resonated with their faith experience and then made contributions to psychoanalysis that incarnated aspects of their religious experience.

Chapter 2

The first movement toward mutual recognition

Theoretical perspectives

IDENTIFICATION IN INFANCY

> As she cradles her newborn child and looks into its eyes, the first-time mother says, "I believe she knows me. You do know me, don't you? Yes, you do." ... [N]ever will she feel more strongly, than in those first days of her baby's life, the intense mixture of his being part of herself, utterly familiar and yet utterly new, unknown, and other.
>
> —Benjamin (1988, pp. 13–14)

> It is important to distinguish between a mother's capacity to identify with her infant ... and the infant's state of not yet having emerged from absolute dependence. Only gradually does the infant separate out the not-me from the me ...
>
> —Winnicott (1959, p. 102)

Before birth

The move from unfettered adult to being a mother whose primary preoccupation is her infant is essentially the move from transcendence to a necessary immanence, from a position of being separate to accepting the prenatal and postnatal confluence of physical and emotional forces and consequent responsibilities that attach mother and infant into a mutually regulating dyadic relationship. This mother–infant relationship was an early focus for Winnicott and Benjamin. Winnicott (1960) describes the process of induction into motherhood in this way:

> Soon after conception, or when conception is known to be possible, the woman begins to alter in her orientation, and to be concerned with the changes that are taking place within her. In various ways she is encouraged by her own body to be interested in herself. The mother

> shifts some of her sense of self on to the baby that is growing within her. (p. 53)

The mother's divesting of separateness is simply the last in a chain of oscillations between transcendence and immanence, the very joining of coitus reflective of a parental unit of two made one, prefiguring the internal courtship that will bring forth another human being. Two alien biological components, egg and sperm, traversing internal continental divides, are driven toward immanence, linking their individual identities to become a new creation.

During pregnancy, mother is not seen by the fetus, but felt and heard. Trevarthen (2009) elaborates:

> There is evidence that the first awareness a human being can have of another is transmitted through the interior of the body of the mother to her foetus—from the periodic contractions of her uterus, the stepping displacements of her body and the pulse and tones of her voice [Trevarthen et al., 2006]. (p. 514)

Trevarthen proceeds to compare the rhythms of the mother's body heard by the yet unborn fetus to music and dance (p. 514).

A developing infant is not seen by the mother, but felt and heard through the aegis of scientific instrumentation. Sight for the mother will be limited to "through a glass darkly" via sonograms, until the day that she can gaze at her infant face to face. Until that time, in thousands of ways the mother is being drawn into rhythm with her infant, into a heightening dance of immanence, the perceptual understanding of whom she is carrying, which culminates in the actual experience of a held baby.

After birth

The mother has heard, the mother has felt, but now she sees: The infant in her arms now captures her gaze as she captures the infant's. Research by Meltzoff has shown the following:

> Infants as young as 42 min can imitate the facial expression of an adult model. The infant perceives the correspondence between what he or she sees in the face of the model, and what he or she feels proprioceptively in his or her own face. How can the infant do this? Through cross-modal matching. The infant can translate between environmental information and inner proprioceptive information, detecting matches, from the beginning of life. The infant can bring its internal state and behavior into a correspondence with the environment. Meltzoff [1985, 1990] argued that this cross-modal matching provides a fundamental relatedness between self and other, between inner state and environment. He

> suggested that it provides the earliest experience of "like me." (Beebe & Lachmann, 1998, p. 488)

One of the fondest memories of my children's infancies had to do with gazing at them. Whether they were serenely nursing with milk drooling down their faces as they fell asleep or were in their bassinet next to me struggling to peek over the edge and explode into a smile to see Mommy's face, the shift from sensing in the womb to seeing with one's eyes was the essence of incarnation, and the prime vehicle of an identification with my infant who was "like me." Schore (2003) confirms the import of these periods of intense mutual gaze. He states: "An infant will smile in response to enlargened pupils. Even more intriguingly, viewing enlargened pupils rapidly elicits dilated pupils in the baby, and dilated pupils are known to release caregiver behavior" (p. 7). Beebe and Lachmann (1988a) concur with Schore, asserting that matching of affective patterns "recreates an inner psychophysiological state similar to the partner's" (Schore, 2003, p. 8). Thus mutual regulation between mother and infant begins in the womb and is intensified, enhanced, and solidified into a pattern of attachment following birth.

In the mind

At the neurological level, the gaze of my infants was accompanied by the firing of our mirror neurons. "Mirror neurons are premotor neurons that fire both when an action is executed and when it is observed being performed by someone else" (Gallese, 2009, p. 520). Gallese asserts that this neurological system is involved in the imitation and replication of intricate behaviors through observation. Thus, intersubjective relatedness at high levels of complexity is operative from birth. Gallese concludes: "The shared intersubjective we-centric space mapped by mirroring mechanisms is likely crucial in bonding neonates and infants to the social world, but it progressively also acquires a different role. It provides the self with the capacity to simultaneously entertain self–other identification and difference" (p. 530).

Presaging mirror neuron discoveries, Winnicott (1960) saw the import of infant/maternal attunement. He writes, "The important thing, in my view, is that the mother through identification of herself with her infant knows what the infant feels like and so is able to provide almost exactly what the infant needs in the way of holding and in the provision of an environment generally" (p. 54).

Though Winnicott coined the phrase "good enough" mothering, he also delineated the myriad ways in which the rhythm could become to greater or lesser extents impinged upon due to maternal deficit or intrusion. These are the times that the infant's own constitutional endowment

(Klein, 1975), the misattunement of significant others (Beebe & Lachmann, 1988a, 1988b), and trauma or the failure to provide what is needed (Balint, 1968; Fairbairn, 1952; Klein, 1975; Kohut, 2000; Winnicott, 1960) inflict intrapsychic damage producing disrupted affect regulation (Schore, 2003) and disturbed capacity for mentalization[1] (Fonagy et al., 2002), with its consequential disturbance in capacity for relationship. In these times, the interpersonal mélange of projections transports the dyad into the height of confused immanence: Mother and infant become enmeshed in an intersubjective "hall of mirrors" (Benjamin, 2004b).

IDENTIFICATION IN ANALYSIS

> In the course of a psychoanalytic journey, patient and analyst ... [g]radually mutually regulate each other's behaviors, enactments, and states of consciousness such that each gets under the other's skin, each reaches into the other's guts, each is breathed in and absorbed by the other. For a while, patient and analyst share a jointly created skin-ego/breathing self.
>
> —Aron & Anderson (1998, pp. 25–26)

> For Winnicott, analytic process, like the mother–infant relationship, is the creation of a transitional space within which the nature of certain contradictory realities is not questioned but instead simply allowed to exist.
>
> —Slochower (1996, p. 29)

Before the first appointment

As an analyst/psychotherapist engaged in the details of administering a practice, the person whose voice I hear on the answering machine from the night before, although a stranger, is someone whom I anticipate with both hope and anxiety. Like mother and prenatal infant, I wonder, "Who will this person be?" "Will I be able to connect to her?" "What will his needs be?" I register clues as I hear the slight tremor in the voice, the hang-ups that preceded that call, the crying children in the background, all hints of who will be entering my office. And the cues are perceived in turn by the prospective patient in my return phone call. The rhythm has begun. Does the caller answer my return call at the time she suggested, or does she immediately give me the sense of having an internal world filled with objects that were unreliable, where no one delivered what was promised? Is he overly annoyed when my call is felt to be less prompt than he would have liked? Does this introduce me to the parent for whom nothing was fast enough or good enough? Vital, but preliminary, notes become catalogued in my mind. These initial interactions become part of the common skin

I share with my patient, part of the pattern that will determine our rhythm, its *on* or *off* quality.

After the first appointment

The hour of the session has arrived and I eagerly look forward to meeting the person behind the voice. Initially, after forms are completed, I ask why they have come. And then I listen. I listen intently. When we have agreed to work together, my very focused listening continues for many sessions, along with my questions that help me understand the complexities of this individual's life and help refine the problem both in my eyes and in the patient's eyes.

With those eyes, I look as well. I search for the source of the pain. I see my new patient looking at me, probing my demeanor, seeing me seeing him. With my gaze I speak words of acceptance and understanding and comfort to her.

Winnicott (1963a) described the functions that a mother performs for her infant, and by extension that the analyst performs for the patient, as falling in two categories: those having to do with her role as environmental mother, and those having to do with her role as object mother. As environment mother I ensure that I am there when I am supposed to be, the room is warm and friendly, the noises are kept to a minimum (except for my two Pomeranians who snore to a rhythm of their own!), and I provide the physical necessities that accompany good therapeutic care. Winnicott referred to this as the provision of a "holding environment," in much the same fashion as a parent would provide for a child. In the early days of treatment such patterns become established, hopefully in ways that calm and bring hope to the patient. The safe frame with reliable times and responses aids in accomplishing this.

As object mother I attempt to provide a nonintrusive, yet alive, responsiveness to my patient, a genuine curiosity about his life, a heart sufficiently unguarded to be touched by my patient's pain. In turn I offer what for some is a rare experience of empathy: a commitment to have faith even when hers is lacking and to care even when a steadfast belief pervades that care does not exist. I strive to identify with the patient and thus narrate her story back in a way that can make sense and can aid in the growth of the patient's own capacity for mentalization (Fonagy et al., 2002). Perhaps even more importantly, I pay attention to the rhythm of my patient.

In the mind

These initial interactions in the process of recognition, as Benjamin (2000) explains, occur through the patient's experience of my mind's beginning to understand his or her mind and might best be described as *identification.* She writes:

> Mitchell rightly picks up on mutual identification as crucial to my understanding of how we solve the dilemma of helping the person who does not yet have her own voice. For long stretches of analysis, recognition may appear to be a one-way street, except that we are moved by our deep conscious and unconscious identification with the patient we aim to recognize. (p. 294)

The concrete listening and speaking are the obvious text of identification, while the maternal functions—affect regulation, provision of a holding environment, attunement—and the patient's response to these functions begin to occur in a particular rhythm that undulates beneath the surface, lulling us into our unique dance of incarnation. Incarnation and identification slowly build through a nudging of one partner by another into roles that are some admixture of the patient's and therapist's old object ties etched within the neurological circuitry. While these identifications will need to be owned by each respective subject, these identifications soon crescendo into what we call *enactments*, which become the focal points for either repetition of old patterns of behavior or for re-creation.

When unresolved enactment or repetition prevails, analysts find themselves behaving at odds with their desired healing intentions. Stephen Mitchell (1997), describing this dilemma, discusses a case presented by Grossman and Stewart (1976). In this case, a patient who had lived out a pattern of masochistic submission to men "submitted" to Grossman and Stewart's denigrating interpretation of her problem. This interpretation became an unwitting repetition of the same type of demeaning interpretation that had hurt her in her previous analysis. The authors of the case, who were highly trained clinicians, making every attempt to be helpful, became the very sort of abusive persons who had previously injured her (Mitchell, 1997, pp. 44–47). Mitchell explains:

> This is a wonderful example of the central problem at the heart of every analysis. ... The analyst makes an interpretation about the way in which the patient eroticizes interactions, and the patient experiences the interpretation itself as a seduction. The analyst makes an interpretation about the way in which the patient transforms every interaction into a battle, and the patient experiences the interpretation itself as a power operation. Or, in this case, the analyst makes an interpretation about the patient's masochism, and the patient experiences the interpretation as a put-down to be agreed to and feel humiliated by. (p. 45)

And so the therapist, making every effort to provide a reparative experience for the patient, often slides into the incarnation—perceived or real—of the bad parent, an aspect of incarnating called *enactment* that will be examined in greater detail in the next chapter.

INCARNATION AS ANALOGUE TO IDENTIFICATION IN HEGEL[2]

> But the man who lives in contradiction is meant to become conscious of this original unity [with God]. ... [I]t is necessary in religion "for man to appear to him as God and for God to appear to him as man" [Hegel, *Philosophy of Religion* XIV, 141]. ... Only in this way does man become certain of the unity between himself and God in immediate tangible terms.
>
> —Kung (1987, p. 367)

> God is the true God, spirit, because he is not merely Father, and hence closed up within himself, but because he is Son, because he becomes the other and sublates this other.
>
> —Hegel (Hodgson, 2005, p. 172)

Hegel's presentation of the incarnation of God in Jesus Christ, which precedes the narrative point at which Benjamin engages with Hegel's theory of recognition, can be seen as an analogue to the first movement of recognition in which mother and infant, analyst and analysand experience one another for the first time and begin a growing mutual identification. We can view the narrative of a transcendent God's incarnation and its analogue in the analyst's relationship with the patient as presenting an immanent, experience-near means of transformation. God is no longer solely a God of the sky, but walks in the rhythm of humanity. Similarly, relational psychoanalysis has brought the analyst from the position of deified authority—the all-knowing analyst—to a position that recognizes the role of incarnation, of asymmetrical mutuality (Aron, 1996). Reading or learning about relationship, or even interpreting it, becomes secondary to experiencing it personally.

Hegel's premises: Before incarnation

Hegel spends much time developing the process of incarnation. For him, there is an originary love that empowers the migration of *Geist* into incarnation through crucifixion and toward resurrection (Hodgson, 2005; Kung, 1987; Werner, 2007; Williams, 1997).[3] This love, Hegel believed, is God himself (Hegel, 2006 [1827 lectures]), and it is through an explanation of

God's subjectivity as a loving being that Hegel begins his elaboration of the process of recognition.

For Hegel, it was necessary that a loving God incarnate into human substance to breach both the primodial rupture that alienated humans from Him, and the internal rupture that alienated each human from the intrinsic godlikeness in themselves and with other human beings. In his 1824 lectures Hegel speaks pointedly of this rupture:

> Evil first occurs within the sphere of rupture or cleavage [*Entzweiung*]; it is the consciousness of being-for-myself in opposition to an external nature, but also in opposition to the objective [truth] that is inwardly universal. ... Abstractly, being evil means singularizing myself [*mich vereinzeln*] in a way that cuts me off from the universal (which is the rational, the laws, the determinations of spirit). (Hodgson, 2005, p. 152)

In order to provide a template from which "being-for-self" and "being-for-others" could be harmonized, Hegel "resurrected the trinitarian conception of God out of the dustbin of discarded relics from the ancient Christian past. ... In so doing, Hegel reestablished the concept of the Trinity as a crucial component in both philosophy and theology" (Grenz, 2001, p. 29). What Hegel advanced was that love existed in the relationships among the persons of the Trinity. In that trinitarian model, intersubjectivity, and thus mutual recognition, arises from the maintenance of sameness and difference through the overarching thirdness of the triune godhead itself. Hegel explains:

> As eternal love God loves Another, who is identical with him and loves him in return, in a Third. All of God is realized in each of these three forms "a game of love with itself" [XIV, 93]. ... "God is Spirit, and we may define him abstractly as self-separating universal Spirit. ... This is what in the Christian religion is called *triunity*" [XIV, 69]. (Kung, 1987, p. 362)

It is in this Trinitarian image that humans were created: capable of experiencing recognition through relationality in the dialectic of sameness and difference. Through this image, the capacity for a dialectic of self and other becomes possible (Powell, 2001). Hegel elaborates:

> When we say, "God is love," we are saying something very great and true. ... Love is a distinguishing of two, who nevertheless are absolutely not distinguished for each other. The consciousness or feeling of the identity of the two—to be outside of myself and in the other—this is love. (Hodgson, 2005, pp. 135–136)

Hegel's premises: After incarnation

In order for humans to regain their humanity-in-godlikeness, God emptied Himself into human form in an act of ultimate self-giving. Only in this act of incarnation could humanity see the dialectic of divinity and humanity held in the humanity of Jesus whom Christians recognize as the Christ. In Christ, humans could gaze upon God, and in seeing Him, see who they were meant to be. Hegel found the doctrine of the Trinity to be an essential basis for the incarnation, one that allowed God to remain transcendent yet become immanent (i.e., human, so that humans might experience their own godlikeness). Kung describes the incarnation as a climactic moment in Hegel's writings:

> At this juncture Hegel's *Philosophy of Religion* reaches its climax. Both the divine and the human here reach their apex. This is "the momentous element," "the most weighty moment in religion": "God appears in human shape" [XIV, 137]! God and man are not different, but one! God and finite matter are not mutually exclusive—this is said against Platonism of every hue. (Kung, 1987, p. 367)

In his 1827 lectures, Hegel (2006) confirms the Biblical narrative that presents Christ as fully human, "a human being in all the external contingencies, in all the temporal exigencies and conditions, that this entails" (3: 316), elsewhere describing Him as expressing human joy, sorrow, anger, and need (Hodgson, 2005, p. 164). However, in spite of the constraints placed upon Christ in his humanity, in the 1821 manuscript Hegel emphasizes Christ's comportment as consonant with who He was. He refers to Christ's role as model and teacher in the Sermon on the Mount. There, He communicated a message to those who had congregated together of the incomparable significance of one's internal state, contrasting inner intentions with outer deeds, and prioritizing relationships of love above stultifying familial attachments (3:117–122). From historical narratives, we also know that Christ was involved in feeding the hungry, providing healing to the ill, and offering a patient and attuned ear to those in distress.

Hegel goes on to conclude in his 1827 lectures that "Jesus speaks not merely as a teacher who expounds on the basis of his subjective insight but as a prophet" (Hodgson, 2005, p. 167). That is, the essential "asymmetry in mutuality" of Christ's earthly existence was evident in His capacity to be fully human yet retain and impart a consciousness of divine realities that exceeded the comprehension and/or vision of His followers.[4]

However, estrangement would ensure that repair of the rupture through incarnation and identification alone would fall short, for humanity would see Christ through the veil of its estrangement. Ultimately, the Christian narrative recounts that Christ to greater and greater extents incarnated as that which

He needed to become in order for reconciliation to take place: the broken and reviled "everyone" who would ultimately restore relationship with God. In Part II, we will see how identification and incarnation must be followed by surrender and crucifixion for the rupture between two subjectivities to be bridged. In that process the Trinitarian idea of surrender to a "third" as a means by which "being-for-self" and "being-for-others" lose their antithetical stances comes to the fore in Hegel and psychoanalytic thought.

INCARNATION AND RELATIONAL PSYCHOANALYSIS

As analysts, we progress from the initial differentiation—or transcendence—that precedes the encounter with the patient, to learning about them at a distance, to seeing them face to face. As analysts, we identify with our patients, and they identify with us as we begin the process of incarnating into the helpers they need us to be. The human dynamic of projection ensures that the process will move from benign identification to a disorienting lack of differentiation—an immanence which will lead to enactments with our patients. Enactments, inescapable and necessary, will bring to our shores the tempestuous suffering of the patient.

Hegel would assert that the identificatory/incarnational initiative of God, and by extension of the parent and of the analyst, is the first movement toward mutual recognition and is made possible through a force for life, a force called love. But that force of love, Hegel and Benjamin would concur, can only be experienced in the crucible of differentiation. G. K. Chesterton (1908) pointedly recapitulates Hegel's distinctively Christian perspective:

> Love desires personality; therefore love desires division. It is the instinct of Christianity to be glad that God has broken the universe into little pieces. ... This is the intellectual abyss between Buddhism and Christianity ... the divine centre of Christianity actually threw man out of it in order that he might love it. (p. 139)

ENDNOTES

1. Fonagy and Target (1998) define *mentalization* (or reflective function) as the "developmental acquisition that permits children to respond not only to another person's behavior but to the child's conception of others' attitudes, intentions, or plans. Mentalization enables children to 'read' other people's minds. By attributing mental states to others, children make people's behavior meaningful and predictable" (p. 92).

2. "The textual situation is complicated: The *Lectures on the Philosophy of Religion* (Speirs & Sanderson, c. 1895) is a translation of the 2nd Werke edition (1840). Lasson reedited the text in the 1920s. The Glockner Jubilee edition is a reprint of the 2nd Werke edition. Kung [likely] used Lasson [for his original German text], and the translator of Kung translated this passage from Kung's text" (Peter Hodgson, personal communication). For any works quoted from Kung's book, I will simply cite Kung. All other quotations from Hegel's works will be from Hodgson's translation, which "is based on a separation of the different lecture series, whereas Lasson is still an amalgam of them except for Hegel's own lecture manuscript of 1821" (Peter Hodgson, personal communication). Thus, the numbering system of the references will differ due to resourcing different translations.
3. Though *reason* has often been stressed as the central feature of Hegel's system, some scholars prefer to focus on the animating force of love (*liebe*), which dominated Hegel's early writings and to which he returned in his later works (Hodgson, Kung, Werner, Williams). My work will follow the interpretation of this latter group.
4. On the 1821 manuscript Hodgson notes: "Hegel continues with an examination of Jesus' self-references as Son of God or Son of Man as found in the Synoptic Gospels. He assumes uncritically that the Gospels provide for the most part a reliable account of what Jesus actually said. Indeed, he warns against an exegesis that attempts to tone down or flatten out these expressions" (Hodgson, 2005, p. 165).

Chapter 3

Introducing Mandy

Clinical perspectives

CHRISTIAN CLINICAL CONSIDERATIONS

A psychoanalysis that recognizes a transcendent spiritual force that propels toward health and renewal is not altogether different, in terms of clinical practice, from its more secular counterpart. What does distinguish the former is a basis for hope that lies beyond our mere technical skills or our theoretical persuasions. For Hegel, and for those who have held to his belief in the active involvement of the Spirit (of God) through the instrumentality of surrendered humans, hope emerges from the faith that therapeutic efforts are undergirded by a transcendent enlivening force. The loving acts of each human are understood as inspired by a force for love that is committed to the enlargement of spheres of goodness within individual hearts as well as in society at large.[1] Such hope was captured by theologian Jurgen Moltmann (1993) in these words:

> God is he "who maketh the dead alive and calleth into being the things that are not." The spell of the dogma of hopelessness—*ex nihilo nihil fit*—is broken where he who raises the dead is recognized to be God. Where in faith and hope we begin to live in the light of the possibilities and promises of this God, the whole fullness of life discloses itself as a life of history and therefore a life to be loved. ... Love does not shut its eyes to the non-existent and say it is nothing, but becomes itself the magic power that brings it into being. In its hope, love surveys the open possibilities of history. In love, hope brings all things into the light of the promises of God. (pp. 31–32)

Such a faith perspective also sets apart a psychotherapy that aims merely at symptom reduction or support, from a psychotherapy that fully engages the prophetic calling of the therapist. From a Christian perspective, practicing a relationally oriented, psychoanalytic psychotherapy most profoundly mirrors Isaiah's anointing to "proclaim the year of God's favor" (Isaiah 61:1–4). In the process of that proclamation, we "bind up the broken-hearted," "free people from captivity," "release patients from the darkness in their lives"; we "comfort those that mourn" and facilitate transformation of their ashes into "crowns of redemptive beauty." From their hours of grieving, we locate an "oil of gladness" that had heretofore gone unnoticed. Clothed in despair, we aid in reclothing our patients in garments of joyful gratitude for life. Whereas our patients come to us feeling as wind-tossed reeds, we offer through our consistent dedication and profound involvement the possibility of a new self-identity: "oaks of righteousness," a planting that reflects the regained image of their strong and resilient Creator. Such a therapy seeks to facilitate all the redemptive possibilities engendered in the sacred space of the counseling room, a space where active participation, that is, incarnation, becomes the precursor to resurrection. In this sacred space "Thy kingdom come" is relationally experienced in a redemptive culture of justice, love, honesty, and hope.[2]

This manifest hope elucidates for me five clinical recognitions of a Christian psychoanalytic perspective, the first of which is as follows:

1. The analyst recognizes that God (Spirit) is love and is the causal force moving humanity toward a pancultural telos of love and actualization.

A second, and related, recognition is that the patient in my office is made in the image of this God. In spite of damage, deprivation, or lack of capacity, the human before me reflects the Creator from whom she was ultimately birthed. Though mortal and human, divinity in finite form resides before me. In concert with Hegel, I can articulate this second clinical recognition:

2. The analyst recognizes that each patient is made in the image of the Creator and is thus imbued with aspects of being that reflect their divine constitution and origin.

Following closely from the second recognition, each patient is worthy of the greatest dignity and care, for he is a finite reflection of an infinite Creator. No one can be deemed unfit, unworthy, unnecessary. A third clinical recognition derives from this second recognition:

3. The analyst recognizes that each patient being made in the image of the Creator is equally worthy of utmost respect and care.

A fourth recognition, flowing from a Hegelian perspective, coincides with a more orthodox Christian perspective. Each patient is part of the whole of God's created universe and has a role in the history and telos of redemption. What will empower each patient is the "work of the negative" (see Chapter 4). Newness and progress emerge from this struggle, yielding a fourth clinical recognition:

4. The analyst recognizes that each patient has a redemptive destiny that is closely related to the very areas of damage in their lives, and this redemptive destiny fulfills the negation[3] and the creative transformation of that damage into something good and new.

A collateral and fifth clinical recognition comprehends the intersubjective, though asymmetrical, relationship of the patient and analyst who surrender to this life force:

5. The analyst recognizes that she and the patient are intersubjectively related; thus the process of redemption and re-creation is at work in the analyst concurrently with the patient.

These five clinical recognitions collectively contribute to a sacred space in which God is intersubjectively related to my patient and me in our work together. With a patient who lives in faith of this mystery, God is recognized and invited to guide from the very first session. With those who have no faith perspective, these principles, though unexpressed, permeate the treatment. Such a clinical manner is consistent with a Christian narrative and is a source of security to a patient who relies on this narrative for hope.

INTRODUCTION TO THE CASE

Mandy had first called my office in 1994, when she was 22 years of age. Having just finished college, she was substitute teaching until she could procure a full-time job and was dating a young man she had known from high school. In this initial contact I experienced her as a thoughtful, mildly anxious young woman, whose dress and manner of speaking were quite conservative.

Mandy had sought treatment before with her church's pastoral counselor, but terminated, feeling that her difficulties were beyond the scope of that counselor's expertise. Her most pressing complaint was of recurring, vivid, sexual images that would tortuously and unpredictably come to mind. She reported that these images had started when she was 19, after witnessing her sister's boyfriend obsessively stalk her and then discovering his subsequent psychological collapse. The images came back in full force when she was 21, in college, and assigned a college roommate with a history of psychotic breaks.

Mandy shared her tragic early history. When she was not quite 6 years old, her mother had been violently murdered at the hands of her father. She was nearby as the murder was taking place, and father's attack on mother turned to an attack on her when she responded to her mother's screams from the adjacent bedroom. Mandy believed there was a connection between her reaction to the more recent incidents and the tragedies of her earlier history, but couldn't quite connect the dots.

As the weeks unfolded, Mandy revealed her more generalized concerns regarding sexuality, which included experiencing an irrational terror that she might accidentally abuse a child. She reluctantly shared her discomfort with experiencing any touch that might stimulate sexual feelings, including performing normal hygiene, which she did as quickly as possible and with the greatest of difficulty. Even receiving a hug filled Mandy with anxiety. What if she had caused someone to feel sexual feelings, or what if she would start to feel them? All of these fears inhibited her confidence both professionally and relationally. As we explored her history, Mandy became more intently focused on the possibility of recovering memories of sexual abuse, perhaps even ritual abuse. If these could come to light, Mandy mused, she would be freed of her symptoms.

FAMILY HISTORY

Mandy was raised in an economically depressed, rural Pennsylvania community. Her father and mother both worked, taking turns caring for her and her younger sister, Trudy. Her nuclear family lived in a house that was also shared with her father's brother Ned, his wife and two children, Paul and Sam, and her paternal great-grandmother, whom she described as slovenly and vulgar. Great-grandmother would "pee" in a bucket that Mandy and Trudy would have to empty, being careful not to drop or splash the heavy, filled bucket as they performed this daily chore. The house had seen a previous tragedy, when 10 years earlier, it burned down, killing Mandy's paternal grandmother. Mandy's father was just a teenager at the time and was called upon to identify the body of his burned mother.

Willy, as Mandy's father was called, caused home life to be lived on a razor's edge of uncertainty. He could unpredictably shift from fun-loving, bongo-drum-playing Dad who took Mandy and Trudy on daring snowmobile rides, and with whom she felt a special bond, to a terrifying monster.

One time he introduced Mandy and her sister to a girlfriend he "kept on the side," swearing them to secrecy. He subsequently took them on a long sailing adventure to which his "girlfriend" Susie was invited. Stowed away in their cots in the hold, they would hear Dad's amorous activities. Initially, Mandy remembered little of her mother, Kathy. She described her as compliant and sad, and Mandy felt no close connection with her. Her few memories of mother chronicled this distance and were recollections of reprimands from mother. Though she expressed sadness for her father's treatment of her mother, Mandy openly wondered if she had ever been special to her in the years that preceded her mother's death.

Apart from Mandy's final and catastrophic memory of incest perpetrated by her father on the day of the murder, the day that changed her life forever, no other clear memories of abuse were recalled by Mandy. However, we became confident even with only fragmented memories that substantial abuse had occurred and eventually found validation in this belief through her sister's recollections of violations and also with Mandy's vivid nightmares of abuse.

One late spring afternoon, when Mandy was almost 6 years old, she remembers lying in bed with Dad, feeling his body against hers, and feeling him touch her. She felt special, but she knew that this was not right. Mom unexpectedly entered the room. Mandy recalls an argument ensuing, which she recalls as having been over a bowl of soup that Mom wanted to bring to Dad. Mandy slipped out of the bed and left the room during the argument. She went downstairs and started watching cartoons. Then, she heard a loud bang. When she looked around the corner, she saw her father come out of the bedroom, shirtless and bloodied, looking angry. She went back to watching cartoons, hoping that if she pretended she couldn't see him, he wouldn't see her. The next thing she remembered was her father choking her and then abruptly dropping her. She was very confused by his behavior and so followed him into the next room. He started attacking great-grandmother. Mandy screamed for him not to hurt her Nana, at which point, he turned the attack on her. When she came to, no one was around, so she went upstairs looking for her mother and father.

By the time Mandy entered her parents' room, Mom, who was nearly nine months pregnant, lay on the floor in a pool of blood. Mandy ran in. She remembered bending down near Mom's unrecognizable face and hearing her muffled breaths. She didn't know it at the time, but Mom's eyes had been cut out, her lips and the tip of her nose bitten off. The baby had been carved out of the womb, his eye cut out, his lips and penis bitten off. All she saw was blood. Mandy described her experience: "I felt totally, utterly helpless." She heard Dad's footsteps downstairs and tried to hide. She remembered that he saw her, but then blocked out what happened next. This time he attacked her as he slashed her body and her face, ultimately plunging his screwdriver into her eye and throwing her across the room. Rescue teams finally arrived on the scene, and life as Mandy knew it was over.

Mandy's torso and face were massively lacerated; she lost her eye, her mother, her almost-born brother, her home, and her father on the same day. After weeks in the hospital, Mandy was finally reunited with her sister, who had been spared from severe physical injury, and the two girls moved in with the maternal grandparents. Grandmother, now a broken woman, did her best, and granddad, diagnosed with bipolar illness, was to be avoided. Mandy became a dutiful grandchild, causing no problems and earning her keep. After an arduous trial and the details of this anguishing event being strewn across national newspapers, Dad was finally committed to a state hospital for life.

CLINICAL NOTES: FALL 1994

She had heard my voice on the radio. I had heard her voice on the telephone. Today she sits before me. We are strangers peering into each other to understand ... to see ... to hope. Mandy shares her life story with me in capsule form. I immediately like her; I am moved by the courage of this woman. She has travelled more than an hour to see me, and yet she decides that she wants to do this every week so she can get the help she needs. In concert with her narrative, and with her permission, I end the first session with a prayer that God would guide in this process of healing.

Mandy returned after her first session stating that she was able to lie down and take a nap for the first time in years. She attributes this to feeling a sense of security as she begins to work with me. Mandy will begin once-weekly psychoanalytic psychotherapy. Her commitment is impressive. Regular time for her has been set. Regular policies have been discussed—office policy papers signed. I am attempting to avoid unpredictabilities and to make the setting comfortable and reliable.

She presents in a remarkably intact manner for what she has been through. She is sharing her story freely, but as is common among survivors of trauma, she tends to relate facts about the tragic events with little affect. However, her dreams are telling a different story. Nightmares, decapitations, gruesome sexual attacks. Blood. Gore. Terror. She has had a recurring dream:

> She is standing someplace and notices that one of her teeth has loosened and fallen to the ground. She is frightened. She puts her hand to her mouth and inexplicably one tooth after another begins to fall out until she has none left.

"Powerless," "defenseless," and "out of control" are the feelings that she ascribes to these dreams. We explore this picture of her internal world.

I learn that the move to life with Mandy's grandparents ushered the beginning of her strong religious affiliations. Since the age of 6, Mandy has been involved with a fundamentalist Christian church. Mandy, in fact, appears to anchor her traumatized life in her Christian faith. It provides for her a basis for hope. I note, however, that what she describes as "faith" feels like more of a rigid adherence to a fundamentalist reading of the Bible, as opposed to a relationship of trust and reliance on the God of that text. Her belief in those texts has, however, provided a much-needed sense of safety.

We are also beginning to explore the intrusive images. They plague her, terrifying her from moving forward in her desire to establish a future with her boyfriend. We spend much time on the nature of the sexual abuse that she may have suffered, guided by her emerging images. I question whether the images are simply dissociated material erupting into consciousness. Perhaps they are. However, they have an obsessive quality as well. I am feeling a tremendous need to do everything right for Mandy—to avoid any possible harm that an oversight might cause. I refer Mandy for a psychiatric evaluation.

Clinical commentary: Centrality of Mandy's faith

Recognizing the role that Mandy's faith played for her was essential to the process of identification and incarnation, and the ultimate recognition of her as a person. Being familiar with her faith perspective aided me in identifying with Mandy's beliefs and incarnating into the person of faith she could attach to and trust, one who could be attuned to her staunch convictions and nurture the flame of hope in her (Ellens, 2007, 2009).

Although Mandy had not begun to relate to God as truly "Other," that is, her experience with God was that of object-relating (see Chapter 5), Mandy's adherence to religious precepts prevented her from enacting the abuses of her corrupt and destructive internal objects. In fact, Mandy treated others respectfully and in a caring fashion: she was honest, responsible, and industrious. While I will later discuss further benefits that accrued to Mandy from her religious convictions, here are a few of the more obvious:

1. Mandy's religious narrative gave her a safe moral structure by which to live. She gave me a journal entry that captured the tragedy of her life, and her desperate need of a dependable environment like the religious structure she embraced. She wrote: "I watched my father cheat on my mother ... I 'cheated' with my father on my mother ... my father 'cheated' on me with my sister and my mother ... do you see how upside down a world like that is? In the world where I come from, nobody can be trusted, not even yourself. Anything can happen." In Mandy's sacred text, the rules for behavior, along with rewards and punishments, were clearly spelled out. For a person emerging from such familial carnage, this provided an inestimable sense of safety.
2. Mandy's religious narrative offered her an alternate identity. Her specifically fundamentalist Christian narrative stipulates that while she has earthly parents, she is truly a child of God. Her identity is therefore to be anchored to that God as her heavenly father/mother. She is no longer an orphan, for the "Lord" is her shepherd. A short journal entry regarding the terminal illness of her grandmother reflected Mandy's deeply held beliefs about this heavenly father. She wrote: "Dear God, Nanny is so sad right now. I don't know why she has to

be here. Please comfort her. Please show her why you have her here. I know you love her very much. May she feel that love now and always. Amen." Mandy was aware of the deep struggle that she had with "feeling" the truth of this belief, yet found in it sufficient comfort.

3. Mandy's religious narrative gave her a new family. Being a child of God, Mandy experienced friendships in her specific congregation and the church at large as being part of an extended family, a network that spans geographic and time boundaries. She became situated in a social context that gave her a sense, as Fromm would describe, of "rootedness" and "relatedness."
4. Mandy believed that even though her experience of God's love was distorted by her history, she could trust that He was involved in her life. This belief hastened the development of the therapeutic alliance with me and gave her hope that she could lead a normal life.

CLINICAL NOTES: 1995

Mandy is growing. The mild antidepressant and the help she is receiving with me have convinced her that marriage is possible. I procure a release to confer with a specialist in trauma to ensure that I am proceeding correctly.

I confer with Dr. X. His recommendation: Her life must be dismantled for about 2 years. Every dissociated aspect of her trauma needs to be addressed before she can be reintegrated and move on.

I am working in the transference but am fearful of stimulating paternal introjects. I study trauma theory, deepen my understanding of object relations. I utilize other nonanalytic tools that will support the work: gestalt and neuro-linguistic programming techniques. I train in eye movement desensitization and reprocessing (EMDR) and spend several sessions working with Mandy, who experiences only mild benefit. Mandy's experience of a safe holding environment appears to have the most efficacy.

Ken has proposed to Mandy. After 5½ years of dating, they are engaged to be married. Mandy and I oscillate between an exploration of her continuing fears regarding adequacy in the "role of wife," and the events of her childhood that have led to these fears. Mandy and Ken will begin premarital counseling with their pastor. They intend to have several sessions with my husband, who is also a psychologist.

We work on her tendency to comply with most of her fiancé's requests. She seems eager to please both him and me. We discuss the role of anger in relationships. She is uncomfortable with that feeling. A connection is made with her fear of becoming like her father. She fears that hidden beneath the woman she is becoming is a psychotic, murderous father who will emerge and destroy anything that she has succeeded in achieving. I endeavor to not enact that role in the transference.

In September, Mandy and Ken have their first conjoint session with my husband, Lowell. They plan to continue briefly following their wedding. I meet Ken for the first time. He presents as a very responsible and devoted man. I feel relieved with her choice of a spouse.

Mandy is joyful about her wedding. She is feeling a sense of responsibility to Trudy, her younger sister, and wants her to feel honored and supported that day as well. September 30, 1995: Today, Mandy and Ken married.

Clinical commentary: Holding of dialectics

"Paradox upon paradox is at the root of psychotherapy. Patients come to us for change, but need to be accepted, they want and need to be believed and yet their most deeply held attitudes and beliefs must be questioned," states Lewis Aron (2004, p. 17), as he applies Ricoeur's hermeneutic of suspicion and faith (see below) to the clinical setting. Was my belief in Mandy's strength and support of her desire to marry simply my naïve denial of the immensity of her difficulties? This is what the specialist in trauma seemed to suggest. However, my experience with Mandy caused me to resist tilting simply toward a *hermeneutic of suspicion* as the trauma expert had. In this instance, I leaned toward who she wanted to be, and by extension, who I needed to be for her: someone who can help her fulfill her dreams and believe in her. A *hermeneutic of faith* was my tentative choice, though I held to it lightly, for Mandy's internal world was still largely unknown to me.

Germane to the practice of relational psychoanalysis is the maintaining of tensions between otherwise complementary positions. Irwin Hoffman's *Ritual and Spontaneity in the Psychoanalytic Process* (1998) among other works (Benjamin, 1988; Ghent, 1990; Mitchell, 1995) stands out as exemplary in this vein. Hoffman (1994) states:

> To think and speak in a dialectical way is difficult and sometimes confusing. Many of our concepts in psychoanalysis imply dichotomous thinking. Fantasy versus reality, repetition versus new experience, self-expression versus responsivity to others, technique versus personal relationship, interpretation versus enactment, individual versus social, intrapsychic versus interpersonal, construction versus discovery, even analyst versus patient. There is a sense that these polarities constitute a series of mutually exclusive opposites. But when we think about the poles within each pairing in dialectical terms, we are challenged not only to recognize their obviously contrasting features, but also to find the effects of each pole on the other, and even aspects of each pole represented within the other. (p. 194)

In a deviation from Hegel's dialectic, which presupposed a synthesis and resolution, Hoffman, citing Ogden (1986), advocates "a process in which each of two opposing concepts creates, informs, preserves, and negates the other, each standing in a dynamic (ever-changing) relationship with the other" (p. 195). The heuristic advantages of such an amended Hegelian use of dialectics were embraced as well by Paul Ricoeur from his perspective of hermeneutic, phenomenological philosophy. In his magisterial *Freud and Philosophy* (1970), Ricoeur applies this philosophical perspective to his study of Freud's corpus, employing a dialectical approach to symbol, myth, and text, and consequently producing an enriching and generative dialogue.

In my work as a relational psychoanalyst, and as a person of Christian faith, I recognize four specific tensions that contain particular clinical salience, for they reflect philosophical and theological tensions that have universal application.

Subjective position of the analyst: Transcendent and immanent

While the terms *transcendent* and *immanent* have theological associations—God as other, and God as one with us—the terms have broader connotations. The terms *transcendence* and *immanence* can describe not only a theological tension but also human tensions, tensions that are alternatively captured in related philosophically based phrases such as "the one and the many" and "unity and diversity."

This philosophical tension re-emerges in our own discipline of psychoanalysis in the fertile discussions about intersubjectivity. In the necessary move away from the solipsism of the Cartesian mind, relationalists have attempted to explain how two subjects, analyst and patient, can mutually and radically influence each other, yet remain subjects in their own right. In short, how can immanence (oneness) and transcendence (otherness) coexist and function? Jessica Benjamin's work on "recognition" addresses the critical importance of the appropriate handling of this philosophical tension as it appears in the analytic situation.

Hermeneutic of the analyst: Suspicion and faith

The French philosopher Paul Ricoeur (1970) developed the phrases "hermeneutic of suspicion" and "hermeneutic of faith" to describe the two prongs of the hermeneutic task. The "hermeneutic of suspicion" focuses on the need for deconstruction whereas the "hermeneutic of faith" tilts toward human potential. While Ricoeur's phrases were chosen to represent this dialectic, there are other apt descriptions to be found in the literature. Foremost would be Stephen Mitchell's (1988) "beast and the baby" or Strenger's (1989) categories of "classical" versus "romantic" visions of psychoanalysis. Akhtar (2000), speaking to these same dichotomies, elaborates:

> Seen and described variously, this schism subsumes the following dichotomies: Oedipal–preoedipal, psychopathological–developmental, one person–two person, verbal–non-verbal, conflict–deficit, and so on. To be sure, each such conceptual pair has its own vantage point, its ups and downs in psychoanalytic history, heuristic accompaniments, and technical nuances. At the same time, these dichotomies do tend to share an important common element. One polarity of these concepts ... tends to tilt the analyst's listening in a skeptical direction and his or her interventions toward a search for hidden meanings in the patient's communications. The other polarity ... tends to tilt the analyst's listening toward credulousness and his or her interventions in an affirmative direction. (p. 266)

My specific privileging of Ricoeur's terms derives from the functions that he designates to these complementary phrases. Ricoeur (1970), in a dense explication, describes the double work of the hermeneutic enterprise. The "negative" can be understood only in relation to something else that gives it definition, most specifically, "the good" or "sacred" (pp. 13–17). Ricoeur describes the opposition of these poles of hermeneutics, helping us to understand how their juxtaposition aids in meaning-making:

> According to one pole, hermeneutics is understood as the manifestation and restoration of a meaning ... according to the other pole, it is understood as a demystification, as a reduction of illusion. ... Hermeneutics seems to me to be animated by this double motivation: willingness to suspect, willingness to listen. ... It may be that this situation, in its apparent distress, is instructive: it may be that extreme iconoclasm belongs to the restoration of meaning. (p. 27)

Epistemology of the analyst: Reason and experience

Conceptualizations of what was transformational in the clinical encounter in the earlier years of psychoanalysis were steeped in modernist thought. Insight, derived from theory-based interpretations on the part of the analyst, was the agent of change of these models. Insight is no longer considered the most important element in the process of change in relational psychoanalysis. We have moved to an understanding of change deriving from an experientially based, mutually influenced, co-construction of our shared patient/analyst realities, which neither relies on a priori structures or rigid diagnostic categorizing (Aron, 1996; I. Hoffman, 1998).

To be honest, we must acknowledge that while one may talk the experience-near talk of Winnicott, one may also simultaneously think the metapsychology of Fairbairn or Freud or Klein. This historic debate resides not only in the academy, but in our minds. And for good cause. This bifurcation is, in fact, part of the dialectical force for life described by Hegel. When recognized, negotiation of this dialectic of reason and experience becomes a gift that moves the therapy forward. In an echo of Ricoeur, philosopher Perinbanayagam (1985) describes this necessary tension thus: "There is structure and process, there is subjectivity, after a fashion, and objectivity, and indeed, both rationalism and empiricism are necessary to solve the great mystery of the beingness of the individual and the actions of the self as ongoing constructions" (pp. xiv–xv).

In my clinical experience, I am mindful of my preferred texts (Ricoeur, 1970), my prejudices (Gadamer, 1989), and my diagnostic categories, to which I continually (though subliminally) refer despite my relational, antifoundationalist stance. As my work with Mandy develops, it becomes increasingly evident to me how I must navigate this dialectic.

Temporal positioning of the analyst: Archeological and teleological

Historically, psychoanalytic work had circumnavigated between present and past: the here and now of transference, and the past of original trauma. In recent times, clinical work has entered the waters of futurity (Bollas, 1979; Cooper, 2000; Loewald, 1972; Summers, 2003). The old, that is, archeology (Ricoeur), is transformed by a view of the future (teleology).

This shift has deep philosophical roots. Beginning with Brentano (1874, 1995),[4] who theorized "intentionality" and was the fountainhead of what became phenomenological philosophy—humans are oriented toward a telos. Husserl developed Brentano's ideas, which Frank Summers (2003) succinctly sketches:

> As first established by Husserl [1904] in his lectures on internal time consciousness, and later elaborated by Heidegger [1926] and Schutz [1932], temporality, the experience of time, does not follow the linear model of objective time as past-present-future. Time is experienced as projected, thrown toward the future, and, as we move toward our future, we encounter the past, and as the past meets us in our project, we live in the present. Each present moment is embedded within some future project, a conception of life's trajectory, and gains its meaning only in that context. (p. 138)

Loewald, having been mentored by Heidegger—in a line descending from Brentano through Husserl—introduced psychoanalysis to this view of time. Time itself is a nonlinear matrix, the past having the full potential of the future embedded within it and orienting the person toward its realization in relational matrices.

CLINICAL NOTES: 1996–1998

In my clinical work with Mandy, I endeavored to hold in mind her latent potentials while also experiencing the blockages in the here-and-now process of treatment. In defining the past that is constitutive of these blockages, I helped Mandy create a narrative (Schaffer, 1992) from which her unique intentionality, or destiny, could become evident. From a Hegelian and Christian perspective, embedded in the unfolding dialectical process of my relationship with Mandy in linear time, is the full potential of *Spirit*. Mandy's existence in time, these narratives stipulate, also transcends time (i.e., is eternal).

Much time is spent processing family relationships, especially with father. We begin to focus on the probability that she had been sexually abused before the day of the murder. This is becoming a repetitive focus. Mandy continues to have little memory of her mother.

We discuss in more depth the little girl who survived the trauma. She writes this description in third person:

> Would you look at her? I can't believe she even comes out in public looking like that. I don't even want to look at her she is so disgusting. Look at her eyes. They don't even match—They look cross-eyed. Her face is all marred—she is so ugly. What makes her think that she can come to our gathering places. She doesn't belong here. She isn't one of us. She'll never fit in. That is so obvious, why can't she see that? She just isn't good enough. I wish she wouldn't look at us. Her eyes freak me out; I can't tell what she is looking at. Sometimes her one eye even closes half way. I'll bet she's some kind of weirdo—like she probably has some kind of mental disorder.

Memories become so painful for Mandy that I encourage her to discuss her experiences in the third person as she had done in her writing. In spite of her distress, Mandy decides to begin to investigate court records, to speak with people who remembered the tragic day. She exhibits a strong motivation to grow, and sees understanding the events of the past as a prerequisite for growth.

We contemplate the possibility of taking a trip together to her home area, and to her mother's grave. We process what this would mean to her. I look for indicators that would signal a negative potential in this. In the transference, she is experiencing me as a mother who is with her in her pain.

In January of 1997 we take a trip to her town. She shows me the home where the murder occurred. We visit neighbors and speak with them about the event and their memories of the family. We visit the cemetery where her mother and unborn brother are buried. She could not find the graves. She is strangely unemotional about this. Her intrusive thoughts significantly increase. We begin to connect her lack of affect with an increase in disturbing thoughts. I note that sadness and anger may be implicated in the torturing thoughts.

Mandy's recurrent dream of teeth falling is beginning to change. Not all of the teeth are falling out of her mouth.

Clinical commentary: Multiple self-states and Trinity

At this point in the treatment, Mandy and I had mutually identified with one another in multiple ways, though Mandy was not cognizant of the extent of my identification. There was a close bond, a working alliance forged by the many intersections of our histories, the shift in her "teeth" dream an exciting confirmation that something was consolidating within Mandy. At a more conscious level some of these fortuitous identifications were: (1) both of us shared a common faith; (2) both of us had attended the same college briefly; (3) I had once substituted as a teacher in the school she had attended as a teenager; (4) she knew at a much more profound level a terror that I also had experienced as a child; (5) her rational capabilities, like mine, had been a prime means of survival; (6) she, like me, had longed for a loving family; (7) we both strove to be excellent at whatever we undertook. Certainly many other strands of identification could have been acknowledged. Mandy and I incarnated into a smoothly functioning mother/daughter dyad, with the additional bonus of my husband offering a role of surrogate father in the premarital counseling. His presence in our office maintained him thereafter in the background role of present and safe father.

In a psychodynamic narrative, Mandy and I spoke in and through our many shifting self-states through which we identified with one another. Frightened child, responsible parent, longing little girl—these and many others were the unseen guests that frequented our treatment dialogue.

Relational perspectives on multiplicity

Relational psychoanalysis, in a departure from the hegemony of modernist thought, has retheorized our intrapsychic or internal worlds. Whereas in times past, analysts would speak of a singular tripartite psychic structure with its system of defense, the internal map has become populated with multiple denizens that we call "self-states" (Bromberg, 1998; Davies & Frawley, 2004; Stern, 2004). Each self-state is constructed through historical occurrences—particularly relationships with significant others—and reflects a specific relational hue, a unique way of being, sometimes a particular chronological age, and becomes prominent for specific tasks. Bromberg (1996) elaborates:

> A human being's ability to live a life with both authenticity and self awareness depends on the presence of an ongoing dialectic between

> separateness and unity of one's self-states, allowing each self to function optimally without foreclosing communication and negotiation between them. When all goes well developmentally, a person is only dimly or momentarily aware of the existence of individual self-states and their respective realities, because each functions as part of a healthy illusion of cohesive personal identity—an overarching cognitive and experiential state felt as "me." Each self-state is a piece of a functional whole, informed by a process of internal negotiation with the realities, values, affects, and perspectives of the others. (p. 514)

Theological perspectives on multiplicity

While Hegel reestablished the doctrine of Trinity to its central role within Christian doctrine, a Trinitarian template for human relationality is a more recent development. By interrogating a narrative that humans are a reflection of their Creator, that is, they are bearers of the *imago dei*, the Trinity is being culled as a source of information about our humanity.

Catherine La Cugna (1991) is an interdisciplinary theologian who describes the Trinity in terms that bear much resemblance to our current psychoanalytic perspectives on multiplicity. Explicating the 4th-century Cappadocian doctrine of *perichoresis*, she writes:

> *[P]erichoresis* expressed the idea that the three divine persons mutually inhere in one another, draw life from one another, "are" what they are by relation to one another. *Perichoresis* means being-in-one-another, permeation without confusion. No person exists by him/herself or is referred to him/herself; this would produce number and therefore division within God. Rather, to be a divine person is to be by nature in relation to other persons. Each divine person is irresistibly drawn to the other, taking his/her existence from the other, containing the other in him/herself, while at the same time pouring self out into the other. ... While there is no blurring of the individuality of each person, there is also no separation. There is only the communion of love in which each person comes to be ... what he/she is, entirely with reference to the other. ... *Perichoresis* provides a dynamic model of persons in communion based on mutuality and interdependence. (pp. 270–271)

Developing and extending La Cugna's thoughts, theologian Pamela Cooper-White (2008), borrowing from the more fluid and generative approaches to the human experience advanced in relational psychoanalysis, utilizes the concept of multiplicity in the theological comprehension of God. She states, "The Trinity is, then, a spacious room—even a *matrix*/womb, in which multiple metaphors can flourish, honoring simultaneously the relationality and the multiplicity of God" (pp. 11–12).

Self-states in Mandy

Relational psychoanalysts now believe multiplicity to be the normative expression of our human experience; dissociation renders unbridgeable the spaces between self-states, providing both a mechanism for survival and prohibiting access to vital, but dreaded, aspects of the self. Mandy's multiple traumas, so overwhelming to her conscious experience, in this relational reading, become relegated to the borderland of her mind, safely beyond conscious awareness. Bromberg (1996) explains:

> The key quality of a highly dissociated personality organization is its defensive dedication to retaining the protection afforded by the separateness of self-states (their discontinuity) and minimizing their potential for simultaneous accessibility to consciousness. (p. 516)

For Mandy, both her actual memories and her associated affects of traumatic experiences were almost entirely dissociated, leaving her a highly functioning but affectively restricted woman. In the dissociated realm of her mind were many self-states. In relation to mother the most dominant self-state was the longing little girl without a caring mother, manifesting concurrently with a depressed mother self-state; there was also an impish little girl with a disapproving mother. There was the bereft, powerless little girl with her dead mother, and the angry child with her absent mother. In relation to her father, there was the special little girl with her fun-loving daddy, the terrified child with the threatening father, the powerless child with the maniacal father, as well as the bad sexual child with the objectifying and abusing father. Finally, one of the most painful self-states was Mandy as an appallingly mutilated girl, having lost an eye, scarred and forever deformed. These self-states manifested primarily through my experience in the transference. I interpreted sparingly, attempting to foster slow, incrementally intensifying affective arousal that would enable Mandy to safely experience those alien parts of herself.

For Mandy to experience recognition, these alienated self-states needed to be experienced and become accessible to her. This would occur through my allowing her experience to resonate within myself, yielding to enactments with these selves, and experientially discovering these selves with Mandy.

Looking at Mandy through the lens of my own experience would help me to understand her, but would also prevent me from seeing her as separate, eventually entangling us both in what Winnicott would call "object-relating," also known in a sociological paradigm as *colonization*. That is, my ability to see her as separate from myself would become hampered as I incarnated through identification with her into the type of therapist that she needed. Reciprocally, outside of my awareness was my expectation that Mandy be the type of patient that I desired.

This lack of ability to critically reflect on the clinical process became evident in several areas. Her seeming disinterest in things pertaining to her mother screamed silently, but prompted by Mandy's distress, I obligingly focused more on the sexual abuse she may have endured, and in that process, foreclosed on her mother by focusing on her father.

In concert with the focus on sexual abuse, I noted a level of compliance that pervaded our sessions. Mandy seemed terrified of any expression of anger, or even of mild annoyance; she was consistently pleasant. I concluded that her fundamentalist upbringing had coalesced with her trauma to render her deadened to spontaneity, fearful of any action that would bring about catastrophe. Aware of the ever-present possibility of enacting the damage of the past, I redoubled my efforts to ensure that Mandy's abusive internal objects and my own rageful internal objects (*My own rageful internal objects ... Yes, Mandy. I do know. Terror. Tears. Aloneness.*) would not succeed in reproducing for her a traumatic experience. Winnicott became even more important at this juncture. The frame must be held very securely: I started promptly; ended promptly; was available, absolutely predictable, and reliable. I needed to be warmly supportive though absolutely nonintrusive. *I would become for Mandy the epitome of the caring mother that she had needed.*

In the midst of the incarnation into this reparative unit, a subtle enactment began to germinate, one related to the fundamentalism of our respective childhoods. We initially were able to identify with the best of her religious aspirations, but we also, as I would later learn, were beginning to replicate an aspect of her faith that had done her harm. This development, I would later come to understand, was at the heart of psychoanalytic enactment.

UNDERSTANDING ENACTMENT

In relational psychoanalysis, *enactment* has risen to prominence as a concept to be understood and utilized in the therapeutic process. Enactment is probably the most crucial clinical construct in relational psychoanalysis. For me, it is what sets the work of relational psychoanalysis apart from all other forms of therapy. But enactment is important to me as well because I believe it provides a contemporary means of understanding Biblical narratives that are replete with examples of enactment from stories and ceremonial rituals of Judaism to the movement of incarnation and crucifixion of the New Testament.

Enactment appears across orientations in the psychological literature. Its usage, however, has variant meanings depending on the orientation. It is often used interchangeably in early literature with *reenactment* and *acting out*, most frequently in group and family therapy. It is also utilized in psychoanalysis and Gestalt work. I will first contextualize the concept of enactment in its historical development in the psychotherapies before describing its specific salience for psychoanalysis.

Enactment in early literature

Family therapy

Salvador Minuchin (1974), structural family therapy theorist, described enactment as the technique by which the therapist asks the family to "dance in his presence." The family is encouraged to play out in the therapeutic setting the patterns that normally occur outside of the office:

> The enactments that are set in motion at the behest of the family therapist are, initially isomorphic to and simulative of the normative family patterns. These simulations can be for purposes of assessment or for making obvious to the family what their normative patterns are, especially when the family therapist directs their attention to them. However, enactment's major use is the alteration of these simulated patterns. (Seeman & Wiener, 1985, p. 145)

Other family therapists such as Virginia Satir, Jay Haley, and Ross Speck regarded role playing as a form of enactment. Sculpting, a particular form of role playing, was used extensively by Satir. Jay Haley (1976) would manipulate physical elements in the office to "enact" stress by initiating a new problem for the family to resolve and then providing for corrective enactments. Thus, to the family therapist, enactment has a dual utility: assessment and correction. It is this intentional contrivance of enactments that distinguishes enactment in other therapies from the psychoanalytic understanding of enactment.

Commenting on the efficacy and widespread utilization of enactment in family therapy, Hamburg (1985) writes:

> Enactment is one of family therapy's most powerful techniques for inducing behavioral and experiential change. The therapist prompts the clients to behave differently in ways they never thought they could. ... The therapist can instigate an enactment in a variety of ways. It can be done directly by specifying the desired outcome and telling the clients to achieve it, as when Minuchin tells an impotent mother to quiet her unruly children and simply enjoins her to "make it happen" [Minuchin & Fishman, 1981]. Or it can be done more indirectly as Whitaker often does it, by manipulating transactions between the clients, or between them and the therapist, so that they are provoked into new behavior almost as an abreaction [Napier & Whitaker, 1978]. (pp. 187–191)

Group therapy

Nicholas (1984), author of *Change in the Context of Group Therapy*, understands group experience as being a

> corrective emotional experience. ... Loosely defined, "the corrective emotional experience" is the reenactment with satisfaction and favorable consequences of an emotional situation which in the past was painful and/or ended unfavorable. Research reported by Yalom (1975) indicates that the corrective emotional experience is a primary curative factor in group therapy. (p. 36)

Nicholas describes healing factors in group therapy as linked to the group transference that emerges. She then states that the corrective "reenactment" taking place in the group process may be accelerated through the use of psychodramatic techniques. Of his technique of psychodrama Moreno (1953) wrote: "There are several forms of enactment, pretending to be in a role, re-enactment or acting out a past scene, living out a problem presently pressing, creating life on the stage or testing oneself for the future" (p. 82).

What distinguishes psychodrama from other group approaches is its phenomenological emphasis. Emanating from its humanistic narrative, the therapeutic outcomes of psychodrama focus on awareness, especially awareness of spontaneously emerging experience. Blatner (1973) refers to psychodrama as "acting-in":

> What emerges is an enactment which turns the impulse into insights. Thus psychodrama facilitates not "acting-out" but what should be called "acting-in": the applications of action methods to the exploration of the psychological aspects of human experience. (p. 2)

Personality theorist George Kelly, developer of Personal Construct Theory, also spoke of the use of enactment in group work. In this approach, however, as contrasted with the phenomenological approach of psychodrama, role playing is part of a "fixed set of sequential activities" (Petrie, 1987, p. 31). Kelly's work clearly distinguishes enactment as an objective role playing, thus narrowing his usage in contrast to the broader definitions of Whitaker and Minuchin.

Additionally, early literature on Gestalt group work is replete with references to enactment. Here, it is also defined very objectively and portrayed as primarily dealing with actual role-playing situations (Petrie, 1987, p. 32).

Psychoanalysis

What appears to crystallize in the psychoanalytic literature is a generic usage of the term *enactment* as representative of all forms of playing out of patterns within therapy. In contrast, references to *reenactment* are primarily specific to historical determinants of behavior (i.e., repetitions of past events or relationships). Such is the case in the early psychoanalytic literature where it was associated with *acting out* either in a negative cast, or positively, in attempts to master unfinished business from the past.

In psychoanalytic literature, acting out has had a pejorative cast. The implication was that acting out is a resistance against remembering and working through, is countertherapeutic, and needs to be transformed into acting in or reenactment within the therapy and the transference. However, an example of the broadened ambiguity of this concept appeared in an article by Tonnesmann (1980):

> As Anna Freud pointed out, in the context of the widening scope of psycho-analytic treatment the concept of *acting out* has undergone a change from denoting resistance against recovering the past to denoting experiential attempts at *re-enactment* or *enactment* in the clinical situation. (p. 24, emphasis added)

Irwin Hoffman (1983), in a prescient acknowledgement of enactment, also interchangeably used the terms. He writes:

> The extent to which the analyst's "objectivity," the tendency which is inclined towards understanding more than *enacting*, the extent to which this tendency will prevail ... is unknown at any given moment not only to the patient but also to the analyst. (p. 413, emphasis added)

Later in the same article he continues: "To think that the analyst will have any special capability in such circumstances to resist neurotic forms of reciprocal *reenactment* would have to be based on an assumption that his mental health is vastly superior to that of the patient" (p. 417).

In referring to similar therapy configurations which others label as reenactment, McLaughlin (1987), in "The Play of Transference: Some Reflections on Enactment in the Psychoanalytic Situation," defines couch behaviors and postures as enactments. While linking the behaviors to the past, he labels them not as reenactments but as enactments.

Stolorow, Brandchaft, and Atwood (1987) reveal disagreement on the use of *enactment*. One can see the beginnings of a shift in the use of the term that they are helping to inaugurate:

> To any such misattunement to Martin's subjective state and to the legitimacy of his underlying motivation, Martin reacted with rage or with an intensification of his staying-away behavior, sometimes accompanied by other *enactments* designed to restore a sense of distinctness. ... Similar *enactments* are frequently regarded by analysts as *acting-out*,

supposedly arising from fears of commitment to the analytic process. (p. 56)

Current thinking on enactment in psychoanalysis

"The analyst who is perhaps most responsible for the introduction and acceptance of the [current use of the] term enactment within the mainstream psychoanalytic community is Theodore Jacobs. Following Jacob's (1986) seminal article, the technical term enactment became a central notion in the reconceptualization of Freudian clinical theory," Aron (1996, p. 198) observes. From its confused beginning, enactment has become a cardinal construct in relational thought and, according to Aron, most often refers to a "discrete and unique" relational transaction between patient and analyst that leads to "mutual and bidirectional, unconscious influence" (Aron, 2003, p. 627).

Enactment and neuroscience

Neuroscience has elucidated the process of enactment even further, through its findings on neural networking. These findings were presaged as far back as David Hume, who championed the "law of association of ideas." In his *Treatise of Human Nature*, Hume (1739) observed

> that our minds are mirrors to one another: They reflect one another's passions, sentiments, and opinions. This "sympathy" or "propensity we have to sympathize with others, to receive by communication [the] inclinations and sentiments [of others], however different from, or even contrary to our own," he held to be the chief source of moral distinctions. (Decety & Chaminade, 2003, p. 578)

Of even greater import to psychoanalysts is the work of Sigmund Freud, whose research in the *Project for a Scientific Psychology* anticipated future revelations about the activity of neurons. In Jones's (1955) biography, he cites Freud's lecture delivered around 1884 entitled, "The structure of the elements of the nervous system," which referred to an anatomical structure he called a "nerve-net" as of "very great importance," and predated Waldeyer's "neurone" theory of 1891 (Freud, 1897, p. 231fn).

Studying under William James at Harvard and Cattell at Columbia, Thorndike (1911) presciently sketches the theme of neuroplasticity. He writes:

> The chief life processes of a neurone concerned in learning [are] reception and conduction of the nerve impulse, and modifiability or change of connections. The connections formed between situation and response are represented by connections between neurones and neurones ... across their synapses. (Lecas, 2006, p. 392)

Experimental psychology picked up Thorndike's theme during the period between the 1930s and the 1960s and studied the human subject as a neural automaton during the heyday of behaviorism. However, according to Lecas (2006):

> Today, it is an old, anti-mentalist doctrine, quite disregarded. For example in his book *Descarte's Error*, Damasio invoked the rise of cognitive psychology as a salutary revolution, following the long night of behaviorism which emphasized the stimulus-response couple. (p. 386)

Lecas continues: "Alternatively, it may be suggested that the 'cognitive revolution' was not so abrupt and that much of the 'old' behavioristic era survives in the 'new' cognitive psychology, now associated with the neuroscience and cognitive sciences. In other words, there is more continuity than discontinuity" (pp. 386–387).

Lecas' critique both chronicles evidence of forerunners of the neuroscientific findings that validate enactment, and reveals the less salubrious trend toward behavioral reductionism. Two theorists of the era of behaviorism are examples of this. Edwin Guthrie's (1952) theory of contiguity stipulated that "a combination of stimuli which has accompanied a movement will on its recurrence tend to be followed by that movement" (p. 23). This phrase captured many associative learning phenomena, including learning without reinforcement and learning from a single experience. If one modernized the phrase to read, "A combination of stimuli which has accompanied *a significant neural activity* will on its recurrence tend to be followed by that *neural activity*," one can see that Guthrie's phrase anticipated modern neuroscience. Amplifying Guthrie's approach, Hebb (1949) came even closer to modern perspectives when he asserted what could be summarized as "cells that fire together, wire together."

The study of operations of the mind shifted from behavior to learning and memory in the decades to come, with the cognitive sciences coming to full bloom in the discipline of neuroscience. Deeply couched within neuroscience is the ever-present enticing error of the early days of behaviorism and its mechanistic, reductionistic approach that belies roots in Descarte's machine animal. Lecas (2006) alleges that "the Neurosciences of 'learning and memory' [were] built up with the substitutive-reductionist approach taken by behaviorists" (p. 396). He continues,

> This new SR reductionism could be sketched as a stimulus-response flowchart composed of a succession of "black boxes" corresponding to the traditional mental functions: perception, memory, decision, motor response. Such a model of mind, inspired by the computer metaphor (a very simplified computer) resembled a machine blueprint. As roughly

> put by Varela: "*computers offer a mechanical model of thought*" [*Invitation aux Sciences Cognitives*, 1989, p. 39]. (p. 396)

The cross-disciplinary work being advanced between neuroscience and psychoanalysis is path-breaking in that the potentially mechanistic models of neuroscience are moderated by a psychoanalysis with its never fully definable mystery of the human subject. While neuroscientific mapping of empathy, dissociation, dreaming, and so on will undoubtedly be invaluable, psychoanalysis will continue to provide the much-needed emphasis on individuality and mystery of the human being, which is not reducible to the black box of empirical data.

This caveat notwithstanding, neuroscience, validating Hume's centuries-old, two-person perspective with the discovery of mirror neurons, has aided psychoanalysis in scientifically validating the process of enactment. "Mirror neurons are premotor neurons that fire both when an action is executed and when it is observed being performed by someone else" (Gallese, 2009, p. 520). Thus, in the process of psychotherapy, though we have as of yet not plumbed the implications of this research, we know that minute behaviors on the part of one subject are observed, registered, and replicated with the other through the process of mirroring. A strong emphasis on visual cues predominates in the literature, beginning with the very first moments of life. Ironically, such an emphasis on visual cues provides for me a pivotal bridge to the writings of Paul Ricoeur, whose work on the evocative power of "symbol" led him to speculate that it is the apperception of "symbol" that gives rise to thought and by extension to feelings. Ricoeur's work provides a bridge as well between the myths and symbols of culture, and the operations of the mind. Meissner (2009) has called our attention to the import of visual cues:

> Reviewing studies on the facial communication of emotion, Lundquist and Ohman (2005) and de Gelder (2005) suggest that the facial expression of emotion elicits corresponding automatic mirror-image neuromuscular facial reactions (so-called "embodiment" or embodied simulation) in observers—happy faces activate a happy display, angry faces an angry display. Even when facial expressions were masked by a neutral masking stimulus, the subjects' facial muscles reacted with the corresponding emotion—and all of this unconsciously. (p. 108)

Rendering the complexity of our neurological mirroring system even more awe-inspiring, animal studies have confirmed the following:

> A subset of these mirror neurons also respond when the final part of an action, crucial in triggering the response in full vision, is hidden, and can therefore only be inferred (Umilta et al., 2001). This finding is compatible with the idea that we understand actions when we map the

> visual representation of the observed action onto our motor representations of the same action [for a recent review see Rizzolatti, Fogassi, & Gallese, 2001]. (Decety & Chaminade, 2003, p. 582)

I will suggest that all behavior might involve an enactment of neurally encoded schemas. How then can we differentiate between enactment as a therapeutic construct and its more universal neurological ubiquity? Ginot (2009), in a well-documented interdisciplinary study between neuroscience and psychoanalysis, offers this perspective:

> A growing body of clinical work and neuroscientific research has demonstrated that what enactments communicate in such gripping and indirect ways are implicit, neurally encoded affective and relational patterns. Patterns formed before verbal memory was fully developed and those defensively dissociated later on by an emotionally overwhelmed sense of self (Bromberg, 1998, 2003, 2006; Bucci, 2007a, 2007b; Mancia, 2006; Pally, 2006; Stern, 2004). (p. 292)

The right hemisphere of the brain is implicated in the storage of highly charged memories, while the left brain is more focused on verbal comprehension and thus initially lags developmentally behind the right. "Wittling and Roschmann (1993), for example, found that in subjects viewing emotional films the right hemisphere indicated stronger affective reactions. Similarly, lateral visual presentations of facial emotional expression coupled with painful stimuli were harder to extinguish in the right hemisphere than in the left (Grawe, 2007)" (Ginot, 2009, p. 293).

It is the affective loading of encoded material that triggers dissociation. This affectively-loaded material is, however, amenable to reintegration through a relational approach that allows the affects to emerge via enactment in the therapeutic milieu. There, the formerly dissociated thoughts and feelings come to have meaning and eventually are reintegrated by the left brain.

> What gets to be empathically known through enactments, then, are relational patterns and self-representations that cannot become recognized through verbal interchanges alone. Indeed, noting the inevitable relational impasses characterizing transference-countertransference interactions, Bromberg sees enactments as nonconscious messages to the analyst to get engaged directly and emotionally with unsymbolized self-states that cannot be otherwise expressed. (Ginot, 2009, p. 293)

Concluding remarks on enactment

I have been interested in enactment since the 1980s when I was trained as a psychodramatist concurrent with my doctoral studies. My dissertation

(M. Hoffman, 1989) focused on enactment and its expression across psychotherapeutic orientations. The definition of enactment that I chose at that time still has applicability. I defined *enactment* as: "The playing-out in therapy of patterns which occur in a person's life which may be either spontaneous or induced."

In psychoanalysis, spontaneous enactments occur during the commingling of dissociated experience (or experience through projective identification) in the patient/analyst intersubjective matrix. What I find important to emphasize is that the working through and meaning-making for the left brain is no less an enactment; it is simply a therapeutic enactment. The affect-initiated behavior, previously carried forward out of awareness, is now mentalized through the mutual processing of the therapist and patient, who function in a fashion akin to Bion's metabolizing mother and infant in a healing, therapeutic enactment. This broadened definition of enactment permits psychoanalysis to then harmonize its theories to the larger body of psychological literature.

For me, there is no more powerful means of producing understanding and change than working in this fashion. The exclusive privileging of left hemisphere, verbal understanding, and the unwitting reliance on mechanistic views of our patients have fallen short. Consequently, many who feel defective and hopeless have been recipients of treatments that target a part of the brain that does not carry the endowment of the tragedy, treatments that often exclude variables not fully reducible to the laboratory such as love and hope.

In conclusion, I believe that an understanding of Judaic and Christian theology may be benefitted by viewing its stories through the lens of enactment such as this study is attempting to do. What has appeared as mystical and archaic may thus be rendered accessible to the 21st-century mind.

CLINICAL NOTES: 1998–2000

Mandy has not had a home of her own since she was 6 years of age, when the murders occurred. She also feels undeserving of having one. During the time of living in her grandparents' home, she had always felt uncomfortable with her achievements, for they were followed by envious treatment from her aunts. We process what it would feel like to finally have a home.

The teeth dreams have radically changed. Mandy's teeth no longer fall out of her mouth.

Accompanying this change, Mandy expresses a desire to progress in her career. She begins to apply for teaching positions, and after several tries begins teaching at a local college. She begins work on her master's degree as well.

Mandy has been talking more about her sorrow over her father. We have been processing this for a while. She relates: "I'm so torn because that same man that I'm angry at is someone I loved very much (tearful). I lost everything in one day: father, mother, home, my eye, security. That same man that I loved is also the one who took everything away from me." We begin to discuss the possibility of more intensive therapy. What follows is a session from the end of this period.

Mandy began the session by discussing a car accident that involved a relative of hers. Every bone in his face was crushed. She expressed great compassion and concern. She was concerned that he was so badly mangled that he would never look normal again. She went on to talk about K's father, who had surgery that left a large scar. She then talked about a little girl who lost her arm, but is now doing OK.

MANDY: I can feel empathy for people in pain more than most people. Now Brenda gets on the Internet and interrupts me, but I can feel compassion for her. When I try to ask how she is, she just gets me to say more and doesn't really connect with me about herself. I feel so sorry for her—she's made so many unwise choices.

MARIE: (Starting hesitantly) I'm not sure if I should say this or not. As you were talking about feeling such compassion for all these people, I was feeling that same kind of compassion for you because in many ways you were that mangled, traumatized little girl. But I also felt the same difficulty that you felt with Brenda. "How do I reach you and connect with you?"

MANDY: I'm unresponsive too!

MARIE: No! You're terrified.

MANDY: (Tearing up) I just wonder what the Bible says about caring for family.... What are our responsibilities?

MARIE: While I could answer that, I am more interested in understanding why you need to refocus on caring for others. It's like I am gazing at you, and you are gazing out the window.

MANDY: (Tearful) It's selfish to focus on yourself. So many times when I was little, I was very excited about something I accomplished. I was belittled and made to feel that I was really only a guest in my home and that I was not a child like my aunts were. It is very difficult to celebrate myself.

MARIE: Is it OK for me to celebrate you?

MANDY: (Tearful) You and my grandmother are two people who have celebrated me most in my life. I know how much you celebrate me. It's just so hard to focus on myself.

MARIE: Is it wrong for an infant to gaze into her mother's eyes and be totally preoccupied with her mother, and for a mother to be totally preoccupied with her child?

MANDY: No ... That's the way it should be.

MARIE: It seems to me that at some level when you lost the gaze of your parents, all you could do was consider it a total loss and gaze at others. You couldn't desire or experience being the one gazed at.

MANDY: (Choking up) It's so hard to lose your parents. I'm so afraid that if you gaze at me you'll see how mangled I am and not like me.

MARIE: I haven't gone anywhere. (On a hunch) How long have we been working?

MANDY: Five to six years.

MARIE: I've known you for almost as many years as your parents had known you. I suspect that this year will hold a lot of deeper connection. We will be passing a milestone.

MANDY: (Shocked) I dated my husband for six years before marrying him as well. Maybe I have to wait that long before realizing someone is not going to go away.

MARIE: (Both gazing at each other with a look of expectancy) These years "in utero" have produced a lot of growth. You've been waiting to exhale....

MANDY: (Taking a deep breath, she smiles and exhales) I never thought of where I am in the years I have been working with you. What happened to me just took away any sense of my identity, and like I've said before, it gave me a sense of "floating in the ocean."

MARIE: Well, I guess I got to get some ropes.

MANDY: And pull me in!

ENDNOTES

1. It is beyond the scope of this volume to elucidate the arguments for or against theism. However, questions may emerge pertaining to human origins. "If we are simply 'fancy animals' ... which have survived based on fitness in the Darwinian model, then the means of our evolution is the conquest and elimination of that which is inferior. This Darwinian/Nietzschean model offers no intrinsic basis for upward evolution apart from what amounts ultimately to brute narcissism. Nor does it offer a basis for virtue or love. Consequently, it privileges 'autonomy' ... over surrender (Ghent, 1990), for surrender based on faith and trust, is the antithesis of conquest" (M. Hoffman, 2006, pp. 83–84).
2. The paragraph noted is extrapolated from the text of Isaiah 61:1–4 (NIV). This text reads: The Spirit of the Sovereign LORD is on me, because the LORD has anointed me to preach good news to the poor. He has sent me to bind up the brokenhearted, to proclaim freedom for the captives and release from darkness for the prisoners. To proclaim the year of the LORD's favor and the day of vengeance of our God, to comfort all who mourn, and provide for those who grieve in Zion—To bestow on them a crown of beauty instead of ashes, the oil of gladness instead of mourning, and a garment of praise instead of a spirit of

despair. They will be called oaks of righteousness, a planting of the LORD for the display of his splendor. They will rebuild the ancient ruins and restore the places long devastated; they will renew the ruined cities that have been devastated for generations.

3. By negation, eradication of the damage is not meant. Future chapters will explain how negation includes but goes beyond what is negated.
4. Brentano's influence on Freud will be addressed in the next section on historical perspectives.

Chapter 4

Identifying the Christian narrative in early psychoanalysis

Historical perspectives

FREUD AND CHRISTIANITY

A robust dialogue with religion had been part of academic discourse for centuries; psychoanalysis—propelled by Freud's Enlightenment thinking—disidentified with religion, seeing it as a vestige of human primitivity. For a brief period during his university years, however, Freud did contemplate the viability of theism. This contemplation would have enormous consequences for the future of psychoanalysis.

During the years 1874 to 1876, Freud, a student at the University of Vienna, elected to take five courses in philosophy (his only nonmedical courses) with a charismatic professor named Franz Brentano (Vitz, 1988).[1] Brentano's other memorable pupils included Edmund Husserl, Franz Kafka, Christian von Ehrenfels, and Carl Stumpf.

As an empiricist, Brentano (1987) both applauded the logical positivism of his day and retained a place for teleology, holding that science and religion may beneficially coexist. In the introduction to his collected lectures, *On the Existence of God* (1987), he avers:

> The knowledge of the universal principal [God] sheds its light upon all things, upon what is, what was, and what will be. The great cosmological questions—whether the world is a unity or a plurality, whether it will ultimately end or continue forever, whether its course is more toward good or evil—they are all to be resolved only in the light of the question of God's existence. (p. 12)

One of Brentano's far-reaching contributions to philosophy was the notion of "intentionality," a construct that suggests that all mental phenomena are intentional, that is, they are meaningful. Furthermore, in presciently relational terms, he asserted that mental phenomena are always object oriented: They are to be understood relationally. Interweaving the philosophical and spiritual, Brentano would add that the ultimate relationship is with the Creator. Therefore, the most sublime object orientation is the human response to a God who created in love. Brentano (1980), in agreement with Anselm, deemed "the love of God to be our highest [human] faculty" (pp. 18–19).

Reflecting on Brentano, who parlayed comfortably in both science and philosophy while feeling at home with the spiritual, Freud, in a letter to Silberstein remarks:

> I, the godless medical man and empiricist, am attending two courses in philosophy. ... One of the courses—listen and marvel!—deals with the existence of God, and Prof. Brentano, who gives the lectures, is a splendid man, a scholar and philosopher.... (Freud & Silberstein, 1990, pp. 70–71)

On March 7, 1875, Freud adds:

> The two of us (Paneth and I) have established closer contact with him; we sent him a letter containing some objections and he invited us to his home, refuted them, and seemed to take some interest in us. ... When you and I meet, I shall tell you more about this remarkable man (a believer, a teleologist(!) and a Darwinian and a damned clever fellow, a genius in fact), who is in many respects, an ideal human being. For now, just the news that under Brentano's fruitful influence I have arrived at the decision to take my PhD in philosophy and zoology; further negotiations about my admission to the philosophical faculty either next term or next year are in progress. (p. 95)

Freud ultimately rejected both Brentano's appreciation of philosophy and his teleological perspective, which derived from his belief in a sublime orientation to God (Gay, 1987; Vitz, 1988). He did appropriate, however, Brentano's conceptualizations regarding intentionality (Wakefield, 1992). Freud, reclothing intentionality in the garb of Helmholtz and Brucke (Ricoeur, 1970; J. Smith, 1976), grounded his development of that theory in an antitheistic, logical positivism that emulated Comte. Wolf (1978) speaking with clairvoyant-like foresight, predicted a return to Brentano's phenomenological trajectory—a return that I will discuss later. In a review of Smith's *Psychiatry and the Humanities, Volume I* (1976), Wolf observes:

> Behind Husserl looms the much neglected Brentano who had also been Freud's teacher. Brentano was the discoverer of intentionality of consciousness. It is instructive to follow how, in contrast to Freud who hid intentionality behind a naturalist science face, the phenomenologists made it the exclusive center of their philosophical and psychological approaches. The time seems ripe now for a new integration. (p. 316)

I believe that shortly after his courses with Brentano, Freud with finality put to rest any latent inclinations toward theistic belief, and accorded full allegiance to the god of science, a choice that Otto Rank later characterized as "man's newest, weakest and most self-defeating deception thus far" (Seif, 1980, p. 59).

PSYCHOANALYSTS INFLUENCED BY THE CHRISTIAN NARRATIVE

In the biographical material to follow, I will identify analysts whose histories suggest influence by the Christian narrative. These analysts are largely unrecognized as having affinity with the Christian narrative that is embedded in their theory and practice. Other noteworthy psychoanalysts who were not observant Christians nonetheless left imprints of their early Christian training in the corpus of their work. Beginning with Oskar Pfister and ending arbitrarily in the mid-1900s, I will make a sweeping review of such analysts (primarily in English-speaking countries). My choices are representative, for an exhaustive list would be a book in itself.

For the sake of organization, I will group analysts in two categories: *adapters* and *reactors*. Adapters are analysts who self-identified as Christians in the course of their lives and whose works reflect either explicitly or implicitly that narrative. Reactors are analysts who were significantly impacted by Christianity through upbringing or conversion, but later repudiated it, and the evidence in their theories belies their reactivity.

Switzerland: Oskar Pfister, adapter

"In his clerical garb and with the manners and behavior of a pastor," reminisced Anna Freud about Oskar Pfister, "[he] was like a visitor from another planet" (Meng & Freud, 1963, p. 11). "His human warmth and enthusiasm, his capacity for taking a lively part in the minor events of the day, enchanted the children of the [Freud] household, and made him at all times a most welcome guest, a uniquely human figure in his way" (p. 11). Born in Zurich in 1873, Pfister first met Freud in 1909, beginning a 30-year friendship lasting until Freud's death, during which time Pfister published prolifically. Pfister's thought differed radically from Freud's views on religion, though he saw Freud as fundamentally striving for their shared ethic of love. Pfister observed:

> It is not the religious creed that is the true criterion for a Christian; in John 13:35 another is given. "By this love you have for one another, everyone will know that you are my disciples." At the risk of being mocked by loose tongues, I dare to assert again that Freud, in the

light of these words, with his view of life, and his life's work has pre-eminence over many a certified church-Christian who considers him a heathen, as he does himself. (Roazen, 1993, p. 578)

Ellenberger (1970)[2] notes that Pfister played a dominant role in vitalizing the Swiss Psychoanalytic Society, describing him as a "a pugnacious personality and prolific writer who published a flow of books and articles on the application of psychoanalysis to the education of normal and abnormal children, to the cure of souls (*Seelsorge*), and problems of art and philosophy" (pp. 845–846). His focus on child psychiatry and pedagogy impacted Jean Piaget, who attended seminars with him in 1918–1919 (Schepeler, 1993).

Pfister's influence burgeoned beyond Switzerland as he became an "apostle of Freud" (W. Hoffer, 1958, p. 616), enriching the nascent psychoanalysis with articles and books on therapeutic technique, pedagogy, pastoral counseling, capitalism, infantile sexuality, lecturing as far as Scandinavia, and organizing a psychoanalytic contingent there. In 1913 he wrote a comprehensive textbook on psychoanalysis (*Die Psychoanalytische Methode/The Psychoanalytic Method*; Pfister, 1917), to which Freud wrote a preface and which was translated into several languages. It is therefore no surprise that the English translation of this text was undoubtedly D. W. Winnicott's introduction to psychoanalysis (Rodman, 2003, p, 387).

England: D. W. Winnicott, adapter

Perhaps no other analyst has been as positively influential as Winnicott with regard to the place of religion in individuals and in culture, and for this reason I will devote more space in Chapter 7 to his work. According to Goldman (1993), Winnicott experienced a "lingering religiosity" (p. 115) that was deeply rooted in his Wesleyan, Protestant upbringing and was reflected in his singing and playing Wesleyan church music to the end of his life (Kahr, 1996, p. 105).

This "lingering religiosity" guided Winnicott to creatively incorporate religious constructs into his writings. The capacity for creativity was of deep interest to Winnicott, whose writings on transitional space linked it to the realm of spiritual experience, a realm with which he was very familiar (Winnicott, 1963b, p. 184). In striking similarity to Winnicott's formative Wesleyan religious narrative, his writings and clinical practices reflect a belief in human goodness. "In his poised, dignified, idiosyncratic, and playful manner [Winnicott] was, fundamentally, what could be called a believer in 'grace'" (Goldman, 1993, p. 28), a grace reflected in his abiding hopefulness, "the fuel by which life may advance" (Rodman, 2003, p. 244).[3]

England: Hugh Crichton-Miller, adapter

Hugh Crichton-Miller, Scottish psychiatrist, founded the Tavistock Clinic in 1920 (Dicks, 1970, p. 14). The son of a Scottish Protestant minister (Miller, 2008), Crichton-Miller's vision for Tavistock was originally as a place where the traumatic effects of "shell-shock" could be studied and remedied, and eventually became a place where suffering outpatients unable to afford private fees could receive psychoanalytic treatment (Dicks, 1970, p. 1). Crichton-Miller embraced a Christian narrative that did not ignore the ills of society, a perspective that many times stood in contrast to observable Christian practice in England of that era (Richards, 2000). In the 1920s he published three works: *The New Psychology and the Teacher* (1922), *The New Psychology and the Parent* (1923), *and The New Psychology and the Preacher* (1924). His Christian perspective is evident in an excerpt from this last work: "When one contemplates the discrepancies between current Christian practice on the one hand and the gospel of the Cross on the other, it is easy to see why the psychologist attacks the former in preference to the latter (Crichton-Miller, 1924, pp. 39–40). Crichton-Miller saw psychoanalysis as a means of "revitalizing" Christianity (p. 65), and thus revitalizing culture. Perhaps most notably, Crichton-Miller endorsed the theme of love, which was beginning to be faintly heard in British psychoanalysis. He writes: "Christianity introduces a new principle—that of love. Society is therefore challenged to substitute for the power principle of biology, the love principle of the gospels" (pp. 78–79). Crichton-Miller drew to Tavistock many more who would share his perspectives on love and spirituality and practice them in a manner that would not negate the sensibilities of those who sought help.

England: John Rickman, adapter

John Rickman was born into a Quaker family in Surrey, England. After receiving his medical degree in 1916 and serving with the *Friends War Victims Relief Unit* in Russia,[4] he returned to England to work at Fulborn Mental Hospital, near Cambridge. In 1920 he went to Vienna to have an analysis with Freud (Simmonds, 2006, p. 132). He returned that year to England and at Freud's recommendation became an associate member of the newly formed British Psychoanalytic Society. In 1928, Rickman journeyed to Budapest to have an analysis with Sándor Ferenczi (Rickman, 2003). Rickman is considered, along with several others—Ella Sharpe, Marjorie Brierley,[5] and Sylvia Payne (Arden, 1987, p. 237)—to have been at the nucleus of the evolution of the Independent Group in the British Psychoanalytic Society, and was analyst to Wilfred Bion, Masud Khan, and Samuel Beckett, among others.

Rickman presented a paper entitled *Need for a Belief in God* to the 15th International Psycho-Analytical Congress in 1938; but it was not published until 1957, and even then was placed in the appendix of his selected works (Simmonds, 2006, p. 132). In the paper, Rickman presented a study of Quaker beliefs, explaining "The Inner Light"—an "indwelling of God in man" as that which "lifts him above the morass of loneliness and lovelessness, of misery and degradation into which he would otherwise sink ..." He then wryly queries:

> Having reached this point, our investigations can take two directions, either we may consider the Inner Light as a symbol for the Divine penis or semen, or we may consider the influence it exerts on the Quaker outlook on the world. The latter has the merit of showing it in action. (Rickman, 1957, p. 385)

England: Wilfred Bion, adapter

Wilfred Bion was born in 1897 in the Punjab region of India into a very religious family whose motto emblazoned upon their crest read *Nisi dominus frustra*, "Without God there is no purpose" (Bléandonu, 1994, p. 7). "A verse from Psalm 127 underscores the theme: 'Except the Lord build the house, they labour in vain that build it; except the Lord keep the city, the watchman waketh but in vain'" (p. 7). Bion's autobiographical work *The Long Weekend* (1982) traced his paternal ancestry to Protestant Huguenots who emigrated from France to England, and missionary fervor dotted his family's history. Bion's parents, however, were not in the employ of a religious organization: His father was a civil engineer, his mother a homemaker. Religious education and discipline were the family standard. Wilfred imbibed the teachings to the extent that "Arf Arfer," that is, "Our Father," "began to turn up, unbidden, in his thoughts, daydreams and nightmares" (p. 12).

At 8 years of age, in keeping with the customs of middle- and upper-class families, Wilfred was sent to the Christian Bishop's Stortford College prep school in England. Bion refers to this time as "ghastly" and "gloomy" (Bléandonu, 1994, p. 15). Prayers, attendance at church services, proper walks, and chapel attendance were all compulsory. Bion wavered between fear of unknown spiritual forces and an absolute detesting of religion.

Graduating from school, Bion joined the war effort in 1916 as a tank commander in France. Attachments were difficult there, but Bion became close to Quainton, "a lively and brilliant man, who was a Quaker, [and who] enabled him to maintain a difficult relationship with God" (Bléandonu, 1994, p. 29). Bion regularly went with him to chapel services, but this friendship was cut short by Quainton's going on leave and never returning.

The year 1919 found Bion at Oxford University. There, Grotstein (1981) notes, he "was much influenced by conversations with the philosopher [A] H. J. Paton" (p. 523). Philosopher H. J. Paton was a Christian of note at Oxford, and a later Gifford Lecturer in the years 1949–1950. In those lectures he warned of the dangers of logical positivism, the necessity of an acceptance of science and spirituality through a "binocular" vision of life, and discussed the pathways to understanding practiced by the mystics. His earlier conversations with Bion most likely touched on these topics, including his ideas about mysticism.

Bion graduated, returned to Bishop's Stortford College to teach, and then returned to his studies, this time to begin medical training for the purpose of becoming a psychoanalyst. In 1930, Bion received his medical and surgical credentials. During his training, he had made the acquaintance of Dr. J. A. Hadfield, a supporter of psychoanalysis and the writer of the preface to Ian Suttie's book, *The Origins of Love and Hate* (1935). As a result, Bion joined the staff of the Tavistock Clinic, where Hadfield was held in high esteem.

While at the Tavistock, Bion was drawn to John Rickman, a Quaker who demonstrated the "moral qualities characteristic of this community: altruism, social responsibility, organizational responsibility, and intellectual openness" (Bléandonu, 1994, p. 46). Bion began a training analysis with Rickman in 1937. In 1938, Rickman gave a paper at the International Psycho-Analytic Congress entitled, "The need for belief in God" (p. 47), Bion feeling quite comfortable with Rickman's shared religious background. This analysis was productive for Bion but only lasted two years due to Rickman's death. Bion would have another analysis with Melanie Klein, which would extend from 1946–1952. During this time Bion would begin his prolific writing career.

His writing career would focus on areas untouched by most other analysts. Grotstein (1997) observes: "Bion incurred the criticism of his colleagues by daring to investigate faith, spirituality, religion, mysticism, metaphysics, and fetal mental life" (no page number). Bion's early structured religion, however, would recede in favor of a mystical approach to spirituality, which infused his life's work. Eigen (1998) describes Bion's mysticism, referring to Bion's symbol for the Eternal Infinite—"O":

> Bion uses many images and expressions from religious and mystical life to portray psychoanalytic processes. But he does more. He filters mysticism through psychoanalysis and psychoanalysis through mysticism. Psychoanalysis may be a special discipline imposed on life, but it is worse than nothing if it does not express and further life. Psychoanalysis is "a stripe on the tiger," a part of larger reality, O, that remains unknown, perhaps unknowable. Yet unknowable O is our

> home. We may not *know* O, we can only be O. We *are* O, parts of O. Even if we try to get outside O, there is nowhere outside to get. We *are* something we can't *know*. (pp. 16–17)

Though Bion's trajectory veered far from orthodox Christianity, he nonetheless retained memories of its stories, using them freely in his writings. In *Attention and Interpretation: A Scientific Approach to Insight in Psycho-Analysis and Groups* (1970), he offers this commentary on Jesus:

> The conflict between the mystic and his group is exhibited in its most exaggerated, and therefore most easily studied form, in the account of Jesus and his relationship with the group. He himself claimed, in a manner typical of many mystics, that his teachings were in conformity with the existing Establishment: "Think not that I am come to destroy the law or the prophets: I am not come to destroy but to fulfill" [Matthew 5:17, AV]. (p. 111)

Concurrent with Bion's interest in mysticism was his theorizing about groups. For Bion, these were not two separate universes, for internal and external, the individual and the group all remained psychically interconnected. His work on groups demonstrated that psychotic processes not only function within the individual, but function in a group as a whole, and that madness and the mystical are linked.

Wilfred Bion died on November 8, 1979. In a memorial tribute, Donald Meltzer recapitulates the major achievements of Bion's life. He recounts a point toward the end of his life when his mathematical approaches lost their creative energy. He writes:

> This brought him to a clear recognition of the similarity between psychoanalytical history and theological history, where the qualities of the clergy and the organization of the Church could be seen to have strangled or crushed the creative power of the theological ideas. He had only to return to his own ideas in *Experiences in Groups* to shift from a mathematical vertex and mode of exposition to a theological one in order to describe his social and internal experiences as a thinker who had been found by new ideas. (1981, p. 12)

England: Michael Balint, adapter

Michael Balint[6] was born Mihály Maurice Bergsmann on December 3, 1896, as the older of two children to an Orthodox Jewish Budapest physician and his wife. He studied medicine at Semmelweiss University in Budapest, where he also earned qualifications in neuropsychiatry, philosophy, chemistry, physics, and biology. In 1914 his studies were interrupted: He was drafted to serve the war effort as a physician in the military on the Russian front and later in Italy (Balint, 1968; Lakasing, 2005; Moreau-Ricaud, 2002). He graduated in 1920 with an M.D. from Budapest University (Sutherland, 1971).

Upon his return to Budapest, he met Alice Székely-Kovacs and they married. Alice introduced Michael to Freud's writings early in their courtship, and Michael was already attending Ferenczi's lectures in 1919. During these years, Michael changed his name from Bergsmann to Balint against his father's will and also converted to the Unitarian church. His "father even ceased all relationship with Michael and his newly founded family because he could not forgive him his conversion to the Unitarian church" (Moreau-Ricaud, 2002). The couple moved to Berlin in 1920, where Michael split his time between a biochemistry laboratory and the Berlin Institute of Psychoanalysis. Both Alice and Michael were in analysis with Hans Sachs. Dissatisfied with their analyses, they returned to Budapest in 1924, where they completed analyses with Ferenczi (Haynal, 1988; Moreau-Ricaud, 2002).

The Balints were active in the Hungarian Psychoanalytic Association and made significant contributions, but left Hungary in January 1939 in the face of growing anti-Semitism. Michael and Alice and their son John settled in Manchester, England, and sadly, Alice died in July of that same year from a ruptured aortic aneurysm. A second tragedy was his parents' suicides in 1945 in the face of their imminent arrest by the Nazis (Stewart et al., 1996). In 1945 Balint also moved to London and established a psychoanalytic practice, shortly thereafter joining the Tavistock Clinic (Lakasing, 2005). There he became very close friends with John Rickman, whom he classified as "of the really highly valuable group of people who represented a standard of civilization, of gentlemanliness, which has gone out of society" (Swerdloff, 2002, p. 411).

Michael would distinguish himself as a major contributor to psychoanalytic thought in the object relations tradition. His progressively developing ideas, beginning with his 1924 paper in Budapest, culminated in his book, *The Basic Fault* (1968). He married Enid Albu-Eicholtz, also a psychoanalyst, in the 1950s, and they were frequent partners in training and teaching of psychoanalysis. In 1968 Michael was elected president of the British Psychoanalytic Society. Michael died at age 74 on December 31, 1970, in London.

Little is known of Michael's disposition toward religious faith. However, André Haynal seems to believe that Balint's conversion was personal and motivated by more than a desire to assimilate into Christian culture (personal communication, July, 2009). An unpublished exception to the paucity of written validation of his religious sensibilities is found in his personal papers archived at the Department of Psychiatry at the University of Geneva.[7] Contained in the archives are approximately 25 library withdrawal tickets from the John Ryland's Library in Manchester, England, the city of residence for Balint. All of the tickets bear the titles of now out-of-print Biblical/theological works including *Peter, Prince of the Apostles*

(1927) by F. J. Foakes Jackson; *The Life of Saint Paul* (1927) by F. J. Foakes Jackson; *The Servants of Jahweh* by A. S. Peake (1931); *The Apocrypha* by Rhodes James Montague (1921); and *Liturgy and Worship* by Clarke-Harris (1932). All of these circulation tickets bear the year 1941 and are contained in an envelope in the archive labeled "St. Paul Religion." Also contained in the envelope are many pages of Balint's handwritten notes compiling his research on these books of theology from the John Ryland's Library. In the absence of biographical evidence documenting Balint's personal embrace of the Christian faith, he was well-studied in that narrative and thoroughly acquainted himself with the theology of Paul, who emphasized love of God and other in all of his extant writings (see especially I Corinthians 13). It is conceivable that the Christian narrative added impetus to Balint's courageous renunciation of Freud's "primary narcissism" and his development of the alternate presupposition of "primary love."

Sutherland (1980) lists Balint as one of the four most influential object relations theorists along with (the British Christians) Winnicott, Fairbairn, and Guntrip and notes that all four "liked and respected each other" (p. 830). Interestingly, Balint's theory of development finds its midpoint between Winnicott's Wesleyan-like optimistic developmental theory and Fairbairn's Calvinist-like pessimistic developmental theory with his assertion of both "primary love" and "the basic fault," the latter of which he believed could be remediated by the "new beginning," an encounter of love in the analytic relationship (personal communication: Lowell Hoffman, November 2009).

Scotland: Ian and Jane Suttie, adapters

Ian Suttie was born in Glasgow, Scotland, in 1889. After receiving his medical degree (with commendation), he joined the staff of Glasgow Royal Asylum, Gartnavel, Scotland, where he met and married Jane Robertson. In 1928, he affiliated with the Tavistock Clinic in London, where Jane and he eventually became full staff members, both also establishing private practices in London (Suttie, 1935).

Ian and Jane worked collaboratively (Dicks, 1970, p. 50), resulting in the writing of *Origins of Love and Hate* (originally published in 1935). The volume was published under Ian's name, Bacal (1987) regarding it "as representing an epistemological break with the traditional psychoanalytic theory of his day" (p. 82), and anticipated the work of Fairbairn, Guntrip, Balint, and Winnicott (Suttie, 1935, p. xxiii). Suttie describes his emendations to Freud as "introducing the conception of an innate need-for-companionship which is the infant's only way of self-preservation. This need, giving rise to parental and fellowship 'love', I put in the place of the Freudian Libido, and regard it as genetically independent of genital appetite" (p. 6). Suttie linked his views with the religious narrative that he dearly embraced, writing that Christianity "offers the conception of social life as based upon Love, rather than upon authority" (p. 140), and describing "the main concern of the Christian teachings to be the cultivation of 'love' as the basis of happiness, mental stability and social harmony" (p. 154).[8] In his preface to Suttie's book, J. A. Hadfield summarizes Suttie's perspective, stating, "The Christian religion has aimed, and often successfully aimed, at the solution of this sense of guilt by its offer of forgiveness, its insistence on the love of God, and upon the love and friendship of man to man as the essence of social life" (p. xlviii).

Scotland: W. R. D. Fairbairn, adapter

Ronald Fairbairn was raised in a Scottish Presbyterian family, his childhood bathed in that church's teachings (Sutherland, 1989, p. 2). This intellectually stimulating environment of Scottish Calvinism left its mark on Fairbairn, who, Sutherland (1989) tells us, took "matters such as religious moral and social questions" (p. 4) very seriously. His contribution is consequently of such importance that, like Winnicott, I will devote Chapter 7 to him.

Fairbairn's religious narrative, which emphasizes the need of humans to be personally related to their Maker, is evident in the shift he introduces to psychoanalytic thought. Humans, Fairbairn postulated, were born to relate. In Fairbairn's view, Mitchell (1988) asserts, "the central motivation in human experience is the seeking out and maintaining of an intense emotional bond with another person" (p. 27). In his theory, Fairbairn creates the conceptual space for a new, good object to meet this longing. Though his works are less clinically oriented and geared more toward theoretical system building, in keeping with his intellectually robust, Calvinist, religious narrative, Fairbairn's works have radically altered the way treatment is conceptualized.

Scotland: Harry S. Guntrip, adapter

Harry S. Guntrip came to psychoanalysis from his earlier profession as a Congregational minister. Having received analysis and then supervision from Tavistock's H. Crichton-Miller, he maintained a private practice as well as conducted research and lectured at Leeds University (Hazell, 1994, p. 2). Several key influences, all Christian, are notable in Guntrip's biography. Of central importance was his period of study with John Macmurray,[9] professor of moral philosophy at London University, and later at Edinburgh University. Guntrip relates Macmurray's view as holding that

> science concerns the relation of persons to things in terms of utility values, whilst religion concerns the relation of person to persons in terms of intrinsic values. He [Macmurray] writes ... "The field of religion is the field of personal relations. ... Its problem is the problem of

communion or community. Religion is about fellowship and community" (Macmurray, 1936, p. 43). Thus the therapeutic factor may be properly described as religious. (Hazell, 1994, p. 84)

Guntrip, in an echo of fellow Scot Ian Suttie, believed that "a true psychotherapy must be a combination of scientific technique for opening up the unconscious, and the parental factor of healing love" (Hazell, 1994, p. 84).

Another key figure in Guntrip's development was Ronald Fairbairn, with whom he also had an analysis. Hazell (1994) comments:

> As the analysis developed with Fairbairn, he [Guntrip] sought to bring together the new orientation with his religious experience in a new book, *Mental Pain and the Cure of Souls* (1956). He and Fairbairn found themselves in agreement that psychotherapy was sterile unless conducted from a point of view that makes the value of the person central, and moreover that those who had been accustomed to regard life from a religious standpoint were more likely to take this view than those whose outlook led them to approach the individual as an organism. (p. 9)

Following Guntrip's analysis with Fairbairn, he entered analysis with Winnicott who, for Guntrip, took Fairbairn's *theory* of need of a good, new object and brought that theory to lived experience.[10] Winnicott's religious narrative had predisposed him to privilege the experiential and thus influence Guntrip in the development of his own integrated theory. Guntrip, according to Dobbs (2005), identifies "the work of both Fairbairn and Winnicott as 'interacting together' and as the 'main stimulus' to his thinking, culminating in his exposition of *schizoid phenomena* as the heart of the problem" (Dobbs, 2005, p. 146). Guntrip (1968) concludes: "*The rebirth and regrowth of the lost living heart of the personality is the ultimate problem psychotherapy seeks to solve*" (p. 12, emphasis in original).

Lack of space, and a need for greater elaboration precludes further discussion of other notable influences.[11,12] However, each of the personages presented above became involved with mentees and colleagues who shared their religious views.

United States: James Jackson Putnam, adapter

It was September of 1909 at Clark University in Worcester, Massachusetts, that James Putnam was seated among the intellectual elite of American psychology—G. Stanley Hall, William James, Adolf Meyer, Franz Boas—listening intently to Freud as he delivered one of his first American lectures (Hale, 1971, p. 23). Putnam promptly invited Freud and his companions, Jung and Ferenczi, to accompany him to his Adirondack retreat, where they continued in conversation. Following the visit, Putnam wrote an article supporting psychoanalysis (p. 24).

By April of 1910, "Freud's 'views' had become 'the cause'" (Hale, 1971, p. 25). In 1921 Freud commented in the preface to Putnam's book *Addresses on Psychoanalysis* (1951) that in America "[Putnam] was able to do perhaps more than anyone for the spread of psychoanalysis ... and to protect it from aspersions" (p. iii). Putnam, the founder of both Harvard's Department of Neurology as well as the American Neurological Association, went on to be the first president of the American Psychoanalytic Association, publishing nearly 50 papers on psychoanalysis before his death in 1918.

James Putnam was both a devotee of psychoanalysis and an unabashed believer in God—a God who can redeem humans through the instrumentality of the discipline that Freud had created. He writes to Jones:

> As regards the question of "religion" ... I feel bound to say my say about it just because the scientific attitude is so recalcitrant or hostile. ... My God by the way is not "in the skies," as of course you know. Furthermore, since the stream cannot rise higher than its source, and since we are "personal" yet have obvious possibilities of further progress, I can see no other possibility than that the universe is personal and may fairly demand a personal recognition [James Putnam to Ernest Jones, Oct. 1, 1915]. (Hale, 1971, p. 293)

Putnam's allegiance to his Christian faith inspired him to support the establishment of the "Emmanuel Movement"—a pastoral counseling initiative which was begun at the Emmanuel Church on Newbury St. in Boston. There, free of charge, patients could receive spiritually sensitive psychotherapy, Putnam providing neurological evaluations. This movement burgeoned throughout the country, though Putnam ultimately saw the lay movement as injurious to his medical profession. Though parting with the Emmanuel Movement, he retained his Christian perspective.[13]

Over the years, Putnam attempted to convince Freud of the importance of spirituality in the care of the soul, sending him books,[14,15] and exchanging letters. Freud, in a spirit of respectful disagreement sent this exemplary reply on March 10, 1910, to Putnam: "It would be a great delight to me to discuss religion with you since you are both tolerant and enlightened. ... 'Just God' and 'kindly Nature' are only the noblest sublimations of our parental complexes, and our infantile helplessness is the ultimate root of religion" (Hale, 1971, p. 97).

United States: Clara Thompson, reactor

Clara Thompson was born in Providence, Rhode Island, in 1893 and lived with her immediate and extended family. Religion was both a central tenet of her family and the cause of strife between her maternal and paternal grandparents (Green, 1964). Some of the literature suggests that Clara was close to her father and at odds with her mother, but material from Ferenczi's *Clinical Diary* (1985) casts doubt on this portrayal.[16]

In her youth, Clara Thompson was very active with her Baptist church and youth group, which was affiliated with the organization *Christian Endeavor*. So committed to her Christianity was she that she intended to become a medical missionary. To that end, upon graduating from high school, Clara entered Brown University and began a premed course of study. While at Brown, Clara moved away from her desire to become a medical missionary and stopped attending church.

Thompson did not lose a core value of her missionary aspirations: a desire to bring change into her world. In an article on Thompson, Capelle (1998) observes: "It is sometimes said that the social scientists of this era—native-born Protestants, for the most part—transferred the fervor of their evangelical faith to this secular crusade. I suspect this was true of Clara Thompson" (p. 77).

Evidence of this transfer can be seen in the group that Clara organized in the early 1930s and which became the prototype for today's supervision groups. Silver (2003) comments:

> She and others had met on Sunday mornings in the early 1930s at her Baltimore apartment to discuss their current clinical frustrations and challenges. Their patients' improvements were so astounding that they named themselves "The Miracle Club." (p. 329)

Clara's group met on Sunday mornings—the day of the week that she once attended church, and bore a group name that reflects her earlier longing to bring spiritual healing. Silver, impressed by her model wrote:

> There should be miracle clubs in every mental health training program. They should include a required case seminar with presentations followed by related readings. I would have future psychiatrists, psychologists, social workers, and other therapists studying together, commenting on each other's case presentations, hearing about the most recent sessions, and thus becoming intimately respectful of each other's areas of expertise. (pp. 329–330)

Thompson began a long-term friendship with Harry Sullivan, who himself was the product of a conflicted Catholic upbringing. She followed Sullivan's advice to have an analysis with Ferenczi in Budapest, and upon Ferenczi's death did not return to Baltimore but moved to New York. Her friendship with Sullivan continued as he moved to a position at Yale. During her years in New York City, she helped establish and direct the William

Alanson White Institute, and she maintained a close circle of friends who would nurture each others' minds. Sullivan named this circle the "Zodiac" group, the core group consisting of Thompson from a Baptist background, Sullivan from a Catholic background, Karen Horney from a Lutheran background, and Erich Fromm from a Jewish background and also interested in religious studies in Christianity and Buddhism. This group would be at the forefront of a psychoanalytic revival where hierarchy was dismantled in deference to mutuality and interpersonal relationship. All of the members of this group respected cultural traditions that nurture people's lives. Thompson's friend, Ruth Benedict, was responsible for publishing "the anthropological best-seller of the century, *Patterns of Culture [1934]*" (Capelle, 1998, p. 84). The major tenet of this book—"the life history of an individual is first and foremost an accommodation to the patterns and standards traditionally handed down in his community" (p. 85)—is consistent with an understanding of Clara Thompson as shaped by her early history and community.

Though little is written about Thompson's religious background, there is a correspondence between her cultural background and her professional career. Her emphasis on relationship and love, in contrast to a restricted positivistic exploration, and her friendships with people of a religious background are well-documented. She wrote book reviews in the journal *Pastoral Psychology* and published two articles in the same: "Towards a Psychology of Women" (1953) and "The Unmarried Woman" (1959). These articles reveal a woman emancipated from a form of religion that had suppressed her, who remains caring to others who may be experiencing their religion in the same inhibiting fashion that she had.

United States: Harry Stack Sullivan, reactor

Harry Sullivan was born in upstate New York, on February 21, 1892, and was "the only Irish Catholic boy in the village school district. Now as then, the remote hamlet is apt to be frightened of the stranger in its midst and to withdraw from him" noted biographer Helen Perry (1982, p. 10). Sullivan's childhood was marred by the injuries inflicted by religion-turned-power structure. In the very rural and Protestant Chenango County, New York, the Irish Sullivans were an anomaly to be scorned. The scourge of religious prejudice had not begun with Sullivan's immediate family. Irish Catholic ancestors on both sides of Harry's family (as opposed to Protestants) had been deprived of the right to own land in Ireland due to religious prejudice from the time of the Penal Laws of 1695 until the Catholic emancipation of 1829. Destitute and attempting to survive the great famine, Harry's grandparents fled to America.

Tragically, the family settled in an area of New York marked by a mystical religious fervor. It was characterized as a

> "burned-over district," that is, the area in which the intensity of religious experience had the quality of a great fire. Chenango County was a part of this phenomenon; the two chief founders of the Mormon religion, for instance, had roots in the County—Brigham Young had once lived in Smyrna township, and Joseph Smith had worked for a while in the southeast part of the County near Afton. (Perry, 1982, p. 42)

Harry suffered this culture of mystification, one that believed that the inherent miseries of Chenango County derived from a curse that had been placed on the land. Of course there were other explanations, such as unfortunate geography, that were the cause of that area's difficulties. The curse myth, related by novelist Carl Carmer, goes like this:

> The story is that a man of God rode into the Chenango Valley and tried to start a church there. He preached loud and he preached long but he could not get the people to give him enough money to build the church. So he mounted his horse and rode on. When he got to the top of the ridge on the far side of Unadilla Creek, that marks the Otsego County line, he turned back in his saddle, lifted a hand and cursed the land of the Chenango. Never, he said, should people gather in the valley, it should never hear the wheels of industry nor feel the happy prosperity of busy cities, it should always dwell darkly in the displeasure of his God. (Perry, 1982, p. 41)

Adding to Harry's mystification was the religious and ethnic ostracism that plagued his childhood. Harry, an only child, grew up lonely. Clara Thompson reports: "The close friends of his childhood were the livestock on the farm. With them he felt comfortable and less lonely" (Perry, 1982, p. 58fn).

"During Harry's childhood, loyalty to the [Catholic] Church was the one parental prerogative that his father continued to assert," notes Perry (1982, p. 87). So,

> by the time Harry was confirmed at St. Malachy's he probably knew all there was to know about St. Francis of Assisi. Whatever else bored him about going to church, he liked the stories of the saints and had considerable knowledge of them; and he appreciated the ancient beauty of the Catholic liturgy. Moreover, the Latin used in church formed a continuum with this interest in the scientific names for geologic formations. (p. 88)

Harry received his medical degree, served a brief time in the Army Medical Corps, and at the age of 30 attended briefly at St. Elizabeth's

Hospital in Washington, D.C. Then, he took up residency at the Sheppard and Enoch Pratt Hospital in Towson, Maryland, a hospital founded by Quaker Moses Sheppard,

> who had been a warden of the poor in Baltimore and a commissioner of the prison ... Sheppard specified that the asylum was to care "first for the poor of the Society of Friends; secondly for such of the Society as are able to pay; and then for the poor indiscriminately; afterwards the Trustees will use their discretion." (Perry, 1982, pp. 191–192)

Sullivan was strongly impressed with the demonstration of Christian charity in his contacts with the Society of Friends. He would later state in a lecture given in the 1940s that the Society of Friends is "the most astonishing demonstration of there being a Christian way of life that I've encountered—in fact, almost the only one" (Perry, 1982, p. 193). At Sheppard Pratt, Sullivan evolved into the legend he came to be.

Following Sheppard Pratt and with the support of many including the Rioch's, missionary children with whom he shared a deep camaraderie, Sullivan began consultation at Chestnut Lodge in Bethesda, Maryland, in October of 1942. He founded the Washington School of Psychiatry in 1943. In 1946, the Washington School's New York branch would become the William Alanson White Institute. Just three years later, Harry Sullivan died while traveling in France. It is noteworthy that he specifically requested a Catholic burial (Perry, 1982).

I have chosen to label Harry Sullivan as primarily a reactor to Christianity, because the corpus of his writings reveals a person committed to demystification, and a rebellion against hierarchical structures. Conversely, Sullivan assimilated an appreciation for the enduring sense of community and the impact of culture that he had gained as a consequence of his experiences in the Catholic Church,[17] as well as a view of the analyst, like God, as participant/observer.[18]

Demystification

Sullivan's early years were spent in a Protestant community that embraced mysticism. If tragedy occurred, it was because "God" was not pleased. If good occurred, it was "God's" reward. A central place for mysticism existed as well in Harry's Roman Catholic Church—in their rituals, in their symbols, in their music, and in the stories of their saints. Learning from his idiosyncratic experiences both religious and familial, Sullivan may have come to believe that this process that he would come to call "mystification," as it occurred in a family unit, was responsible for much of the confusion and difficulty of patients.

Edgar Levenson (1981) captures the radically here-and-now, demystified approach of the interpersonal school founded by Sullivan. He writes:

> [Sullivan] developed a psychology which was apple-pie American empiricism, rooted in real experience. Mead, Cooley, Peirce, Adolph Meyer were his forebears and the linguists Sapir and Korzybski, his working colleagues. His case material shows his unstinting search for the detailed event, his attention to nuances of cultural experience, his emphasis on what Laing—out of Marx—called "mystified" experience (Laing, 1967). "People come to me to get their lives untangled," he said. Not, you will note, to have their fantasies deciphered. (p. 487)

In a contradiction of Freud's language, Sullivan established a different theoretical language more keyed to empirical observation than to metapsychological constructs. He focused on in-the-moment interactions that illuminated the patient's difficulties. He was guided by pragmatism and utility, not by psychoanalytic "doctrine."

Rebellion against hierarchical structures

Sullivan refocused psychoanalysis on the social field. As a result, he addressed the hierarchical structure of the all-knowing analyst (surely influenced by the background object of the all-knowing church) and the isolated patient (an isolation with which he was all too familiar) with his/her problems. The analyst, according to Sullivan, is a participant/observer. Artificial divides between priest and laity, analyst and patient, Protestant and Catholic, are no longer valid.

Invalid as well is the papacy, whether Roman Catholic or psychoanalytic. Freud would not be the sole arbiter of psychoanalytic "truth."

Appreciation for the role of community

As a result of Sullivan's painful years in his parochial home area, he appreciated the decisive role that community can play for better or for worse. Thus, interpersonal psychoanalysis was the study of the interactions of real people, present and past, and not the cross-currents of drives and fantasies. At the heart of Sullivan's inter*person*al psychoanalysis were the interactions of persons.

He also could value the role of religious community, a sentiment echoed in the words of his son Jimmy regarding his preference for a Catholic burial. Jimmy wrote, "Like psychiatry, religion has its use in the world and, again, like psychiatry it sometimes does more harm than good" (Perry, 1982, p. 422).

The analyst as participant/observer

In his early years, Sullivan was steeped in Christian theology and in the sense of a spiritual realm that coexisted with human life. Concepts like prayers to God and to the saints who are participants/observers, as well as the mystical union of the church that is united yet diverse, may have predisposed Sullivan toward a refocusing on intersubjective realities that were burgeoning as well in British psychoanalysis.

United States: Heinz Kohut, adapter

Though some European Jews converted to Christianity to avoid anti-Semitic attack, there were those whose assimilation into Christianity grew well beyond the initial pragmatic decision. It is believed by some that Heinz Kohut was one of the latter.

Kohut was born in Vienna in 1913 to Jewish parents; his father was a more background figure to his deeply involved mother, Else. His mother's religious history is complex, for there is evidence that at some point she identified with Catholicism (Strozier, 2001, p. 7). Strozier remarks:

> As Thomas Kohut [her grandson] sees it, her Jewish origins and life and involvements seemed not to fulfill her spiritual yearnings, and in some way she connected with Catholicism as a girl. That made her, in the eyes of her grandson, a Catholic by belief in a world that came to insist she had to stand up and be counted ethnically as a Jew ... (p. 7)

A repudiation of this viewpoint by other sources close to the Kohut family reflects the complexity of the matter.

Kohut completed his medical training at the University of Vienna. However, as the war exploded, Kohut and his mother fled Vienna, and on March 5, 1940, after a year in a staging camp in England, Kohut arrived in Chicago. Following a medical internship, Kohut specialized in neurology, and during this time—the mid-1940s—formally associated with the Unitarian Church. "It was also in these years, it seems, that Kohut decided he was a Christian by belief" states Strozier (2001, p. 75), who paints a conflicted picture of Kohut's relationship to religion. Strozier goes on to comment that "Unitarianism was the perfect compromise for a spiritual man torn by his Jewish and Christian identities who had come to embrace Jesus as the religious figure of paramount significance in his life" (p. 75).

After an analysis with August Aichorn and later Ruth Eissler, Kohut was accepted into the Chicago Institute for Psychoanalysis in 1946, and he also shifted his interest from neurology to psychiatry. In that decade as well, Kohut's mother changed her spiritual orientation. Strozier (2001) summarizes:

> But something was happening to her spiritually. A customer, Eleanor Roth, became Else's closest friend. Roth, a Catholic, talked to her of God and faith and introduced her to her own church in Huntley, Illinois, near Woodstock, northwest of Chicago. Sometime in the late 1940s Else decided to convert and was sponsored by Roth in her church. (p. 88)

An enduring shift away from a Jewish identity and toward a Christian one, though one cannot be certain of the reasons, continued in Heinz's life as well. In 1948 while teaching a case seminar, he met and later married Elizabeth Meyer, who had ironically studied in Vienna and had even been a student of his former analyst Aichorn. Elizabeth, a social worker of German descent, was born in Wisconsin and was a Christian. As their family grew to include their child, Thomas, and relatives of the Meyer family, Kohut became bolder in his association with Christianity. Strozier (2001) continues: "He felt it was important for Thomas to have a Christian upbringing and become familiar with the Bible. He became good friends with the pastor of the Unitarian Church, John (Jack) F. Hayward, and occasionally even gave a sermon" (p. 115).

Corroborating Kohut's move toward a Christian identity, his son Thomas confirms that this was important to him and he was "quite open about this: He was not Jewish. He was a Christian" (Strozier, 2001, p. 115). Commenting on Kohut's denial of his Judaism, Aron (2007) elaborates: "Whereas Freud was 'the Godless Jew' (Freud, cited in Gay, 1987) Kohut denied his Judaism but championed religious belief: religion was an important theme in his life and work" (p. 416). This is evident both in his writings and in his interest in pastoral psychotherapy (Goldberg, 2003). Kohut's embrace of religion followed the theological predispositions of the Unitarian Church, which did not accept the Christian concept of Trinity, valued the teachings of Christ as central to Christian faith, and emphasized Christ's humanity. Kohut's own incorporation of religious themes reflects, more often than not, an undifferentiated religious perspective.

Influences in Kohut's writings

Kohut's theory provides support for a belief in God in several ways. Aron (2007) delineates three specific dimensions in which the criteria of human need theorized by Kohut is met through belief in God: "the self-object needs for idealization, mirroring, and twinship" (p. 416).

First, there is the self-object need for idealization: "People need to have something to idealize, something perfect, something to live up to, something uplifting. Kohut related this need to the infant's early experience of being lifted up by the big, calm, powerful mother who soothes and comforts and with whose power the infant merges" (Aron, 2007, p. 416). The

God that is encountered in sermons, songs, traditions of the holidays, music, and nature, Kohut felt, touches something deep within the human soul. However, Kohut did not make a reductionistic tie between self-object experiences and God. For Kohut, "Religion is not, as it was basically for Freud, a rather mundane human institution but rather a complex interplay of human psychological need and the deeper workings of the divine" (Strozier, 2001, p. 330).

Second, there is the self-object need for mirroring: Humans are fractured, yet in their fracture there is a basic image of God that remains. "In the Judeo-Christian traditions, the concept of *imago dei* (i.e., the claim that humanity is created in the image of God) derives from the book of Genesis and can be regarded as one of the most fundamental claims to being God-like," states Rector (2000, p. 268), as she presents a self-psychological perspective on religious belief. Accepting this core, divine-like aspect of human self-hood, grace (see Aron, 2007), through many sources including the therapist, mirrors back to a patient the invaluable worth of his humanity.

Third, there is the self-object need for twinship: The incarnation of Christ is the consummate proof of human God-likeness. Rector (2000) relates Kohut's perspective:

> Kohut (early 1970s) referred, inadvertently, in his observation of the tragic figure's "incarnations in the myths of organized religion" (p. 214) to theological concepts of incarnation and suggested these beliefs are directly related to twinship needs. God takes on a human form, becomes like, and as a result knows what human beings experience. For some Christians, Jesus, the incarnation of God, becomes a companion, one who suffered as a human being and who identified with the lowly and the oppressed. (p. 269)

Kohut believed the need for twinship was met within the community of a sacred environment or church, where incarnation is the spirit of communal experience, where all are gathered in the same spiritual quest. Strozier (2001) reflects:

> Within the sacred space of the church you become more like your neighbor. You abandon the extraneous and emphasize the essential. The human bonds deepen in this circle of reflected sameness. And that is enormously reassuring. You become one of God's children in a powerfully shared experience. (p. 333)

At the end of his life

Kohut died on October 8, 1981. His memorial service on October 31 was held at the First Unitarian Church on Woodlawn Ave. at 57th Street in

Chicago. Rev. John F. Hayward, minister and longtime friend of Kohut, presided at the service. There was no mistaking the Christian identification of Kohut, though his Jewish colleagues were dismayed by his final directive:

> The service ended with everyone singing "A Mighty Fortress Is Our God" by Martin Luther, the words and music to which were included in the program. Kohut had been insistent with his son that the service end with this moving and classic Christian hymn. (Strozier, 2001, p. 380)

United States: Erik Erikson, adapter

Erikson was born in Germany in 1902, to a mother of Danish/Jewish heritage who separated from his father during her pregnancy. She subsequently settled in Germany and married her son's attending pediatrician, Dr. Homberger. Mother confided to an adolescent Erik that she had read him numerous books by the Danish philosopher Søren Kierkegaard while pregnant and during his infancy (Coles, 1970), and "urged her son to revere the existential core of Christianity" (Carveth, 2008, p. 109).

"Teased by Christian classmates for being Jewish, and at temple school for being tall, blond and blue-eyed—a 'goy'" (Mooney, 2010, p. 4), he eventually became a wandering artist, landing in Vienna in his 20s. There he was introduced to psychoanalysis and was analyzed by Anna Freud. Vienna not only introduced him to psychoanalysis, but there he also met and fell instantly in love with Joan Serson, a Canadian-American and a daughter of an Episcopalian minister. They married and had two children. Erik completed his psychoanalytic training at the Vienna Psychoanalytic Society shortly thereafter in 1933 (Coles, 1970, p. 24). By Christmas of that year, the Eriksons departed Austria due to the accumulating storm clouds of war and settled in Boston, Massachusetts, Erikson becoming its first child psychoanalyst.

In 1936 the Eriksons moved to New Haven for Erik to teach at Yale Medical School, where he embarked on what was to be pivotal field research at the Pine Ridge Reservation in South Dakota. Erik's interest in working with war veterans subsequently took the family to California, where they resided for more than a decade. During these years Erikson's ideas coalesced to form his eight-stage theory, which was presented in *Childhood and Society* (1950).

Erikson's psychosocial perspective of psychoanalysis was markedly interdisciplinary, and bore the imprint of anthropology, art, and religion. His religious interests expanded over his lifetime, largely through the influence of his wife, Joan, who facilitated his extensive involvement with the Episcopal Church and their joint friendships with Paul Tillich and Reinhold

Neibuhr (L. Friedman, 1999). Erikson wrote numerous psychoanalytically informed religious works that demonstrated his thorough-going knowledge and utilization of Christian history and doctrine.

Young Man Luther (1958)

Erikson's desire in his monumental book *Young Man Luther* was to present both how a clinician might work with a troubled person of faith, and how humans as a whole might emancipate themselves. Erikson would take Luther as his literary "patient"—"in the very broadest sense of the word—a sense that Erikson's fellow Dane Søren Kierkegaard had sanctioned when he called the great German Protestant 'a patient of exceeding import for Christianity'" (Coles, 1970, p. 204). Donald Capps opines that:

> *Young Man Luther* is one of the most impressive psychoanalytic clinical case studies extant, rivaling Freud's own clinical case studies of "Wolf Man," "Rat Man," and "Dr. Schreber" (Freud 1963b), and it is especially valuable as a clinical study of an individual whose psychopathology was both precipitated and ameliorated by religion. (Jacobs & Capps, 1997, p. 134)

Erikson oscillates between psychoanalysis and history as he studies the not-so-uncommon struggles of Luther, who was plagued by divine directives and demonic condemnation that swung in an erratic, bipolar rhythm. Erikson chronicles Luther's attempts to hold himself together and utilizes the case to illustrate shifts in Luther's identity, as well as to portray the impact of false religion. Erikson (1958) carefully traces a momentous shift for Luther, one that revolutionized his view of Christ, who was no longer

> ... an ideal figure to be imitated, or abjectly venerated, or ceremonially remembered as an event in the past [but as] today, here, in me [as] what works in us [and hence] the core of the Christian's identity. ... For a little while, Luther, this first revolutionary individualist, saved the Savior from the tiaras and the ceremonies, the hierarchies and the thought-police, and put him back where he arose: in each man's soul. (p. 212)

In a manner familiar to psychoanalysis, Luther's poignant realizations would fade and return. Not until Luther surrendered to the vulnerabilities of life was he able to secure a core identity, that of a child. Referencing Jesus' welcome to the children that gathered around him (Matthew 18: 1–4), Erikson (1958) concludes:

> In this book, I have described how Luther, once a sorely frightened child, recovered through the study of Christ's Passion the central meaning of the Nativity; and I have indicated in what way Freud's method of introspection brought human conflict under a potentially more secure control by revealing the boundness of man in the loves and rages of his childhood. Thus both Luther and Freud came to acknowledge that "the child is in the midst. ...
>
> The Reformation is continuing in many lands, in the form of manifold revolutions, and in the personalities of protestants of varied vocations. (p. 253)

"The Galilean Sayings and the Sense of 'I'" (1996)

Walter Capps (1996) notes that Erikson told him "on several occasions that he had been thinking about the life of Jesus throughout his career" (p. 226). In his treatment of the deity and humanity of Jesus in his final publication, entitled "The Galilean Sayings and the Sense of 'I,'" Erikson prefigures the relational construct of intersubjectivity. After commenting on Erikson's different literary style, Paranjpe (2000) suggests several other salient features of the essay:

> [2] Its direct reliance on the Bible and scriptural exegesis; [3] its emphasis on mysticism and on the "healing" aspect of Jesus' ministry, in contrast to the emphasis on "ideological" aspects of religion typified in his work on Luther; [4] its discussion of the contrast between Jesus' "ethnic" background on the one hand, and the pan-human compassion of his healing hand on the other; and [5] its attempt to interpret God's enigmatic expression to Moses: " I AM that I AM."
>
> In his critical study of Jesus' first ministry, Erikson saw the "son of man" going well beyond Gandhi in transcending the human-made group boundaries. As "son of God," Jesus' sense of identity was not that of a Jew; it manifested itself in a self that knew no boundary between "self" and "other" and hence His sense of "I" could be expressed only in His Being: "THAT I AM." (p. 288)

For Erikson, religion was at the center of formative life events and possessed a power to inspire both noble achievements and human tragedy. For better or worse, religion is part of each person's individual historical tapestry and as such, Erikson (1969) believed, "we cannot lift a case history out of [a person's unique, individual] history" (pp. 15–16).

United States: Karen Horney, reactor

Karen Horney[19,20] was a spirited but "gentle" rebel in psychoanalysis and even earlier in her upbringing in Germany. Born in Hamburg in 1885,

Horney was reared in a staunchly Lutheran family. She was surrounded with, intrigued by, and questioning of the religious doctrines that daily were presented to her both by her sermonizing father and her Christian school instruction (Hitchcock, 2005; Quinn, 1987). Mother, many years Father's junior, was the target of his rages, a victim like Karen, of his disparagement of the female sex. Of the father Rubins (1978) elaborates:

> His feelings toward the children could also have been influenced by his attitudes toward the two sexes—defined in part by religious beliefs. Did not the Bible declare the woman to be secondarily created from the man; was she not subject to temptation in the Garden and thereby the source of evil? What was permitted in the male could not be tolerated in the female. (p. 11)

Adolescent diaries

After elementary school, Horney attended a convent school where heavy emphasis was placed on religious instruction. Perhaps the best insight into her early relationship to Christian faith is obtained through her adolescent diaries (Horney, 1980), which were discovered many years following her death. Below are several excerpts:

> 28 June 1899: ... There's a bone of contention between Tuti and me: Lisbeth H ... Tuti is always too harsh with her and then I feel morally obligated to protect her. That makes Tuti angry with me. I am really very sorry for Lisbeth: I act according to, "What Jesus has given me is worthy of love." (p. 7)
>
> 9 March 1901: Religion Lesson: ... One can imagine: God, the original creative power; Jesus, divinity manifest, bringing salvation; the Holy Ghost, guardian, reigning in the heart. But they are just as much one as the *various* powers in a person are one, as: willing, feeling, perceiving, etc. (p. 33)
>
> Reinbeck, 3 April 1901: ... I feel too weak to follow Christ. Yet I long for the faith, firm as a rock, that makes oneself *and others* happy. I hardly dare to love Christ, he who was love, the pure one, although he stands before me as a glorious ideal. ... Only one thing can I plead for, like a cry from the deep: "Lord help me" or "give me understanding," but I am too listless to believe—there are so many things to think of. (p. 38)
>
> Reinbeck, 29 April 1904: *The first moral law: Thou shalt not lie!* And the second: thou shalt free thyself from convention, from everyday morality, and shalt think through the highest commands for thy self and act accordingly. Too much custom, too little morality! (p. 82)

> New Year's Eve 1904–1905: ... I long for one thing more: to learn how to listen to the delicate vibrations of my soul, to be incorruptibly *true to myself* and fair to others, to find in this way the right measure of my own worth. (p. 102)

Beginning with late adolescence, and burgeoning in the years of her medical education and marriage to Oskar Horney, Karen commenced a trajectory in which her doubts about Christian religion would lead to her embrace of Buddhism by the end of her life. She would, however, maintain relationships with Christian friends throughout her adult life; and as her daughter, psychoanalyst Marianne Eckardt (1984), would note, Horney's work would have "A very strong Protestant ethic hidden in her system" (p. 241).

However, similar to "protestant" Martin Luther who nailed the 95 theses to the Wittenburg door, Karen Horney was a "protestant," a trait that carried into her years in psychoanalysis. And also like Luther at the Diet of Worms, Horney was censured at the April 29, 1940, annual business meeting of the New York Psychoanalytic Society whereupon she fell into

> a dead silence. Karen rose, and with great dignity, her head high, slowly walked out. Thereupon Thompson, Robbins, Ephron and Sarah Kelman rose and followed her out.... And then they marched jubilantly down the [82nd] street, arm in arm, following Thompson's lead in singing Karen's favorite spiritual: "Go down, Moses, Way down in Egypt land. Tell old Pharaoh, to let my people go." (Rubins, 1978, p. 240)

Her formal letter of resignation from the Society asserted, "The New York Psychoanalytic Society has steadily deteriorated. Reverence for dogma has replaced free inquiry; academic freedom has been abrogated. ... Under the circumstances we have no alternative but to resign, however much we may regret the necessity for this action" (1978, p. 240). This protest against dogma would inspire a reformation within the psychoanalytic community.

Significant adult Christian relationships: Bonhoeffer, Tillich

Horney's adult history reflects her attraction to spirituality. Such was the case in her medical training. European requirements for completing medical studies included writing a thesis, and there was no more enviable sponsorship in Berlin than the neuropsychiatric inpatient service of Karl Bonhoeffer.[21] Horney applied, detailing her childhood religious environment, which might have been of interest to Bonhoeffer, who was a Christian.[22] Rubins (1978) observes: "Perhaps he was influenced by her early religious background which she had described in her application and interviews" (p. 44). Bonhoeffer agreed to sponsor Horney's thesis.

Karl Bonhoeffer's approach was presciently interpersonal, antedating "Sullivan's similar concepts by some forty years" (Rubins, 1978, p. 43), as evidenced by the following vignette:

> Professionally, he [Bonhoeffer] had a special feeling for, and humane way with, the schizophrenic patients on his ward rounds, which the students admired. He could easily interview even the most disturbed patient. Once one of the younger students accidentally locked herself in an isolation room with a violent, agitated patient and could not get out without her forgotten passkey. After she was let out thirty minutes later, Bonhoeffer asked whether she had been afraid of the patient. She responded that she had not, whereupon he gave a lecture on the relationship between doctor and patient, stressing the psychotic's intuitive—or unconscious—awareness of interpersonal attitudes. (Rubins, 1978, p. 43)

In addition to her many theologically inclined friends, Horney developed an enduring and intimate relationship with Protestant theologian Paul Tillich, whom she referred to as "Dear Paulus" (Paris, 1994). Tillich and Horney became intellectual catalysts to one another; Tillich's work in many ways was mirrored in Horney's later writings. Tillich's perspective was as follows:

> Life is a process of actualizing potentials, whether in the organic psychological, spiritual or historical dimension. The historical differs from the others in that it would include the element of fulfillment as well and implies a process in a particular direction. The individual is the bearer of history, the reality in which history occurs. (Rubins, 1978, p. 200)

In the above passage, Tillich's impact on Horney is capsulized. Rubins elaborates:

> These were some of the concepts he had expressed before 1940, the early period of his contact with Karen. The relevance of these concepts to her theory is evident. Attention to the culture, the role of historical development, actualization of one's potential, the need to be involved (in therapy) all appeared. (p. 200)

Paul Tillich remained Karen's friend to the end of her life and gave her eulogy: "She knew the darkness of the human soul, and the darkness of the world, but believed that what giveth light to any one suffering human being will finally give light to the world" (Tillich, 1953, p. 13). The eulogy is reprinted verbatim in the May 1953 issue of *Pastoral Psychology*. In the introduction to this issue honoring Karen Horney, and in a poignant recognition of her lifelong religious interests, the editor acknowledges her involvement with the birth of that journal: "Dr. Horney was interested and participated in the planning of the launching of our journal, *Pastoral Psychology*" (Editor, 1953, p. 8).

Protest against dogma and patriarchy

Horney's early exposure to a rigid form of Christianity, as well as its presentation via her doctrinaire father, may have contributed to a life course that culminated in her courageous stand against dogma and patriarchy (Sayers, 1991).

> Quite radically for the time, Horney exposed the biases and phallocentric views that contributed to the various theoretical suppositions of that era. She was able to articulate how it was in the male society's interest to accept and support particular views of women and their development. She proposed that the psychoanalytic theory of the day was driven by male reality and was not necessarily informed by girls' or women's experience of their femininity. (Miletic, 2002, p. 287)

In so doing, Karen Horney presaged the contemporary relational theorists in their opposition to what had been an almost exclusively phallocentric psychoanalysis. She went on to publish numerous essays on feminine psychology, challenging Freud's concept of penis envy, but also advancing new interpersonal perspectives on motherhood, female development, and sexual development (Westkott, 1986).

Appreciation for the interpersonal/cultural

Horney not only challenged certain dogmas, but "more significantly, she introduced to psychoanalysis a way of thinking in which not only intrapsychic factors, but cultural and political ones play crucial roles" (Miletic, 2002, p. 288). Like Thompson and Sullivan, both from a Christian background, an interpersonal emphasis prevailed in Horney's theories. Horney, along with fellow Zodiac Club members—Sullivan, Thompson, and also Fromm—according to Ingram, "assisted the shift in psychoanalysis from the instinctivistic to the interpersonal/cultural. ... Their impact on conventional Freudian thinking encouraged the rise of ego psychology, the evolution of object relations theories, and the development of transcultural psychiatry" (Horney, 1987, pp. 10–11). Her attention to cultural issues even included her observations regarding religiously committed people. Horney specifically voiced her concerns regarding the "effect on the personality of the conflict between the ideal of Christian unselfishness and the ruthless pressures of competition in our modern world" (p. 8).

Horney ultimately was on the vanguard of the move toward egalitarian relations in culture at the political level, in gender relations, and between analyst and patient. Her interpersonal, mutual style is evident in this final excerpt:

> A colleague might say, "I don't understand this—why does the patient say this and then this?" Or, a supervisee doesn't understand why a patient dwells on some particular point. Very often, under these circumstances, I will say, "Why not ask the patient?" Present the problem to the patient. Sometimes he can even answer it. And you're saying, "I don't understand, could you say what occurs to you?" will stimulate his own associations. So through a real cooperative effort, we get further understanding. (1987, p. 69)

ENDNOTES

1. Franz Brentano, considered the father/grandfather of phenomenology, was full professor of philosophy at the University of Vienna. In disagreement with the doctrine of papal infallibility, he left the Catholic Church, resigning his position, but continuing both in his faith and his mentoring as a *Privatdozent* in Vienna.
2. Henri Ellenberger was an analysand of Pfister (Micale, 1993).
3. I will elaborate more specifically on Winnicott's contributions in the next chapter.
4. Rickman's Quaker beliefs prevented him from participating in the war, and he served in this humanitarian capacity instead (Rickman, 2003).
5. Though it would be natural to include Marjorie Brierley in our review of Christians in early British psychoanalysis, there is no clear statement of Dr. Brierley's persuasions. She became a full member of the British Psychoanalytic Society in 1930, yet little is known of her history. Evidence of her interest in Christianity appears throughout her work, Simmonds (2006) asserting that Brierley was "unwittingly ethnocentrically biased toward Christianity" (p. 132). In 1947 and again in 1951, Brierley argues in revised versions of the same paper ("Notes on Psycho-Analysis and Integrative Living") for incorporating religious understandings into psychoanalysis. She reviewed many works of a religious nature including articles by the Sutties, Mortimer Ostow, Erich Fromm, and Gifford lecturer Sir Charles Sherrington.
6. I wish to thank my husband, Lowell, for researching Balint's history and encouraging me to include this section.
7. I am indebted to André Haynal and Maud Struchen for their generosity in permitting me access to the archives for review of the Balint papers.
8. Suttie, like Crichton-Miller, differentiated between Christianity as it was *intended* to be in the teachings of Jesus in the Gospels and how it was *practiced* in the context of a religious power structure.

9. Guntrip studied philosophy under Professor John Macmurray at University College, where he also studied psychoanalysis under J. G. Flugel (Dobbs, 2005, p. 135).
10. An interesting correspondence exists between Fairbairn's theory-bound Calvinism and Winnicott's experientially oriented Wesleyanism. This will be addressed in Chapter 7.
11. Frank Lake (1966) was a major figure in the founding of psychoanalytically oriented pastoral counseling in the United Kingdom, though his written contributions fall somewhat later than the time period being covered in this study. Those interested in his comprehensive work can resource his book, *Clinical Theology: A Theological and Psychiatric Basis to Clinical Pastoral Care.*
12. Psychoanalysis in Ireland: Jonathan Hanaghan came from England and settled in Dublin during World War II (Skelton, 1983, p. 183). He had just been analyzed by Douglas Byron, a member of the London Psychoanalytic Society, and brought some of his own followers from England with him to be psychoanalyzed. He trained a small number of analysts in Ireland, forming, in 1942, the Irish Psychoanalytic Association (IPAA), the oldest psychoanalytic organization in that country.

    Hanaghan was unique in that his approach was radically integrative of Christianity and psychoanalysis. Called the "Monkstown Group" (Skelton, 1983, p. 183), anyone who wished could come to Hanaghan's home on a Saturday night for an informal talk on psychoanalysis and the New Testament by Hanaghan. Hanaghan published several books, though he did not publish any articles. In that Hanaghan and his colleagues were lay analysts, they were not recognized by official psychoanalytic bodies.
13. Anton Boisen is considered the actual "father" of the American pastoral counseling movement. His influence there as well as in hospital chaplaincy is noteworthy. I have chosen not to include him in these biographical commentaries because his relationship to psychoanalysis is ambiguous. While in certain ways embracing psychoanalysis, he did not consider himself primarily allied with the discipline (Meserve, 1993).
14. See Caird (1893). Caird was a Scottish philosopher and Gifford lecturer.
15. See Harris (1895).
16. We learn from Ferenczi's *Clinical Diary* (1985): "As a child, Dm. [initials for Clara Thompson] had been grossly abused sexually by her father, who was out of control; later, obviously because of the father's bad conscience and social anxiety, he reviled her, so to speak" (p. 3).
17. One might ask if his later affiliation with Quakers might not have provided further appreciation for the importance of community.
18. I thank Linda Barnhurst for this observation in her review of my manuscript.
19. I am indebted to Audrey Atkinson and Katie Maslowe of Regent University for allowing me to resource their research.
20. I also wish to express appreciation to Dr. Marianne Eckardt, Dr. Horney's daughter, who first drew my attention to the influence of the Christian narrative on her mother's work at a conference where I presented a paper on religious narratives in Fairbairn and Winnicott.
21. Rubins (1978) notes: "Numerous Jewish assistants were accepted on his staff, an exception to the explicit or implicit anti-Semitism of most of the faculty" (p. 44).

22. Karl Bonhoeffer's Christianity met its ultimate tests in the Nazi regime, both personally and in the life of his son, Dietrich. Dietrich Bonhoeffer, a promising theologian appointed to Union Theological Seminary in New York, voluntarily returned to Germany against the strongest remonstrances of his colleagues, to risk his life in opposition to the Nazi regime. He formed the "Confessing Churches" and was hanged by direct order of Hitler in 1945 just days before the fall of Berlin.

Part II

Surrender/Crucifixion

In Part II, I am working with surrender in psychoanalysis (the second movement toward mutual recognition) and its analogue in crucifixion (the second movement of Hegel's system).

In Chapter 5, I trace the path of recognition in psychoanalysis from identification to differentiation, from differentiation to negation, and from negation to surrender in infant/mother and patient/analyst relationships. In this second movement toward mutual recognition, both the infant/mother and the patient/analyst dyads progress from a state of "negation," of "doer-done to," complementarity with its destructive attacks, toward mutual surrender to a "moral third." I define *negation* as two opposing forces each pressing for respective needs to be met. Infant and mother, patient and analyst become mired in this necessary process of negation that is fueled by projections leading to enactments. Resolution occurs through survival of the destructive attacks within the enactments and mutual surrender to the "moral third," which facilitates mutual recognition of separate subjectivities. I also detail the differences between surrender and submission, linking submission to Winnicott's object-relating and Biblical idolatry. I draw a parallel between Hegel's portrayal of Christ's survival of destruction in His crucifixion and His surrender to the process of redemption, and the mother and the analyst who repeatedly resurrender to the process of growth. Christ's survival of destruction affirmed a mutual recognition of divinity and humanity (i.e., transcendence and immanence).

In Chapter 6, I examine a stagnation that developed in my treatment with Mandy, contrasting submission versus surrender in our relationship, and exploring the fears that motivated the avoidance of surrender in both of us. I explore the enactment that revealed the avoidance and describe the resumption of a more alive treatment that proceeded through negation and survival of our fears of destruction. I then describe a second point of impasse that involved a deeper level of pain having to do with dead maternal objects and consider the work of André Green. I revisit the concept of the "third," which through its "oscillating function" resolved the enactment, and trace its history to work on creativity in Arieti and Winnicott. Surrendering to the process of growth, Mandy and I experience a greater sense of our individual personalities, potentials, and needs. The chapter contains verbatim dialogue, clinical commentary, and a dream.

In Chapter 7, I return to theorists Ronald Fairbairn and D. W. Winnicott, whom I had briefly discussed in Part I. I present them as exemplars of theorists who had been influenced by the Christian narrative, and whose theories—in part flowing from that narrative—formed a negation to aspects of Freud's theories. The complementarity between religion and psychoanalysis that had existed since Freud, encountered its own negation in these two theorists, whose embrace of both psychoanalysis and the Christian narrative found a third in relationality. In this chapter, which is a revised version of one previously published (M. Hoffman, 2004), I detail the Christian influences in the childhoods and adulthoods of Fairbairn and Winnicott, which I demonstrate in their personal writings. After reviewing the philosophical climate of Great Britain, which nurtured a Christian perspective, and describing the theological polarities in the Christian narratives of these men, I turn to their writings, where I explicate the interpenetration of the Christian narratives with their psychoanalytic theories. Blazing the path of mutual recognition in psychoanalysis, Fairbairn and Winnicott penetrated the complementarity between the Christian narrative and psychoanalysis by pressing through the negation/crucifixion of the respective narratives to mutual surrender. Out of their surrender, a paradigm shift toward relationality was inaugurated.

Chapter 5

The second movement toward mutual recognition

Theoretical perspectives

SURRENDER IN INFANCY

> In his discussion of the conflict between "the independence and dependence of self-consciousness" Hegel showed how the self's wish for absolute independence conflicts with the self's need for recognition.
>
> —Benjamin (1990, pp. 189)

> If a baby cries in a state of rage and feels as if he has destroyed everyone and everything, and yet the people round him remain calm and unhurt, this experience greatly strengthens his ability to see that what he feels to be true is not necessarily real ...
>
> —Winnicott (1949, p. 62)

A time comes in "good-enough" parenting when the infant's illusory "omnipotent control" of mother must come to an end. The movement toward mutual recognition propels the relational dynamic between infant and mother from mutual identification—the earliest phase of recognition—toward a reality in which mother is recognized as having her own center of subjectivity. This shift matures the infant's capacity for awareness of its own and others' limitations but also confronts the infant with the painful fact of its own dependence on mother both for physical and emotional survival, as well as for recognition (Honneth, 1995). Only from a position of being differentiated will the infant be able to experience recognition and "use" what mother offers. This difficult transition from mother as an extension of the infant to mother as a person in her own right was most notably described by Winnicott in his famous paper "The Use of an Object and Relating Through Identifications" (1968). He writes:

> In clinical terms: two babies are feeding at the breast. One is feeding on the self, since the breast and the baby have not yet become (for the baby) separate phenomena. The other is feeding from another-than-me

source. ... In the sequence one can say that first there is object-relating, then in the end there is object-use; in between, however, is the most difficult thing, perhaps, in human development; or the most irksome of all the early failures that come for mending. This thing that there is in between relating and use is the subject's placing of the object outside the area of the subject's omnipotent control; that is, the subject's perception of the object as an external phenomenon, not as a projective entity, in fact recognition of it as an entity in its own right. (1968, p. 221–222)

Identification and differentiation

To explain the process that moves the infant from identification toward recognition of the mother's difference, Benjamin extends Winnicott's emphasis by referring to Sander's (2002) notion of rhythmicity. Initially, in identification, mother and infant create a shared pattern together. This pattern is a kind of nascent or energetic third[1] of mutual regulation and accommodation at the preverbal level. It is called a third because it constitutes something more than the behavior of two partners of the dyad; it is a "dance" created by both, for which neither is wholly responsible. The notion of "rhythmicity" allows mother and infant to experience the necessary "oneness" while the mother retains her subjectivity. Benjamin (2004a, p. 17) notes:

> When the significant other is a recognizing one who surrenders to the rhythm of the baby, a co-created rhythm can begin to evolve. As the caregiver accommodates, so does the baby. The basis for this mutual accommodation is probably the inbuilt tendency to respond symmetrically, to match and mirror; in effect, the baby matches the mother's matching, much as one person's letting go releases the other. (p. 17)

But like Gallese (2009), Benjamin simultaneously creates a berth for differentiation and leaves room for the mother's subjectivity. Benjamin introduces into her narrative of the developing dyad the concept of a different kind of third, the "third-in-the-one." This third in the mother's mind helps her to be both present for her baby's experience but also retain a sense of her own stability in the face of disruption, her own needs in the face of many demands, her own awareness of what is vital or threatening that is more sophisticated than an infant's raw reactions to *cold*, *wet*, *hungry*, *tired*. This differentiation is exhibited through "markedness" (Aron, 2006), a concept originally developed by Gyorgy Gergely, adapted by Fonagy et al. (2002), and further developed by Benjamin (2004a). Aron (2006) explains:

> No matter how well attuned a parent is to the infant's state, her mirroring facial and vocal behaviors never perfectly match the infant's behavioral

expressions. Mothers, and other adults, "mark" their affect-mirroring displays (that is, they signify that these responses are reflections of the other's feelings rather than being expressions of their own feelings) by exaggerating some aspect of their own realistic response. The mother "marks" her mirroring response to her child to signal, so to speak, that it is *her* version of *his* response. The marking (the exaggerated affect display) is meant to differentiate the response from what would have been her own "realistic" response. It is markedness that indicates that it is not mother's affect display, but her reflection (her understanding, her version) of the infant's affect. The exaggerated quality provides a personal stamp or signature, signifying that it is neither a perfect reflection of the other, nor a completely natural response of the self. The infant recognizes and uses this marked quality to "decouple" or to differentiate the perceived emotion from its referent (the parent) and to "anchor" or "own" the marked mirroring stimulus as expressing his or her own self-state. (pp. 357–358)

Differentiation and negation

Benign difference first experienced as "markedness" ultimately augments into more crucial differences to the infant and to a battle of wills. The infant, attempting to maintain a grandiose control over mother, asserts its demand for recognition through held breath, raucous tantrum, wearing-out or withdrawal, as a result of its utter affective disregulation during mother's inattention or absence. It does not recognize mother's status as benefactor of life and goods. Or, perhaps feeling that her status gives her so much power and makes it so helpless, it believes it either has to give up self or give up the needed source of goodness.

This clash of subjectivities is actually indispensible if the infant is to arrive at the capacity for experiencing the mother as a person separate from itself. Benjamin (1988) turns to Winnicott in elaborating this conflict, and also to Hegel. She states: "In his essay, 'The Use of an Object', which is, in many ways, a modern echo of Hegel's reflections on recognition, Winnicott presents the idea that in order to be able to 'use' the object we first have to 'destroy' it" (p. 37). Central to Benjamin's thesis is this Hegelean idea of "negation," which she wed with Winnicott's idea of "destruction of the object." To Benjamin, negation refers to a state of opposition, of what she terms as a "doer"/"done-to" complementarity, as the infant's demands crescendo to attack the mother.

Negation and surrender

The move from identification to surrender entails the painful process of the infant giving up its sense of omnipotence, and surrendering to the process of growth. What is crucial for the infant in the viewpoint of Benjamin (and

Winnicott), is that the mother survives the infant's attack without retaliation or damage. In the process of attempting to destroy mother and finding that she survives, the infant is dissuaded of its own omnipotence, and begins to develop a capacity for recognition of the mother, that is, her "otherness."

Specifically, what the infant is surrendering to is a higher principle of rightness, one paralleling mother's surrender to the sacrificial process of motherhood that perseveres in spite of the infant's demands and attacks. Benjamin (2004a) describes this internal quality that motivates toward a relational, higher good, stating: "This intention to connect and the resulting self-observation create what I would call moral thirdness, the connection to a larger principle of necessity, rightness, or goodness" (p. 26). The establishment of such a "moral third" Benjamin traces to universal patterns of lawfulness and reliability that become forged in this infant-mother relationship.

Avoidance of negation through submission

However, Benjamin (1988) adds a new dimension to the developing process:

> At the same time, the awareness of separate minds and the desire for attunement raises the possibility of a new kind of conflict. Already at one year the infant can experience the conflict between the wish to fulfill his own desire (say, to push the buttons on the stereo), and the wish to remain in accord with his parents' will. Given such inevitable conflict the desire to remain attuned can be converted into submission to the other's will. (p. 31)

Benjamin's reference to submission introduces the work of Emmanuel Ghent, whose contributions on "submission" and "surrender" will be elaborated further in the next section. In his classic paper "Masochism, Submission, Surrender: Masochism as a Perversion of Surrender" (1990), Ghent resonates with Benjamin's cautionary note. If the infant's desire for attunement and recognition with the mother does not encounter some component of mother's negation, its omnipotence remains intact in a submission that is the look-alike for surrender, but is in fact an extension of the infant's sense of omnipotence through the good behaviors that will control mother's responses.

The infant in this scenario learns that submitting to the parent is the way to fulfill its desires, but in so doing it gives up its own agency and spontaneity. The parent must also recognize the subjectivity of the infant. The infant might be understood as saying, "I am a subject; I have my own desire. Recognize that I want something you don't want, then I can give in to your setting limits without erasing myself."

SURRENDER IN ANALYSIS

> Freud knew about what he called action, and also about repetition. He said that no one could be slain in effigy or absentia. But unfortunately, he never came to grips with the intersubjective manifestations of repetition. He proposed that the analyst can stay clean, can be like the chemist handling dangerous chemicals. This denial that we too are chemicals only contributed to the combustion ...
>
> —Benjamin (2004b, p. 752)

> As analysts we repeatedly become involved in the role of failure, and it is not easy for us to accept this role unless we see its positive value. We get made into parents who fail, and only so do we succeed as therapists.
>
> —Winnicott (1962, p. 239)

From the beginning of treatment the analyst sensitively adapts to the emerging needs of the patient, respecting that patient as a human being who has dignity and significance. Over time, the disparate needs of analyst and patient begin to conflict. The march toward a confrontation takes shape in a process called "negation," one that is necessary to move beyond mere identification of analyst and patient to a recognition of others beyond the therapy room. In this process, the analyst, who had been experienced by the patient in a more or less idealized fashion, begins to be experienced as bearing similarity to painful figures in the patient's past. Through negotiating this disruption both analyst and patient emerge to a new awareness of the unique subjectivity of each other, and the patient gains the opportunity to address past wounds.

Identification and differentiation

I make every attempt to identify with, recognize, and adapt to my patient. A specific time is more suitable for the mother with school-aged children during the school year, but needs to be changed during the summer. Or, one patient prefers to pay for sessions once a month; another at each session. Another patient prefers to address me as *Marie*, while another would not think of calling me anything other than *Dr. Hoffman*. These are common and very benign adaptations. The sliding of the analyst into incarnation of the bad parent happens in very subtle ways initially, moving from simple differences to more profound repetitions of deleterious past relationships, before culminating in negation. For instance, if the mother of school-aged children began to expect a change in schedule every month, I would begin to feel imposed upon, perhaps in the same way that she felt imposed upon by a mother who was unpredictable and demanding. I might then become too unyielding to requests and incarnate into the rigid father who detested mother's unpredictability. If the patient who prefers to pay for sessions once a month neglects to pay even at that time, I would begin to feel used and might unwittingly respond as the irritated parent that demanded obedience, failing to discuss the lapse as an aspect of the treatment with the patient. With the patient who prefers to call me *Marie*, I might err toward assuming too great a closeness and neglect to be sufficiently attending to needs that lie behind the familiarity, echoing the patient's neglect by mother. Imperceptibly, both I and the patients begin to assert our individualities in ways that incarnate painful and enslaving past relationships. In essence, both therapist and patient begin to colonize each others' minds and see one another through a rigid lens of personal history.

Differentiation and negation

These distorted perceptions and the feelings that lurk within catapult us into enactments, enactments fueled by painful, unacknowledged, unmourned memories (Mangis, 2007). The mother who is desirous of continuous changes in schedule, when met by a more unyielding response from me, begins to be unyielding herself and might cancel sessions. In this, we both experience previous unmourned memories of feeling unheard and being rejected. The person who failed to pay at the end of the month might respond to my demands for payment with an angry outburst and an accusation that I am just like the father that only cared about his money, bringing to the treatment the memories of angry and selfish parents. And the patient with whom I have become too at ease might respond with a cool withdrawal and compliance that hides a seething anger at my neglect, similar to the quiet but unrelenting anger and neglect we both might have encountered in childhood. Each of these developments becomes part of the process of opposition between two people called *negation*, one that ultimately defines the contours of each individual subjectivity and promotes the establishment of mutual recognition.

Pizer (2003), paraphrasing Russell, describes the process this way: "Good therapy or analysis provides a crucible for emotional growth. It puts *both participants* in touch with a pain that they have not felt before, a pain that enables *memory* as opposed to repetition … [memories of] loss of what once was or should have been … memories that must be borne and grieved" (p. 173).

Negation and surrender

The therapist, realizing the healing necessity of bringing past into present, surrenders to a process in which he or she will at times experience joy but at other times endure pain with the patient. The patient's surrender to the process not yet understood is no less painful and is sometimes frightening. For each, a surrender to a process, a third, with belief in its ultimate benevolent goal, carries the treatment forward.

Earlier in this chapter, I introduced the work of Emmanuel Ghent (1990), who eloquently elaborated the construct of "surrender," and contrasted it with "submission." Ghent connects Winnicott's idea of destruction of the object (the parent) with the patient's surrender in faith to the process. In that surrender in faith, the patient finds that the object, that is, the therapist, survives the destructive attack. Ghent says, "One might imagine the subject saying to the object, 'I went all out, completely vulnerable, in the faith [or surrender] that someone was out there—and it turned out to be true, as I could only have known by destroying you with all my might, and yet here you are. I love you'" (p. 109). Ghent supports this view of surrender by referring to Michael Eigen's (1981) work on the area of faith in Winnicott, Lacan, and Bion. There, Eigen describes the experience of "stepping out" in faith, writing, "I mean to point to a way of experiencing which is undertaken with one's whole being, all out, 'with one's heart, with one's soul, and with all one's might'" (Ghent, 1990, p. 109).

Avoidance of negation through submission

Ghent (1990) proceeds to differentiate surrender from submission. For Ghent, "Submission, losing oneself in the power of the other, becoming enslaved in one or other way to the master, is the ever available lookalike to surrender" (p. 115). In accord with Winnicott, Ghent asserts that the most important factor in distinguishing between surrender and submission is the extent to which the object of surrender is truly outside the area of one's omnipotent control—is not an extension of the self—and therefore available to be utilized. In the next section, I will continue to develop Ghent's ideas, connecting them with the concept of thirdness.

CRUCIFIXION AS ANALOGUE TO SURRENDER IN HEGEL

> Death accomplishes the process whereby the divine idea has divested itself, divested itself unto the bitter anguish of death and the shame of a criminal, and thereby human finitude is transfigured into the highest—the highest love. That is the deepest anguish, this the highest love.
>
> —Hegel (Hodgson, 2005, p. 171)

> When the world shook and the sun was wiped out of heaven, it was not at the crucifixion, but at the cry from the cross: the cry which confessed

> that God was forsaken of God. And now let the revolutionists choose a creed from all the creeds and a god from all the gods of the world, carefully weighing all the gods of inevitable recurrence and of unalterable power. They will not find another god who has himself been in revolt. Nay (the matter grows too difficult for human speech), but let the atheists themselves choose a god. They will find only one divinity who ever uttered their isolation; only one religion in which God seemed for an instant to be an atheist.
>
> —Chesterton (1908, p. 145)

I have been drawing an analogy in this book between the therapist's efforts to incarnate, or identify with the patient, and Hegel's depiction of Christ's story, in particular His incarnation and death. We experience with our patients both the potential of relationship as we mutually identify with one another, and the incarnation into roles patients impose on us that seemingly negate that potential in the process of sharing these identifications. As we surrender to a process that will lead to unavoidable enactments, we experience firsthand the devastation that our patients have been forced to live through. At times we suffer unjustly for the crimes of others, a morass that echoes Freud's (1910b) remark to Pfister that "the transference is indeed a cross" (p. 39). At other times, the limit of the analogy between the therapist and the sinless Christ becomes evident as our own old object ties unconsciously propel us to engage in enactments for which we will suffer crucifixion.

Identification and differentiation

The basis of differentiation in Hegel's narrative begins with Trinity. There, three persons in one form the template that links transcendence with immanence, self and other—the basis of intersubjectivity. It is noteworthy that Benjamin's theorizing of *the one in the third* and *the third in the one* bears a distinct resemblance to Hegel's vision of humans made in the image of the Trinitarian God (Gunton, 1997; Stratton, 2006). So close is Benjamin's language to Christian theology that one may hear its echo in an excerpt of an early Christian poem attributed to St. Patrick entitled "St. Patrick's Breastplate":

> I bind unto myself today
> The strong name of the Trinity,
> By invocation of the same,
> *The Three in One and One in Three.*
>
> (9th century, Book of Armagh, emphasis added)

From Hegel's perspective, Christ, the second person of the Trinity, fully human in his needs, dependencies, longings, and disappointments, was not shielded by his divinity. Moreover, Christ progressively experienced the alienation that humans had experienced as he spoke of the mysterious "kingdom of God" that portrayed a community of people living in harmony through love rather than political conquest. Instead of enacting the projected images of what a powerful deity would do, a human, vulnerable God moves toward His necessary destruction. He became sin though He was God and had not sinned. Not only did God desire humans to see that they are related to God, but God needed to experience the suffering of humanity, looking "*at Himself from the (distorting) human perspective*" (Zizek, 2009, p. 82, emphasis in original).

Differentiation and negation

In *Phenomenology of Spirit* (1807/1977) Hegel first sets out his grand system which moves from incarnation through negation [crucifixion] to resurrection. His work became more systematized and would be presented in subsequent lectures such as his 1827 lectures on religion in which he reviewed his entire system. Hegel (2005) summarizes the first two movements of his system in these 1827 lectures [3:273-4]:

> 1. First, in and for itself, God [is] in his eternity before the creation of the world and outside the world.
> 2. Second, God creates the world and posits the separation. He creates both nature and finite spirit. What is thus created is at first an other, posited outside of God. But God is essentially the reconciling to himself of what is alien, what is particular, what is posited in separation from him. He must restore to freedom and to his truth what is alien, has fallen away in the idea's self-[diremption], in its falling away from itself. This is the path and the process of reconciliation. (Hodgson, 2005, p. 128)

In both *Phenomenology of Spirit* (1807/1977) and in the 1827 lectures, Hegel articulates the concept of a redemptive God who confronts the alienation of humanity and through Christ mediates a reconciliation.The reconciliation between humanity and God and in turn within and between humans, of which Hegel speaks, operates through the "work of the negative." Hegel presents that work as an indispensible aspect of the establishment of mutual recognition. For Hegel (1807/1977), the apex of the "work of the negative" is Christ's crucifixion, and this becomes the exemplar from which he draws his philosophical conclusions. He writes:

> But the life of Spirit is not the life that shrinks from death and keeps itself untouched by devastation, but rather the life that endures it and maintains itself in it. It wins its truth only when, in utter dismemberment,

> it finds itself. ... Spirit is this power only by looking the negative in the face, and tarrying with it. This tarrying with the negative is the magical power that converts it into being. (p. 19)

Christ freely surrendered to a process in which He became totally "other" to God the Father in His crucifixion and death, relinquishing God's infinitude for the utmost human finitude in death. He became the receptor of humanity's distorted projections, dying in a state of utter alienation from God and humans. Yet, His surrender was to a God of love who ensured that destruction would not have the final word and that Christ would survive the destruction through a negation of negation, resurrection to new life. Christ's survival of destruction demonstrated his divinity in humanity and initiated the reconciliation of relationship between God and humans, within humans themselves, and between humans. Hodgson (2005) clarifies this sequence in Hegel's system:

> The world has fallen away from God and "fixated itself as finite consciousness as the consciousness of idols". ... To desist from this separation is to turn back to God" (3:65). ... The 1824 lectures spell this out more fully: "Reconciliation begins with differentiated entities standing opposed to each other [negation]—God, who confronts a world that is estranged from him, and a world that is estranged from its essence. ... Reconciliation is the negation of this separation, this division, and means that each cognizes itself in the other, finds itself in its essence. [1824 lectures 3:171-2] (Hodgson, 2005, p. 97)

Hegel's system thus becomes the template from which intersubjectivity is drawn. Hegel chronicles God's recognition (consciousness) of Himself in humanity first through incarnation, then through a confrontational negation of Himself in Christ's death, and later through the negation of that negation in the resurrection—that is, Christ's survival of destruction—which culminated in Spirit and humanity becoming one, and opened the possibility of intersubjective, loving relationship to God and each other.

In Hegel's theologically conceived movements, we can perceive the analogous process of the therapist, who will endure crucifixions during the course of treatment. Through a surrender in faith to a force for life that survives destruction, the therapist's and patient's differentiated subjectivities are validated and a unity in the thirdness of their shared journey is established.

Negation and surrender

Idolatry

Idolatry is the submissive "look-alike" to surrender, for the idol, created or chosen by the person, is an extension of the self. In Ghent's writing on surrender, it is not coincidental that he refers to Biblical passages concerning idolatry as he explains Winnicott's concept of object-relating. Ghent quotes part of a passage in the Torah, Deuteronomy 6:5 (Tanakh), as Eigen (1981) had previously. The full passage reads, "You shall love the LORD your God with all your heart and with all your soul and with all your might." That is, one's omnipotence is to be negated as one surrenders to a life force that is beyond one's control.

It may help to place this passage in its Biblical context. From the opening words of Deuteronomy, Moses is communicating God's message to Israel. He reminds the people of God's provision, protection, and guidance. He rehearses the Decalogue. In verse 5 of Chapter 6, after cataloging God's goodness to them, Moses relates God's injunction that they surrender to Him: "You shall love the LORD your God with all your heart and with all your soul and with all your might." The framing of this surrender is that He alone is to be worshipped and loved as God. He is the only true God; nothing else was to be worshipped, for this would constitute idolatry. What would be worshipped would be a production of one's own mind imputed to the object or personage of worship; idolatry in Winnicott's terms is object-relating. Erich Fromm, in *You Shall Be as Gods* (1966), eloquently summarizes this concept. He writes:

> The contradiction between idolatry and the recognition of God is, in the last analysis, that between the love of death and the love of life. … Again and again the prophets characterize idolatry's self-castigation and self-humiliation, and the worship of God as self-liberation and liberation from others. … Idolatry, by its very nature, demands submission—the worship of God, on the other hand, independence. (pp. 37, 39)

Love of God is thus a relinquishing of omnipotence and a surrender to His process of growth in life. It is a surrender in faith to a benevolent life force that is ours to use; it is a courageous, passionate, and whole-hearted path of living (Ghent, 1990). The creation of idols, in contrast, is a submission to extensions of the self. Through Moses and the Torah, the idea of surrender to a transcendent Other available for object usage was juxtaposed against idolatry, a prefiguring of object relating, submission, and perversion.

Avoidance of negation through submission: Fundamentalism

As a cultural phenomenon, legalistic submission to God is understood as an aspect of fundamentalism; in Ghent's understanding, submission is a perversion of surrender. An authentic longing to surrender to a God who gives meaning and purpose can fall prey to a false surrender, or submission, to a perverse God representation (Jones, 1991; Rizzuto, 1979). Freud desired to exclude religion from psychoanalytic discourse because of his astute recognition of religious falsehood, a falsehood he had suffered both personally and culturally. But Freud's renunciation of perverse theism evolved from his personal views (as he stated), to an implicit, nearly institutional *shibboleth* in psychoanalysis with regard to theism. This unconscious "reversal" dismissed even the consideration of a salient goodness in authentic theistic narratives. Currently, this historic psychoanalytic reversal may be contributing to the rapidly escalating acrid complementarity between theism and atheism that is burgeoning into a cultural-wide enactment. Having no third of humility or agnosticism, I believe this complementarity of theism/atheism may unwittingly be promoting fundamentalist zealotry in theists and atheists alike, for that which is repressed or dissociated returns with vengeance. Theists would do well to humbly acknowledge that Freud (1927) was right: *That* "illusion" didn't deserve a "future." Likewise, atheists would do well to recognize Pfister's hope in a theism transformed by the very process of rupture and survival of destruction, and in so doing humbly acknowledge a mystery which is beyond human control.

THE LONGING TO SURRENDER

Ghent suggested that there is a universal longing to surrender. In the Christian narrative, the longing to surrender is the spiritual cry of the human soul for relationship with God and neighbor. Such surrender anticipates an enlivening experience of faith and reliance on a loving, but at times mysterious, God.

Surrender to the relational, Trinitarian God facilitates our recognition of His trace in our neighbor (Vitz & Felch, 2006; Watson, 2007). This connection is supported in both Hebraic thought (e.g., Deut. 6:5; Lev. 19:18, Tanakh) and in the gospel narrative as seen in this question posed to Jesus:

> Master, which is the great commandment in the law? Jesus said unto him, Thou shalt love the Lord thy God with all thy heart, and with all thy soul, and with all thy mind. This is the first and great commandment. And the second is like unto it. Thou shalt love thy neighbor as thyself. On these two commandments hang all the law and the prophets. (Matthew 22:36–40, KJV)

The words of Jesus and Moses suggest that surrender to God is surrender to Him as transcendent subject, and as immanent subject in my neighbor in whom God's image radiates. Thus, surrendering to God in the therapeutic encounter would mean surrendering to a process that one cannot control, but a process that can be trusted. Surrender to this God is a surrender out of love and to love; thus, it is an eminently relational surrender (Barsness, 2006; Parlow, 2008). The God apprehended by Christians suffers for and with "others," in a *telos* of reconciliation as we have seen in Hegel's thinking.

Recognition of the scandal of an involved and suffering God was not inaugurated by Christianity and is found to have deep Hebraic origins. Abraham Heschel (1959), Jewish theologian, described the theology of the Tanakh as a "theology of the divine pathos" (1959) refuting the notion of an apathetic God who does not respond to the pain of his creation. Heschel believed that God, in fact, dwells in the suffering and persecution of His people.[2] Christian theologians including La Cugna (1991), Moltmann (1981), and Zizioulas (1997), in concert with their Jewish cohorts, believe that the ubiquitous human need to surrender finds its fulfillment in a relational matrix that includes both a suffering God and one's suffering neighbors.

Dueck and Goodman's (2007) portrayal of the analyst may further an understanding of a Christian view of surrender and its ethical implications for analysts with their patients. Referencing Lévinas they write: "In an encounter with a client, we have before us an individual exposed, nude, vulnerable, and with a history of being psychologically murdered. In seeing the face before us, we lay down our lives before the patient. We expiate for the murders performed" (p. 612).[3]

THE THIRD: THE EMPOWERING AGENT OF SURRENDER[4]

For Ghent it is not the *event* of negation and subsequent survival, but the overall *process* of healing and growth made possible through surrender that bears striking resemblance to Hegel's description of the Spirit's dialectical action in history. The longing to surpass submitting complementarities and move toward an experience of surrendering mutuality would be understood by Hegel as the force for growth, Spirit.

In Trinitarian theology, this is the Spirit, the third person of the Trinity,[5] the sacred liaison between the transcendent God who is "Other" and the immanental God in ourself and our neighbor. The analogue in psychoanalysis to Spirit is a transcendent moral third who disjoins and liberates our complementarities and the immanental "analytic third" (Ogden, 1986) who conjoins and celebrates our communion (Lowery, 2006; Parker, 2008). Hegel's inviting Spirit who is love, life, creativity, comfort, and hope is at the same time the differentiating illuminator of law and ethics who beckons the human spirit toward communion and away from destructiveness. This Spirit provides both law and love in conjunctive and disjunctive movements of thirdness (see Chapter 6).

During the phase of crucifixion and surrender, the Spirit moves toward differentiation, toward disjunction from the projections that mire in complementarities. Surrender to this Spirit of lawfulness in the Christian narrative corresponds to surrender to Benjamin's "moral third," a surrender that disjoins a dyad stalled in projective processes. Surrender to the "moral third" in the Christian narrative and in psychoanalytic practice is achieved and lost repeatedly, a pattern of disruption and repair reflected in all human relationships. I will revisit the subject of thirds in Chapter 6, where I will examine its clinical context.

Having survived destruction, the experience of *we*-ness can return in a conjunctive thirdness of Spirit. In Part III, I will examine this function of the Spirit that inspires and celebrates communion.

ENDNOTES

1. Earlier writings of Jessica Benjamin used the phrase "one-in-the-third" to depict this concept.
2. Lewis Aron (2004b) explores the relationship of Heschel's theology to psychoanalytic ideas in his paper "God's Influence on My Psychoanalytic Vision and Values."
3. Ghent (1990) refers to the role of the therapist in similar terms; however, his view is that it potentially reflects a longing for surrender that has taken a masochistic turn, as opposed to a surrender to a relationship with a redemptive God, the trace of whom the therapist sees in the patient.
4. Alexander Kojève, in his interpretation of Hegel's master/slave dialectic, popularized an almost exclusive, secular focus on this segment of *Phenomenology*, resulting in what some feel is a distortion of Hegel's project (Williams, 1997). For Kojève, the resolution of this dialectic is the abolition of all oppression, including what he perceived as oppression emanating from faith in a divine Master. He writes: "To overcome the insufficiency of the Christian ideology to become free from the absolute Master and beyond, to realize freedom and to live in the world as a human being, autonomous and free—all this is possible only on the condition that one accept the idea of death, and consequently, atheism" (O'Neill, 1996, p. 64).

   An understanding of Hegel's master/slave dialectic should be apprehended only in the context of the whole corpus of his writings. Contextualized in this fashion, Hegel does not, in fact, prescribe the resolution of the dialectic through a destruction of belief in God. Rather, Hegel addresses the necessary destruction of God as *abstraction* or idolatrous projection (in much the same fashion as object-relating). He notes, "The death of the Mediator [Christ] is the death not only of his *natural aspect* or of his particular being-for-self… but also of the *abstraction* of the divine Being [*Phenom. of Spirit* 476]" (Kung, 1987, p. 219). God appeared in the particularity of Christ's human finiteness, the very negation of a transcendent God's infinitude. Hodgson (2005) explains: "This death is the highest love, for love is the consciousness of the identity of the divine and the human, and the finitization of the divine is carried to its extreme in death. Precisely in this monstrous picture we find an envisagement of the unity of the divine and the human at its absolute peak. Love entails a supreme surrender of oneself in the other, and the death of God in the death of Christ is the highest expression of divine love" (p. 171).

Thus God as idol and abstraction is destroyed, allowing for the possibility of mutual recognition based on separateness—God encountering the alterity of God, and humans experiencing the God/man. This mutual recognition replaces the idolatry and submission of the master/slave. The path of surrender is instantiated through the sacrificial death of Christ in which God as absolute ruler is put to death and emerges as surviving other in loving recognition. Commenting on his translation of this aspect of Hegel's writings, T. M. Knox affirms Hegel's *telos*: "The unity of life here is broken by the relation ... of bondage to an objective Lord, and equally broken by the sub-ordination of the individual to a universal end in which he has little or no share. The only solution to this discord is love, not the attenuated love which might be supposed to unite all Christians, but a genuine living bond, a true unity of opposites" (Dubose, 2000, p. 218).

5. This ongoing force that motivates toward surrender arises, according to the Christian narrative and in keeping with both Hegel's and Winnicott's theorizing, by Christ's survival of destruction, which allows "other than me substance" to impact the fabric of human relatedness. The "other than me substance" (Winnicott, 1968) constitutes for the Christian the sacred third, the Holy Spirit.

Chapter 6

Surrendering to the third with Mandy

Clinical perspectives

In the initial years of treatment, I had provided a transitional space in which Mandy could know a sense of safety (to the extent possible) in the world. I incarnated into what she needed me to be, and she became a patient who worked with deep commitment to herself, to the process, and to the belief that her life mattered to God. Mandy was a remarkable young woman. In those few years she achieved so much: marriage, a college teaching position, purchase of a home.

Her disturbing thoughts had become much less intrusive, though we still were not certain of the etiologies of the images. Though her marriage seemed to be going well, I continued to see a pattern of compliance that made her actions both with her husband and with me feel less than spontaneous; her connection, less than vital.

As the initial phase of treatment came to a close, I sensed a growing impasse in spite of the much-deepened ties. I could only describe the impasse as a feeling that we were both avoiding something that needed to be dealt with. With the help of a new supervisor, I discovered that not only had Mandy been relying on her rigid fundamentalist structure to give her an illusion of omnipotent control in her life, thereby avoiding feelings of terror and pain, but I, too, had unwittingly been guilty of the same illusion.

RECOGNIZING ENACTMENT

I began work with a new supervisor who conceptualized Mandy's case from a fresh perspective. He raised the question as to why I was spending so much time trying to find out the "truth" of the sexual abuse, in contrast to the amount of time I was spending about the loss of Mandy's mother. Mandy and I had, of course, talked repeatedly about that horrific event and its consequences. These conversations always seemed to lack energy. The sessions would regularly turn to a discussion of the extent of sexual abuse, and to the diminished yet still troublesome intrusive thoughts. The sexual focus seemed quite valid, and Mandy felt very supported in her pain and confusion, yet it too always seemed to come to a dead end.

As a result of a series of supervisory sessions, I developed the awareness of a powerful enactment deploying in Mandy and me. I had begun my work with Mandy as a spontaneously responding analyst who wished to incarnate the best of a maternal presence. As I entered the space in Mandy's world where the hideous evil had wrought Mandy's trauma, the ghosts were terrifying and I grasped for firm moorings, a predictable and reliable protector. No longer was I surrendering to an enlivening process of growth with Mandy, but I was dogmatically embracing a static religion of "Winnicottian holding" (and unconsciously eliding the last tenet of the Winnicottian "sacred text," i.e., "surviving destruction"). I was now colluding with Mandy to avoid the experience of our shared terror and fantasied annihilation, an experience that could move us from object relating to object usage, and thus to mutual recognition.

My identification with Winnicott disintegrated into theoretical idolatry. Winnicott was my savior of boundless love. Clinging to his mantle and obeying his "commandments" allowed me to dissociate my own fears of being destroyed by the horrors of what lurked without and what prowled within us both in the form of paternal objects. Abiding by the rules of a collapsed Winnicottian narrative, we were falsely feeling omnipotent control in the treatment, a feeling that was all too readily desired by Mandy and me. I began to realize that not only had I been projecting a dissociated, frightened part of myself on to Mandy,[1] but we both were employing Fairbairn's (1952) "moral defense"[2] by assuming that our "good behavior" could be an adequate response to such devastating trauma. In short, my understandable though idolatrous bid for omnipotence through perfectionism was preventing my deeper and necessary move into incarnation and crucifixion (L. Hoffman, 2010). For me to have expected that I would be able to handle such obliterating trauma without these defensive countermeasures may have been further manifestation of my therapeutic omnipotence.

Enactment and intersubjectivity

Paralleling the work that Mandy needed to do with respect to her dead mother was my reality that my mother was in the final stages of Alzheimer's dementia and would soon die.

The caring maternal role I had cultivated specifically to avoid becoming either of our unpredictable and destructive fathers had unwittingly morphed me into becoming a fundamentalist, dead maternal figure, a dynamic duo of my mother and Mandy's mother. I was forced to recognize that the impasse we were experiencing was our coconstruction to avoid apprehension of these painful maternal identifications. My working through of my own resistances to dealing with issues pertaining to my mother enabled me to accompany Mandy more authentically in her own work. Thus, this period of work with Mandy nudged us both closer to mourning the emotional and physical deaths of our mothers.

CLINICAL NOTES: 2000

The opportunity to experience these stronger feelings readily presents itself. In the session following her unexpected cancellation for what appeared to be less-than-critical reasons, with great trepidation, I spend most of the session attempting to explore whether Mandy might have been upset with me. After quite some hesitation, Mandy becomes frank about some frustrations she is feeling regarding the therapy. She pauses then becomes terrified. Would I still want to work with her? Had she grievously hurt me? The session ends with neither her fears nor mine fully allayed. However, I ask her whether she felt we had both survived the confrontation. She says, "Yes." While in most treatments this minor fracas would seem inconsequential, for Mandy it is a major step.

Next session: The crazy woman dream

Mandy arrived a half hour early for the next session and midway through the hour related this dream:

> I am at my old home, and Uncle Ned and my cousins Paul and Sam were there. There was a crazy woman. She was totally out of control. I shot at her or someone else shot at her. It didn't stop her. What was really odd is that the shooting happened but there was no blood. I looked at the woman and there were just old scars. She had to be subdued. She came downstairs. Then I felt something happened to me. I had been in the dream before, but now I felt I was just watching a video. Two guys captured her and tied her up. One of the guys performed oral sex on her (she was tied up so she could do nothing). Right then in the dream I felt like I was having sexual feelings. I didn't want to. It felt like the same kinds of feelings that I have when I have those horrible, repulsive images that come to my mind.

MANDY: I felt awful. What kind of dream is that? It's so weird! What's really weird is that this dream is different from the last one I had like it. Do you remember when I had the dream that Uncle Ned was actually doing this to me and it was evil?

MARIE: Yes.

MANDY: Well, in this dream what these men are trying to do is protect me from her. It wasn't evil. They were trying to distract her so she would be stimulated and then not be violent.

MARIE: So you're saying that this repulsive act was actually benevolent in nature?

MANDY: Yeah, I guess you could say that. They were really wanting to distract her so that she wouldn't be violent.

MARIE: How did you feel when you saw her in the dream?

MANDY: I was terrified. I was glad they were subduing her.

Recognizing the importance of this dream and how close we are to the end of the hour, I decide to attempt to bring clarity to what appears to be the message of the dream.

MARIE: So, you're saying that there is this woman who is filled with aggression and who terrified you. She's shot at but there is no blood, only old scars. Then as she gets closer to you, you back away, out of the dream. Then these men distract her from her aggression with this sexual behavior. You experience both relief that the aggressive woman is subdued, as well as revulsion at the act. Is this right?

MANDY: Yes.

MARIE: What are your thoughts about the dream, in particular, the fact that what felt like a repulsive sexual act actually protected you?

MANDY: I'm wondering if that doesn't have to do with my repulsive thoughts, that they are actually covering something I'm even more afraid of.

The session ends shortly after. We both are experiencing a greater aliveness and an awareness that we can confront some of the stronger emotions that we have been avoiding. I reconfirm my own commitment, however, to not overwhelming or retraumatizing her. The vitality of her lived life must always be kept in mind.

Clinical commentary: Insight from enactment resolution

As a result of my supervision and the dream that emerged in this session, I began to conceptualize more creative understandings of the dynamics of Mandy's symptoms. Were Mandy's religious standards not only providing a sense of omnipotent control, but also serving a secondary defensive function? What kind of alarm could ring so loudly in her mind to distract her from an agony, a despair, a rage that could potentially annihilate her? Sexual abuse as a parallel trauma, with the consequent intrusive thoughts, could be invoked as a distracter from affects of a more potent trauma that neither she nor I desired to experience. With Mandy's sacred text's prohibition of sexual sin, and my sacred text's emphasis on adequate holding, we were avoiding the more painful affect adhering to death, loss, and absence. If this deeper affect could be accessed, perhaps the need for the intrusive, distracting sexual images would diminish. Our surrender to an alive, though painful, process, coupled with a faith in ourselves and in a force for life, could allow for stronger feelings that we could survive.

The resolution of this enactment also clarified that, particularly in cases of trauma, destructiveness in the treatment is measured relatively. For Mandy, merely questioning her dissatisfaction felt threatening, as evidenced by her subsequent dream. Negation, destruction, crucifixion, and surrender are variably defined depending on the particular individuals in the dyad, and survival is never guaranteed. Thus a healthy respect for our own and our patient's vulnerabilities and for the volatility of the process will lead us to supervisory thirds who can help navigate the shoals of such enactments.

My breakdown in holding of dialectics had led to impasse. First, the dialectic of *suspicion* and *faith* was abdicated due to my fear that further investigation would destabilize a conveniently predictable therapy. What I thought to be faith was really my clutching an alluring idol in much the same fashion as a fundamentalist would cling to dogma in lieu of true faith. Second, I was ignoring the *experience* of stagnation as I clung to a *theory* that supported my need to experience omnipotent control. Third, I was misguided in my *archeological* exploration, shrouded in my own theoretical and emotional bias, and was thus impeded in moving toward any *telos*. Finally, I was locked into a position of *immanence*, in which projective processes prevented me from seeing ourselves as *transcendent*, separate subjects. While I was mired in an omnipotent loving of Mandy that would provide all that she needed, Mandy pursued the role of a perfectly submissive patient, both of us believing we were in control of the outcome of our work. Both of us were submitted to respective fundamentalist patterns of controlling our interactions. Beneath our efforts to control was a longing both in Mandy and me to surrender to a more vital process. Ghent suggested that the perversion of "submission" subverts that very longing.

THE WORK OF THE THIRD

In my work with Mandy, our lack of surrender because of our need to retain an illusion of our omnipotence and an avoidance of pain resulted in inhibited progress and a deadening of our work. However, the force for life, the ultimate "background" third, operated through the recommendations of an astute mentor as well as through my own analyst, who helped me deal with my own resistances. I could be reflexive once more as we surmounted the impasse and reexperienced creativity.

Oscillation and the third

My diminished capacity for reflexivity with Mandy was demonstrated by my failure to hold the dialectics of suspicion and faith, theory and experience, archeology and teleology, and the subsequent collapse into immanence. Recent literature on the goals of successful psychoanalytic therapy has emphasized the critical role of self-reflexivity, which is produced through the oscillation between various states and positions. Aron (2000) explains: "Self-reflection, from this point of view, is based on the capacity for internal division, healthy dissociation, 'standing in the spaces' between realities (Bromberg, 1998), building bridges (Pizer, 1998) the *transcendent, oscillating, or dialectical function*" (p. 677; italics added).

Loewald (1988) described this same process in different terms (see Altman, 2002). He saw a most fundamental oscillation between primary-process and secondary-process thinking, between thinking that flows from a position of merger/immanence and thinking that emerges from a position of separateness/transcendence: Loewald believed that living in a dialectic with both was necessary to healthy functioning.

Drawing on Aron's and Loewald's views, current theories of information processing (Lichtenberg, Lachmann, & Fosshage, 1992; Bucci, 1997; Boston Change Process Study Group, 2010), other relational theorists (Daniel Stern, 1985; Beebe & Lachmann, 1998, 2002), and Fonagy and Target's (1998) concept of mentalization, I propose that the central function of oscillation is to produce movement from the immanence of projective identification (primary process) to the transcendence of self-reflexivity (secondary process) and back again to a reconstructed unity.

The binding into recalcitrant complementary roles, which so defines paranoid/schizoid functioning, has required that theorists conceptualize another aspect of a psychoanalytic theory of mind that would account for the ability to move to a space of reflection. In this space one could birth creative alternatives, rather than simply rehearse current primary and secondary process schemas. Attempts to conceptualize and catalyze this emergence of creativity have yielded the hypothesis of a *tertiary process*.

Oscillation and tertiary process

Tertiary process[3] is a concept elaborated upon by Arieti (1976) in his landmark work on artistic creativity. Apart from the earlier work of André Green (1974), this concept did not impact psychoanalysis for some time, although creativity is most certainly present in psychoanalytic work. *Tertiary process* may be defined as a mental system that integrates data from primary and secondary process systems, is highly imagistic, and enables creativity. It is associated with artistic production and spiritual experiences and appears optimally geared toward the reorganization of parts into wholes, and thereby into new, life-enhancing creations. Ironically, Arieti (1976) never referenced Winnicott's contributions in the area of creativity, so we are left wondering about the interplay of transitional (or potential) space with the tertiary process, two concepts that seem to deal with similar phenomena in creativity and play. Schecter (1983) suggests:

> In summary, I would like to propose that the transitional illusionistic world of the child is both an anlage and pre-condition for the Tertiary Process described by Arieti. The transitional world brings together "subjective" and "objective" experience; the Tertiary process combines primary and secondary process. (p. 198)

Oremland (1985) offers this amendment:

> The creative process can be thought of as a developmental recapitulation begun by regressive dedifferentiation that progresses into transitional functioning [differentiation]. But creativity requires a third step. The transitional experiencing must give way to a different tertiary process as the object on a more cognitive level is worked on, over, and with until it becomes the art piece. Developmentally, creativity is a progression and intermixing of infantile, childlike, and adult functioning. (p. 420)

Green (2004) both repeats the preceding views of tertiary process and adds, without comment, a new component:

> It is also the lack of such processes or their impairment, described by Bion (1962), that accounts for the absence of progress in analysis. A similar circumstance was described by Winnicott (1971a) as the inability to play or the lack of a transitional area seen in some patients. (p. 108)

What Green has added is his juxtaposition of Bion's (1962) work on "alpha functioning" with Winnicott's (1971a, 1971b) work on lack of transitional space. Here, for the first time, we see the tertiary process linked with both the intrapsychic movements of primary and secondary processes and the movements within the intersubjective space of the clinical dyad—that is, the move from immanence to transcendence, which creates transitional space. I believe that the tertiary process may be redefined in a more comprehensive fashion to include intrapsychic functions (integrating of primary and secondary processes, including spiritual aspects) and intersubjective functions (creation and negotiation of transitional space) that prompt oscillation into and out of immanence/merger states.

Oscillation in summary

A fundamental oscillation in the therapy with Mandy involved the movement from object-relating immanence to object usage transcendence. This movement, I would assert, occurred through the prompting of the tertiary process, which operating in concert with the force for life, facilitated the intersubjective (between Mandy and me) emergence of transitional space. This space was created through the tertiary process action of a disjunctive third (thinking of theory, my supervisor, a book, a dream) that promoted new and creative treatment possibilities. The tertiary process action unbalanced the static complementarity that had solidified between Mandy and me, and it opened space for creative development, which led to a renewed experience of a conjunctive "analytic third," and relaunched us in our development of mutual recognition.

CLINICAL NOTES: 2000–2001

Sessions have become more vital. Mandy is talking directly about her fears of upsetting me with her feelings. She is also beginning to explore in more depth the relationship with her mother that predated the murder. We have both realized Mandy's longing for Mother's approval, and Mandy's feelings of not being known as Mandy by her mother. Mandy has come to the conclusion that Mother was depressed due to the intolerable living situation.

Mandy is focusing repeatedly on the agony of the loss of her eye. If I were to see her without her eye, would I be repulsed, she asks. Her tone in sessions is laden with greater sadness.

Mandy's grandmother is placed in a nursing home. She wrestles with guilt. She is able to experience feelings without being overwhelmed by them. She encounters difficulties with husband, relatives, and colleagues and is able to assertively respond, though she continues to doubt herself.

Mandy has been hired for a full-time teaching position at a college. She has also succeeded in publishing some articles. She begins work on her doctorate.

Alarming news comes that her father is pursuing his release from the mental institution where he was supposed to remain for life. Mandy is terrified at the prospect.

Session: April 10, 2001

MANDY: I took a walk yesterday and fell. I'm OK but achy. Everything is going well, but I had a strange reaction to a show last night—an ER-type show. The plot was that the husband had an affair with his wife's sister, and then they separated. He wanted to come back, but then he had another affair. I think it reminded me of having felt jealous before we were married. I was jealous of anyone he spent time with or gave time to.

MARIE: You felt threatened that you might not be the only one or that he would leave you.

MANDY: Last night I had to get rid of the feelings after the show. I was going to journal them. I got worried that something is going to overwhelm me. When that happens, I get afraid of having a breakdown.

MARIE: What were the feelings?

MANDY: With my dad—I always "cheated" on my mom by being close to Dad. I got out my baby book. Found something I didn't see before—a short letter to Mom from Dad. He wrote, "The one I love doesn't trust me. It breaks my heart." Of course she shouldn't have trusted him.

MARIE: How do you see yourself as part of all this?

MANDY: As a child I could sense the pain of my mother that my father cheated on her.

MARIE: With whom?

MANDY: A lot of women. He took us with him.

MARIE: How do you feel that impacted you—being placed in a situation where you are aware that Mom is being betrayed?

MANDY: I guess I compartmentalized.

MARIE: How did that work?

MANDY: I must have not thought about Mom. I wonder if Mom was aware of it. I wonder if she was hurt.

MARIE: So Mandy, if there were feelings to be frightened of in this conversation, what might they be?

MANDY: I guess…guilt?

MARIE: About what?

MANDY: Not telling my mother what was going on.

MARIE: Why would you not have wanted to tell Mother?

MANDY: I can't imagine—most kids say everything. I guess I didn't want to upset her. Maybe she would be mad. Because I don't consciously remember trying to hide things from her.

MARIE: So I'm wondering if some of what you were feeling after the show was connected to your own history.

MANDY: Hmm. Sadness for Kim in the show. It must be related to my mother. I guess I don't know where to put Mom. In my mind if she can see me I would never … Well, she knows how much I love her. But there's nothing I can do about it.

MARIE: We're going to have to stop. This is pretty loaded material. How are you feeling?

MANDY: I don't know where to put Mom. My instinct is to put it away.

MARIE: You don't need to. You can call and we can talk.

Session: April 17, 2001

Mandy began the session by disclosing that she kept putting off calling me about last week. She was afraid I would be upset.

MARIE: Can you explore with me what you were afraid I would say or do?

MANDY: Anytime I am in a conflict about doing something, I don't want to be the "bad girl" and hurt anyone. I got so depressed last Thursday but I couldn't figure out why. My crazy thoughts increased so much. I would never actually hurt myself, but I did fantasize briefly about taking drastic measures.

MARIE: Do you have any idea of why you would want to do that?

MANDY: I just wanted to stop the thoughts.

MARIE: I wonder if there is another reason. Do you remember our last session when you became very sad about the loss of your mother, and you said you would deal with it by just shutting it off instead of contacting me? Then there was the session before that where you talked about being caught in a conflictual situation between Mom and Dad on the day of the murder. You felt like a "bad girl" that day.

MANDY: Maybe I felt guilty. I was afraid of Mom's anger. I remember a dream in the hospital after she died, that she was angry at me. I really think I decided never to lose control of my feelings because it meant catastrophe. Getting close meant catastrophe. Getting someone angry meant catastrophe.

MARIE: And you probably fear that if you allow yourself to feel now and lean on me, I will not be there.

MANDY: (At this point she had been crying for 20 minutes.) I do want to lean on you, and I'll call instead of just taking care of myself.

Mandy and I are allowing the therapy process to flow with far less restriction. Mandy is moving away from the initial focus, which was fear of Father, and beginning to deal with the greater pain, which has to do with Mother.

Mandy discovered her baby book and read over it with me. She seemed touched by her mother's love that was apparent in it. The sessions that just occurred are rare in her expression of feelings regarding her mother.

On April 28, 2001, shortly after the above session, my mother passed away. My clinical notes from the sessions upon my return are as follows.

Session: May 8, 2001

We discussed how she went to a funeral of a former friend of her mother and cried over her death. She went on to discuss sadness over my mother's death and over the loss of her own mother. She spoke of the fears of her grandmother's impending death.

Session: May 15, 2001

Mandy appeared to recognize that she renders me dead in an identification with her dead mother, an identification for which my history provides a valency. She becomes the little girl who keeps her dead mother "frozen in time" and does not have to mourn her death nor deal with the potential pain of attaching to me and losing again. We discussed how I felt like the little girl as well who wanted an alive mother but experienced the deadness in her. I acknowledged to her that my own relationship with my mother was making it easy for me to identify with her dead mother.

Clinical commentary: The dead mothers; the mothers who died

André Green (1983) wrote his classic work *The Dead Mother* depicting the relationship between child and depressed mother, whose preoccupation with her own mourning has rendered connection with her child impossible. In his treatise, Green specifically outlined the dynamics that inhered when the child's mother was physically alive, though emotionally dead. Such was the case for Mandy. For before the physical death of Mandy's mother, Mandy had experienced her as a "dead mother" emotionally. In the transference then, an interplay of deadened mothers and yearning children was often present. Jed Sekoff (1999) poignantly describes this interplay:

> Yet, the common body of the dead mother complex elaborates an object that is less between two subjects, than within each of their skins. At any one time in Nina's treatment, either of us might occupy the terrain of the dead other or of the captive self, the yearning subject or the frozen object. It proved imperative to be attentive to these psychical movements lest the stasis binding Nina remain misrecognized as a one-dimensional process, rather than as the mutual construction of a beckoning object and a responsive subject. (p. 115)

However, in my relationship with Mandy, her mother was both emotionally and physically dead, rendering the treatment more complex. Mandy's memories of her mother were of a depressed and absent woman who had little time for her. Though her memories seemed to be categorically negative, from time to time when affect regarding her mother's loss emerged, there was deep sadness. Mandy read her baby book with amazement at the love that seemed to pour from her mother's detailed accounting of her early life. Mandy had not experienced enough of Mother's care and had experienced Mother's gruesome death and her fantasied role in her mother's death. Together, these experiences perpetuated a dissociation of affect that eclipsed most feelings of love for her mother. Intersubjectively, Mandy and I enacted our "dead mothers," while we were engaged in mourning the actual deaths of our mothers; Mandy's mourning was a very complicated grief indeed.[4]

Green (1983) depicts the path of healing for the frozen child who clutches to the "entombed" mother within. He suggests that

> by using the setting as a transitional space, [this approach] makes an ever-living object of the analyst, who is interested, awakened by the analysand, giving proof of his vitality by the associative links he communicates to him. (p. 5)

My task with Mandy was to remain alive to my own feelings and to hers, so that an alive attachment could recommence for Mandy. In this process, the survival of destruction would be of a different sort: I would need to experience and wrestle with the feelings of being her dead mother, her dead self, and at the same time through my faith and love believe that resurrection was possible. But what would resurrection look like? How would it happen?

CLINICAL NOTES: 2002–2003

Mandy begins twice-weekly therapy.

Mandy's father's request for discharge from the hospital was denied. Mandy is greatly relieved.

Her grandmother passes away. Memories of times past are processed. Memories of her mother do not seem to emerge, though interest in exploring her history has increased. Mandy has made trips to visit relatives to ask for details about her childhood. She has revisited her mother's grave and found it. Mother's Day becomes an anniversary of feeling sadness over Mom. She died during that time of year.

Mandy is commanding great respect as a professor. She is feeling more strength in her marriage as well. She is more comfortable with a variety of friends, even those who are opposed to her religious persuasions. Her faith is becoming something that she wishes to study and understand. She will be teaching a college course in the Bible as literature. She is already talking about the ways that she values the Bible, but also sees it as subjected to many different interpretations. She begins to want to dialogue about how faith can also embrace reason, but remain relational.

Mandy gives me permission to present her case at American Psychological Association's Division 39 conference.[5] I am amazed at her growing desire to have her story make a difference in people's lives. No longer is shame her only reaction to her story.

Clinical commentary

Therapeutic work proceeds through many layers of enactments, most often the less threatening appearing first. Though I had rightly attempted to avoid one enactment—turning into Father—I had fallen into another that was even more frightening. "Surviving" the initial confrontation, small though it was, fortified both Mandy and me to endure further struggles with even deeper agonies. Having begun to work through the self-state that embodied shame in relationship to her father, I was pleased to see that she was beginning to experience something generative as a result of her trauma. I was seeing, in our working through of enactments, encouraging manifestations in Mandy of transformations of her trauma into something redemptive. Peter Shabad (2001) puts words to my experience: "The recognition and acceptance of our unique offerings engenders in us a sense of worth or personal dignity of having a special part to play within the whole" (p. 38).

ENDNOTES

1. Complementary and concordant identifications: Issues often present themselves from the least painful to the most. Mandy and I had initially focused on her father's rage. In order to understand the transference that ensued, it was useful to appropriate Racker's (1988) ideas regarding complementary and concordant transferences.

   In brief, Racker posited that roles emerge in the therapeutic process that are connected either to the subject herself or to the significant objects in the subject's life. For instance, if as therapist I were seen in the role of the angry father, I would be occupying a complementary transference position, that is, complementary to the subject, my patient. She in turn would be in the concordant role; that is, she would assume the position of the frightened child that was terrified of Father's rage. That role was concordant with who she was.

   Throughout much of the first segment of our work, I had perceived myself as attempting to control the eruption of aspects of Mandy's father in me, for my own experiences with my father gave me a valency for enacting hurtful behavior. I would not treat Mandy as I had been treated. Mandy, on her side, was also fearful of the rageful father in her and restricted her behaviors and requests so that she would not damage me or catapult me into being a rageful father. In addition to these internal fears, the reality of Father's true evil loomed over the treatment. The consequence of all of this was that we both became deadened and imperceptibly drifted into enacting a more hidden agony, that of the dead mothers that we both harbored.

2. Fairbairn's (1952) "moral defense" entails the child's imputing goodness to a bad parent and internalizing the parent's badness, with the net effect of experiencing some omnipotent control over one's life. His well-known saying is, "Better to be a sinner in a world ruled by God, than to live in a world ruled by the devil" (p. 67).
3. I cite from my previous work: "It is as a result of the work of the tertiary process that thirds evolve. 'Thirds,' a construct most commonly associated with Ogden's (1994) writings on the 'analytic third,' is a term difficult to define adequately and is used variously in the literature. Most often it describes any experience or idea that emerges in the context of a binary polarization and that moves it from its fixed nature to one in which dialogue is possible. I believe that the many thirds described in the literature ultimately are of only two major types: conjunctive and disjunctive. In essence, rather than defining thirds by the location from which they emerge, the dyad or the individual, they may be defined by their function: Do they serve to move toward immanence or toward transcendence; toward merger or toward separateness? Aron, describing the space created by the tertiary process (although he does not refer to it this way) from which emerges the 'third,' depicts that space as being used for precisely this purpose. He describes it as part of a process of creation of 'a psychic space within which to think together about ways in which patient and analyst are similar and different, merged and separate, identified and differentiated from one another' (2006, p. 363).

   "Thirds, then, may derive from virtually any source and are designed to unbalance a static system, toward a creative shift that culminates in a sense of 'oneness,' or Ogden's 'analytic third.' This creative shift will serve to reconfigure the process again in the endless series of ruptures and repairs that the literature has well documented" (2008, pp. 467–468).
4. Space will not allow elaboration on a concept developed by Ferenczi called "Orphic" functioning. This aspect of personality emerges from severe trauma; is geared toward survival, not regeneration; and is experienced as an affectless intellectual component of the personality. "Orphic" functioning was elaborated upon by Nancy Smith (1998a, 1998b, 2001, 2004), for whose research I am grateful. Sadly, Nancy Smith passed away in 2009. She had ironically been a part of my life during college before her training in psychoanalysis. We reconnected many years later around our love for Ferenczi's works.
5. Randall Sorenson was chair of this panel, and this event marked the last time I would see him before his tragic and untimely death in 2005.

Chapter 7

Destruction and survival of the Christian narrative in Fairbairn and Winnicott

Historical perspectives

The middle of the twentieth century saw a beginning shift in the way that the Christian narrative became woven into psychoanalytic thought. The complementarity between religion and psychoanalysis that had existed since Freud encountered its own quiet negation by theorists whom I detailed in Chapter 4, though two stand as exemplars: W. R. D. Fairbairn and D. W. Winnicott. Influenced since childhood by the Christian narrative, Fairbairn and Winnicott did much to "use" it to great benefit for the psychoanalytic community, surrendering to an embrace of both psychoanalysis and the Christian narrative through the "third" of relationality. I will explore the role of religious narratives in the lives of these two theorists, whose work ultimately contributed to tectonic shifts in the geography of psychoanalysis.

RELIGION IN THE LIFE HISTORY OF FAIRBAIRN

In the early years

Born in 1889, William Ronald Dodds Fairbairn was the only child of Thomas and Cecilia Fairbairn. Thomas came from a Calvinist background of Scottish Presbyterianism, and Cecilia was Anglican. Ronald was raised in the Presbyterian tradition, his mother strictly upholding the father's preferences "to the point of being a martinet in bringing her son up to conform to the formalities of their class, religious and otherwise" (Sutherland, 1989, p. 2). According to Sutherland (1989), compulsory, weekly Sunday morning and evening church attendance with his parents did not seem to bother Ronald. The "story of God" was delivered in ample doses through the preaching of the "Word of God."

Scholarly sermons could last more than an hour, and Ronald would enjoy thoughtfully analyzing their content. Music from the psalter, a hymnal divided into segments teaching specific doctrines gleaned from the Psalms, was another powerful instructional tool. Most certainly, memorization of catechisms and Scripture was standard fare throughout his youth, as well.

In the adult years

Fairbairn carried into adulthood his interest in understanding the "serious matters such as religious, moral and social questions" (Sutherland, 1989, p. 4). He enrolled in the study of philosophy at Edinburgh University and he decided to become a minister during this period. His decision was probably influenced by the university faculty who, though renowned in philosophy, sought to integrate the new findings of science with the Christian faith. "The metaphysical content of Fairbairn's first degree was strongly influenced by the interests of Professor Andrew (Seth) Pringle-Pattison (1850–1931) in the philosophies of Kant and Hegel" (Scharff & Birtles, 1994, p. xiv). Pringle-Pattison, a scholar in the works of these German philosophers, was deeply interested in issues of faith as well. Contiguous to Fairbairn's years at Edinburgh (1907–1911), Seth Pringle-Pattison delivered the Gifford Lectures (1912–1913) under the title of "The Idea of God in the Light of Recent Philosophy" (1920). This series of lectures was essentially an apologetic for a belief in God that should be enhanced, not eradicated, by modern philosophy. In his final lecture, Pringle-Pattison (1920) passionately articulated a concept that is central to the Christian narrative, redemption by atoning love:

> No deeper foundation of Idealism can be laid than the perception ... of the spirit's power to transform the very meaning of the past and to transmute every loss into a gain. ... This is the real omnipotence of atoning love, unweariedly creating good out of evil; and it is no far-off theological mystery but, God be thanked, the very texture of our human experience. (p. 416)

Fairbairn did pursue an intermediate degree in divinity at the London University and then, at age 25, returned to Edinburgh, where he began his theological training in the Presbyterian Church. These studies, however, were interrupted by World War I, Fairbairn serving in the army for 3½ years. During this time Fairbairn's career interests shifted from religion to psychology. Fairbairn completed an analysis with an Australian businessman-turned-psychoanalyst named E. H. Connell. Connell, who had come to Edinburgh to study medicine, was analyzed by Ernest Jones. According to Sutherland (1989), Connell "was a very full-blooded Christian" (p. 7). Shortly after this analysis, and upon the death of his father, Fairbairn joined the Anglican Church and his religious beliefs became an exceedingly private matter. While noting in three separate passages in his biography of Fairbairn that he remained active in the church to the end, Sutherland also adds, "One matter he never raised was his continuing religious convictions" (p. 31).

In extraprofessional writing

The intensity of Fairbairn's Christian faith and his sense of mission are clearly evident in the following diary entry, dated August 11, 1910. Fairbairn, at 21, was contemplating Christian ministry and was troubled by the dualism that he believed was incapacitating the church.

> August 11th, which is notable as the 21st birthday of that humble servant of King George V, Ronald Dodds Fairbairn. Not only a humble servant of King George, I hope, however, but also of Jesus Christ; for, at a time such as this, it is well to be serious for a moment, and to pause at this great turning-point of life to take a breath of heavenly air, before plunging into the work and stress of manhood. It is hard to combine in the right mixture the jollity and the seriousness which are both essential for a presentable life. ... The ideal man, in my opinion, is one who, while realizing the seriousness and responsibility of life, yet sees life's whimsicalities and joys as well. But, how few of such there are! ... The serious side must never be neglected, but what I call full bloodedness must be remembered too. It is neglect of this, for one thing, that alienates modern youth from the Church. ... Is the religion of the average Church of today of a nature to capture and mould the full-blown life of the healthy-minded young man and woman? Or does it only provide for one type of mind? Is it only suited for half of the individual's life? True Christianity ought to satisfy every legitimate instinct and aspiration. It ought to be a working and workable philosophy of life for man and boy, matron and maiden; it ought to be adaptable to the condition of schoolroom and football field, of office and golf course, of factory and home. God give me strength to do my share, however little, to effect that unspeakably desirable consummation. I have decided to devote my life to the cause of religion; but may it be a manly, healthy, whole-hearted strong religion, appealing to enthusiasm of youth, as well as to the quiescence of old age—in other words may it be a Christlike religion. (Sutherland, 1989, pp. 6–7)

RELIGION IN THE LIFE HISTORY OF WINNICOTT

In the early years

Religion formed a central cultural framework for Donald Winnicott's early life. His father, J. Frederick Winnicott, was a study in English Wesleyanism. His Wesleyan ancestors had descended from the Midlands in the 1700s, settling in what was to become the geographic center of non-Anglican faith, Plymouth, Devon. Donald's father, later knighted and twice mayor of Plymouth, was an active member and Sunday school teacher at the King Street Wesleyan Church (Rodman, 2003, p. 383) and a founding member of the Wesleyan church on Mutley Plain. There he filled numerous functions, including serving on the synod (Rodman, 2003, p. 383) and singing in the choir (C. Winnicott, 1989, p. 8). Elizabeth, Donald's mother, an Anglican before marriage, supported her more dominant husband's denominational preference. Clare Winnicott referred to Donald's entire family as "leading lights in the church" and "profoundly religious" (Goldman, 1993, pp. 116–117). Frederick Winnicott took his religion (Wesleyan Methodism) very seriously, a religion that demanded a practical outworking of faith in civic responsibility and social action. He insisted that his son be raised according to the values taught in the Bible. In reflecting on this emphasis, Winnicott wrote:

> My father had a simple [religious] faith and once when I asked him a question that could have involved us in a long argument he just said: read the Bible and what you find there will be the true answer for you. So I was left, thank God, to get on with it myself. (C. Winnicott, 1989, p. 8)

One of the most prominent forms of education in the Wesleyan Church was music. Charles Wesley composed more than 6,000 hymns for his church. These hymns were a catechism set to music. Barbara Dockar-Drysdale, a lifelong friend of Winnicott, disclosed to his biographer Brett Kahr (1996) that "Winnicott loved to sing to himself whenever he walked up or down the stairs, preferring the church hymns of his Wesleyan Methodist childhood" (p. 105).

At the first appearance of "childish frivolity" (when, at age 14, Donald used the word *drat*), Donald's father enrolled his son at the Leys School, a Methodist institution founded for the express purpose of integrating faith with academic scholarship (Rodman, 2003, p. 23) and a school where daily chapel attendance and participation in evening prayers was required. The school's founding headmaster, William Fiddian Moulton, a Biblical scholar of international note, made Bible study a mandatory aspect of school life, a Christian school life augmented by a religious choir that Donald joined.

In the adult years

Winnicott faithfully attended the Methodist (Wesleyan) Church until he was 27 years old, at which time he converted to the Anglican Church, which his first wife attended. Concurrently, he became involved in psychoanalysis. He was introduced to psychoanalysis through reading a book by the Swiss pastor and Christian friend of Freud, Oskar Pfister. Winnicott's Christian belief is wryly couched in a letter to his sister, Violet, in which he attempts to explain psychoanalysis: "I shall probably be accused of blasphemy if I say that Christ was a leading psychotherapist" (Rodman, 2003, p. 43).

Another telling reference to Winnicott's religious beliefs is found in a letter sent to him by Joan Riviere, who at this point had been his analyst for at least 5 years. In it she states, "I don't share your demand for everything to be spontaneous in the sense of inspired. ... In other words, perhaps I do believe human beings can sometimes make something good and not that it always has to be God doing it!" (Rodman, 2003, p. 88). Rodman comments, "Her mention of his supposed insistence that everything must come from inspiration, which means it is God that is the ultimate source, is an extreme one. Nonetheless, his confidence in the power of internal sources ... is by this time very great" (p. 88).

Winnicott became an influential writer regarding the place of religion in culture, and though his church involvement declined, he continued to hold to "what can be characterized as a lingering religiosity" (Goldman, 1993, p. 115). This "lingering religiosity" is detectable in Winnicott's essay "Some Thoughts on the Meaning of the Word 'Democracy'" (1950), in which he states, "It is certainly helpful when the reigning monarch quite easily and sincerely ... proclaims a belief in God" (p. 255). Winnicott's second marriage was to Clare Britton, a child and grandchild of Baptist ministers and a very religious person herself (Rodman, 2003, p. 96). She attested that he "was only too thankful if anybody could believe in anything" (Goldman, 1993, p. 115).

Toward the end of Winnicott's life his resurgent interest in religion may have been, according to Clare Winnicott (1989), a negotiating of "his own [impending] death" (p. 3). In 1969, just two years before his death, Winnicott became interested in John Wycliffe and the Lollards. In a letter he characterized himself as "a natural Lollard [who] would have had a bad time in the 14th and 15th centuries" (Goldman, 1993, p. 119). The Lollards were a devout, dissenting group of Christians who suffered greatly for their views, an identification that Winnicott may have felt fit him as well.

According to Rodman (2003), "From at least the mid-1940s to the mid-1960s, Jesus Christ was clearly a figure with whom he identified" (p. 291). Yet Winnicott's interest became even more evident in these final years. The books *King Jesus* and *Nazarene Gospel Restored* fascinated him (Dodi Goldman, June, 2003, personal communication), and he corresponded with their author, Robert Graves (Phillips, 1988, p. 29). Winnicott's fascination with Jesus occurred concurrently with his final and influential work, *The Use of an Object* (1968), which details the destruction and survival of the object.

In extraprofessional writing

In the final decade of his life, Winnicott composed an enigmatic poem, "The Tree." Though some have interpreted the poem as referring strictly to Winnicott's need to enliven his depressed mother, I concur with Rodman (2003), who viewed the poem as also reflective of Winnicott's general identification with the figure of Christ, who suffered and gave of himself to bring life to others. The poem is presented in the form composed by Winnicott. I have added the bracketed Scripture references to denote Winnicott's verbatim usage of Biblical texts in the poem, which is written in the first person singular in identification with the recorded experiences of Jesus.

The Tree [Written November 4, 1963]

Someone touched the hem of my garment [Matt. 9:20, 14:36]
Someone, someone and someone

I had much virtue to give [Mark 5:30, Luke 6:19]
I was the source of virtue
the grape of the vine of the wine [John 15]
I could have loved a woman
Mary, Mary, Mary [Mark 15:40–41]
There was not time for loving
I must be about my father's business [Luke 2:49]
There were publicans and sinners [Matthew 9:10–11]
The poor we had always with us [Matthew 26:11]
There were those sick of the palsy [Matthew 4:24]
and the blind and the maimed [Matthew 15:30]
and widows bereft and grieving [Luke 7:11–15]
women wailing for their children [Jer. 31:15, Mt. 2:18]
fathers with prodigal sons [Luke 15:11–32]
prostitutes drawing their own water [John 4:7–30]
from deep wells in the hot sun

Mother below is weeping [John 19:25–27]
weeping
weeping

Thus I knew her

Once, stretched out on her lap
as now on a dead tree [John 19:17–25]
I learned to make her smile
to stem her tears
to undo her guilt
to cure her inward death

To enliven her was my living

So she became wife, mother, home
The carpenter enjoyed his craft [Mark 6:3]
Children came and loved and were loved [Matthew 19:13–15]
Suffer little children to come unto me [Mark 10:13–16]

Now mother is weeping
She must weep

The sins of the whole world weigh less than this
woman's heaviness [John 1:29]

O Glastonbury [Legendary first English church]

Must I bring even these thorns to flower? [Legend of the thorn]
even this dead tree to leaf?

How in agony
Held by dead wood that has no need of me
by the cruelty of the nail's hatred
of gravity's inexorable and heartless

pull
I thirst [John 19:28]

No garment now [John 19:23, 24]

No hem to be touched [Matthew 9:20]
It is I who need virtue [Luke 6:19]
Eloi, Eloi, lama sabacthani? [Matthew 27:46]

It is I who die [Luke 23:46]
I who die
I die
I (Rodman, 2003, pp. 289–291)

RELIGION IN THE CULTURES OF SCOTLAND AND ENGLAND

Christianity has enjoyed a long and comfortable habitation in the British Isles. References are made to Christians in Britain by Tertullian and Origen, dating back to about 200 CE. Names such as Pelagius, St. Alban, St. Patrick, the Venerable Bede, and Johannes Duns Scotus are luminaries of a British Christianity in which church and academy were interrelated.

The Christian narrative and the British enlightenment

The British Enlightenment differed from that "high" Enlightenment most associated with the French. In France, the *philosophes* revolted against all that was religious. Voltaire, writing to Diderot, stated, "'Religion must be destroyed among respectable people and left to the *canaille* large and small, for whom it was made.' [Diderot agreed, responding] 'The quantity of the *canaille* is just about always the same'" (Himmelfarb, 2001, p. 8). Total rejection of religion as relic for imbecilic masses was "the ultimate expression of rationalism as the *philosophes* understood it: a rejection not only of institutional religion, not only of religion per se, but of the religious conception of man—man who is truly human simply by virtue of being born in the image of God" (p. 10). In contrast, the Enlightenment in England and Scotland remained closely allied with religion as a "moral philosophy ... that was to be a distinctive feature of the British Enlightenment" (p. 2). As Roy Porter (2000) elaborates, "Enlightenment in Britain took place within, rather than against, Protestantism" (p. 99), an Enlightenment of interpenetration of philosophy and religion which tested and reconstructed without destroying the other.

Common beliefs, historic tensions

In Christianity as in philosophy in general, tensions are rarely, if ever, perfectly held. Transcendence and immanence, determinism and human agency, the "one" and the "many," reason and experience, form and freedom—these tensions were variously privileged by theological tilts in the churches of Great Britain, rendering wide divergence of belief and practice that were but complementary aspects of the Christian narrative. Fairbairn and Winnicott respectively matured in divergent polarities of British Christianity.

Scottish Presbyterianism

Scottish Presbyterianism is the child of John Knox and grandchild of Jean Calvin, a religious scholar trained at the University of Paris who protested certain doctrines of the Catholic Church. Calvin introduced what he felt were correctives to the Catholic Church. Two of the correctives that he advanced were as follows:

1. The basis of doctrine is not human tradition and hence at the whim of self-interest; instead, doctrine should be based on *sola scriptura*—scripture alone. Understanding should be derived from a reasoned and thorough exploration of the written Word, and achieved without priestly interpretation.
2. The basis of salvation is strictly grace. No human works, for example, no paying of indulgences, can bring favor with God.

John Knox (of Edinburgh, Scotland) was attracted to Calvin's teachings, and after living in Geneva with Calvin returned to Scotland and is credited with beginning the Scottish Reformation. Scottish Presbyterianism reflects Calvinism's views on the "nature of God" and the "nature of humans."

In their battle against what they perceived as the Roman Catholic Church's exploitation of people by its demands that they perform good works (particularly penance and the purchase of indulgences), Calvinists focused on human nature as it had been corrupted by the Fall. Humans, being thoroughly ravaged by sin, had no ability on their own (i.e., good works) to redeem themselves. They were hopelessly in pursuit of "the bad." The Canons of Dordt express it this way:

> Man was originally formed after the Image of God. His understanding was adorned with a true and saving knowledge of his Creator, and of spiritual things; his heart and will were upright; all his affections pure; and the whole man was holy; but revolting from God ... he forfeited these excellent gifts and on the contrary entailed on himself blindness of mind, horrible darkness, vanity and perverseness of judgment, became wicked, rebellious and obdurate in heart and will, and impure in his affections. (Hanko, Hoeksema, & Van Baren, 1976, p. 8)

Calvinists believe that only God as truly "Other"—transcendent and separate from the human condition—can sovereignly take the initiative and bring about human salvation. For Calvinists, God's love is the ground from which the more dominant figure of His sovereignty springs. With its intellectually robust and exhaustively systematized body of theology, Calvinism privileges a perspective of God as transcendent "Other" and sovereign; while emphasizing a view of the nature of humans as fallen from God's grace, and therefore totally depraved,[1] in bondage to sin, and separated from God and from others, therefore incapable of their own salvation.

English Wesleyanism

The forces that birthed Scottish Presbyterianism were not at all the same forces that brought about English Wesleyanism, also called Methodism. If John Calvin was interested in reforming Christianity, John Wesley was more interested in enlivening it. He was trained in classical languages and literature before going to Oxford at age 16. Wesley did not have the same problem with Catholicism that Knox did.

Henry VIII had seen to it that Protestantism entered England through the political gate. John Wesley, therefore, was very well read in Catholic literature, including the mystics, as well as in the non-Western thinking of the Eastern Orthodox Church. While sympathizing with the doctrines that the

Calvinist reformers fought for, his battles were different from theirs, and the emphases that derived from his battles were different as well. Wesley offered a corrective to the Calvinists on one hand, and to the Anglicans whom he believed had accommodated to deism on the other. Wesley's correctives to Calvinism were as follows:

1. An emphasis on experience as equally indispensable as reason
2. A view of humans that allowed for the presence of goodness
3. A focus on God's love as more central than His sovereignty

The remote God of deism was counterbalanced, as well, by these emphases. Wesley's good God was involved in His world (immanent) and desired that humans be experientially involved with Him.

Wesley's theology has been aptly called a theology of love (Wynkoop, 1972). His passion in speech, writing, and thinking is succinctly captured in the following excerpt:

> The distinguishing marks of a Methodist are not his opinions of any sort. His assenting to this or that scheme of religion, his embracing of any particular set of notions, his espousing the judgment of one man or of another, are all quite wide of the point ... "What then is the mark: Who is a Methodist, according to your own account?" I answer: A Methodist is one who has "the love of God shed abroad in his heart by the Holy Ghost given unto him"; one who "loves the Lord his God with all his heart, and with all his soul, and with all his mind, and with all his strength." God is the joy of his heart, and the desire of his soul. (Piette, 1937, p. 426)

While not denying God's sovereignty or humanity's sinfulness, Wesley emphasized God's love, love that not only created humanity in goodness, but also in goodness saw to it that even after the Fall, humans retained a capacity to seek Him. In contrast to Calvinism, Wesley's scholarly (albeit profoundly experiential) theology privileges a perspective of God as immanent and loving, and emphasizes a view of the nature of humans as yet partaking of God's grace, therefore still in the image of God and potentially inclined toward maturation and connection to God and to others.

RELIGIOUS NARRATIVES IN THE WORK OF FAIRBAIRN AND WINNICOTT

Nature of the parent: Fairbairn

Strains of the Calvinist narrative are detectable in Fairbairn's conceptualization of the role of the "good object"—the parent, in relationship to the infant. That narrative commenced with humans specifically created to desire relationship with their Maker. In like fashion, Fairbairn, in a monumental departure from Freud's instinct theory, postulated that the infant is born with the innate inclination to seek the parent—born object-seeking not simply for survival in the Darwinian sense, but for relationship. Heralding the dawn of a new era in psychoanalysis, "Fairbairn was suggesting that object-seeking, in its most radical form, is not the vehicle for satisfaction of a specific need, but the expression of our very nature, the form through which we become specifically human beings" (Mitchell, 1988, p. 117). In Fairbairn's system, an implicit aspect of the function of the parent is related to the concept of determinism: The child does not choose to be born object-seeking; she comes hardwired or predestined by virtue of her genesis from the parental object to seek relationship. The parent, as good object, in essence bequeaths to the child the innate capacity for this desire.

It is here that Fairbairn's religious narrative is first recognizable. Theologian Loraine Boettner (1983) speaks to the issue of hardwiring in Calvinist theology, stating, "The basic principle of Calvinism is the sovereignty of God. ... He appoints the course of nature and directs the course of history down to the minutest details" (p. 2). Calvinist doctrine further asserts that humans are not only deterministically designed, but are also designed to relate. In his commentary on the book of Romans, Calvin remarks: "[Every human being] is formed to be a spectator of the created world and given eyes that he might be led to its author by contemplating so beautiful a representation" (Lane, 2001, p. 1). Lane adds, "Calvin knew that human desire at its best is but a mirror of God's own desire for relationship ... [through which He is] inviting and exhorting us to the imitation of himself" (p. 9).

In short, the early religious narrative to which Fairbairn was exposed held that a sovereign God created humans in His image, capable of love and desire, first toward Him and then toward each other, beings who by their very nature desire to relate. Fairbairn proceeded to depict the initial stage of an infant's life as one of primary identification with the parent, one that entails total dependence. He then presented this portrait of early life with the repeated qualification that "such total parental availability is an impossibility" (Greenberg & Mitchell, 1983, p. 181). Fairbairn's initial stage of relatedness, therefore, quickly becomes background for the unfolding drama of decline, a decline that is the central focus of much of Fairbairn's work and the stage for the construction of his theory of endopsychic structure.

Fairbairn specifically trains his lens on the effects of the rupture between parent and child, a rupture that not only structures the internal world but also enshrines the good object as "other" and outside the internal, unconscious realm. Neil Skolnick (1998), commenting on Fairbairn's theory, elaborates: "Fairbairn's idea [was] that the internal unconscious world of objects is devoid of good objects. ... Identifications with good objects are, conversely, accorded express tickets to heaven, the celestial realm Fairbairn (1944) dubbed the Central Ego" (pp. 139–141).

Fairbairn's depiction of the role of the good object in development and then in pathology, in which the good object exists permanently separated from the child's unconscious world, echoes Calvin. While initially depicting the loving relationship with God for whom humans were created, Calvin radically refocuses on the Fall and its effects. He copiously documents intrapsychic human fracture and a concomitant separation from God, a God whose dominant post-Fall posture vis-à-vis humans becomes transcendent "other" (i.e., a good object out of human reach). The emphasis in Fairbairn as in Calvin is on the good object that is no more. For both men, at the deepest levels, humans become separated from the good and are attracted to the bad.

Nature of the parent: Winnicott

The Winnicottian parent, specifically the mother, is a "good enough" mother. Winnicott's writings are replete with evocative and poetic descriptions of the many aspects of a mother's role and the centrality of her immanence and her love that are predominantly addressed here. In her immanence, Winnicott's mother is depicted both as one with the infant and as felt presence; in her love, the infant becomes mother's "primary maternal preoccupation." Winnicott's parent is far different from Fairbairn's parent, who is transcendent "other." For Winnicott, parent and child are the very definition of immanence. To Winnicott (1960), the mother and infant are inseparable, a psychosomatic partnership reflected in his classic statement, "There is no such thing as an infant" (p. 39). Scharff and Scharff (1998) elaborate, "The self of the object becomes the integrating function of the infant self. Winnicott does not assume that the infant is ever separate from the mother" (p. 105).

Winnicott's mother and infant are a union that both draws life and creates life. Union with an immanent God for Wesleyans is the felt experience of the human's being in Christ and Christ's being in the human. Charles Wesley memorializes this doctrine of unity with Christ, one that produces growth and transmission of nature, in a didactic hymn composed in 1749 and surely well known to Winnicott:

Jesus, United by Thy Grace

Up unto thee, our living Head
let us in all things grow;
till thou has made us free
indeed and spotless here below.
To thee, inseparably joined,
let all our spirits cleave;
O may we all the loving mind
that was in thee receive.

Winnicott believed that if a mother is reliably and quietly present while her infant is essentially alone, that child will develop the capacity to be alone. The mother's felt presence will provide an experience of quiet relatedness, one that will imbue the child with a sense of safety. Goldman (1993) speaks to the religious correspondence: "The capacity to be alone in the felt presence of the mother—parallels the traditional idea of the Presence of God as being both intimate and ultimate" (p. 123). Another Charles Wesley hymn (1747) surely known and sung by Winnicott poetically articulates this capacity:

> Thou hidden source of calm repose,
> thou all sufficient love divine,
> my help and refuge from my foes,
> secure I am if Thou art mine;
> and lo! from sin and grief and shame
> I hide me, Jesus, in thy name.

For Winnicott, the loving, immanent relationship between a caretaker and an infant is strongly in the foreground, and the mother's "otherness" (as seen in her hatred and her own subjectivity) is retained as background theme. Whether one speaks of Winnicott's "holding environment," "good-enough mothering," or the "facilitating environment," this foreground good object who is loving is analogous to the Wesleyan loving God, one whose grace is abundant and whose provision is bountiful.

Nature of the child: Fairbairn

"For Fairbairn (1944) the establishment of the endopsychic structure, while universal and inevitable, represents a fall from grace" (Skolnick & Scharff, 1998, p. 141). How human beings "fall," or fragment from an initial pristine ego, is the prime target of study for Fairbairn. According to Rubens (2000):

> Virtually all psychoanalytic theories have accepted a metaphor for psychic growth which has been borrowed from biology: "Growth" is defined as movement through progressive levels of structural differentiation and complexity. ... In his most radical departure from the mainstream of psychoanalytic thought, Fairbairn maintained that, far from being the necessary condition for psychic growth, structural differentiation is a defensive and pathological process in human development. (pp. 160–161)

Fairbairn's major theoretical contribution in terms of structuralization of the psyche reflects a directionality of process that is declining, in keeping with his religious narrative. He interweaves the infant's innate object-seeking orientation with the very process from which internal structure is derived. Calvin's core sequence of being born to relate yet fallen as distinguished by a fallen human nature that is totally depraved, in bondage to sin, and (consequently) separated from God and from others, becomes the template for Fairbairn's endopsychic structure. "Indeed, for Fairbairn our unconscious exists as a kind of intrapsychic hell, populated only by split-off pieces of bad objects (either exciting or rejecting) along with the fragments of ego structure they abscond with," states Skolnick (1998, p. 141). Skolnick here relates Fairbairn's graphic portrayal of the corrupting of the infant's good need to relate by its attaching to the exciting and rejecting morsels offered it by its caretakers. Though Fairbairn's theory departs somewhat from Calvin's blameless God by implying that parental figures are culpable, Fairbairn reharmonizes with the Calvinist narrative by painting a Dantean landscape of the infant's totally bleak internal world, filled with longing, rage, and torment and uninterrupted by any ray of potentially redemptive light.

In a continuation of the nightmarish internal condition, Fairbairn goes on to give psychological definition to what Calvin called the "bondage to sin." Fairbairn (1952) asserts "that libidinal 'badness' should be related to the cathexis of bad objects ['sin' always being regarded, according to Hebraic conception, as seeking after strange gods and, according to the Christian conception, as yielding to the Devil]" (p. 74). Fairbairn, in this formulation of the concept of cathexis to bad objects, reinterprets the compulsion to repeat as a derivative of the need to remain connected to parental objects. Humans, he felt, need to persist in their maladaptive behaviors, because such repetition maintains a connection to early caregivers. In effect, Fairbairn (1952) here conceptualizes (in modern psychoanalytic terminology) how the mechanism of the Biblical pronouncement "visiting the iniquity of the fathers upon the children" (Exodus 20:5) becomes enacted. Fairbairn underscores this bondage in behavior and will by stating that "the deepest source of resistance is fear of the release of bad objects from the unconscious" (p. 69). Indeed, confirming Fairbairn's views, Mitchell (1988) adds, "Psychopathology is more than an absence or fearful avoidance of good relatedness. We often observe not just an avoidance of the positive, but a fascination with the negative" (p. 162).

Fairbairn (1952) continues by representing the task of the therapist as aimed at this expulsion of bad objects, in contrast to simple interpretations aimed at the superego level. He states, "It becomes evident, accordingly, that the psychotherapist is the true successor to the exorcist, and that he is concerned, not only with 'the forgiveness of sins' but also with 'the casting out of devils'" (p. 70). Of the therapist's Herculean task, Hirsch (1987) observes:

> Fairbairn clearly ... realized that the analyst was not simply a welcomed rescuer. He knew that the patient was not passively waiting for him to provide a benign experience. From what can be determined, he was inclined to make explicit the patient's attachment to the bad objects and their efforts to convert him into, or see him as one of, the bad objects. (pp. 211–212)

The consequence of this internalized condition of badness is alienation, a tenet of Calvin's theology. As humans become separated from God, they inevitably become separated from their neighbors. In 1738, Jonathan Edwards (1852), an American Calvinist Puritan, reflected (echoing Calvin):

> Before, his soul was under the government of that noble principle of divine love, whereby it was enlarged to the comprehension of all his fellow-creatures and their welfare. ... But so soon as he had transgressed against God, these noble principles were immediately lost, and all this excellent enlargedness of man's soul was gone; and thenceforward he himself shrank, as it were, into a little space, circumscribed and closely shut up within itself, to the exclusion of all things else. Sin, like some powerful astringent, contracted his soul to the very small dimensions of selfishness; and God was forsaken, and fellow-creatures forsaken, and man retired within himself, and became totally governed by narrow and selfish principles and feelings. (p. 158)

This extension of inner darkness into the interpersonal sphere is addressed in Fairbairn's study of "schizoid phenomena." Fairbairn viewed "the schizoid position as far more basic and universal [than the depressive] ... the position that underlay all of human psychopathology" (Rubens, 1998, p. 219). Fairbairn provided a theory that has "for contemporary relational analysts, become the all-important interface where intrapsychic and interpersonal relations meet and together construct a world vision" (Davies, 1998, p. 66).

That world vision, which brings the darkness of the cacophonous voices of the interior into the intersubjective space of relationship, details the mechanisms by which a person becomes locked into a mausoleum of projected internal drama, a drama that effectively isolates him or her from contact with another as truly other. Moreover, the person, seeing his or her love through the filter of internal badness, comprehends love as destructive and, guaranteeing further alienation, chooses rather to destroy by hate "which is overtly destructive and bad, than to destroy by love, which is by rights creative and good" (Fairbairn, 1952, p. 27).

Ending his essay "Schizoid Factors in the Personality," Fairbairn, in describing the hopeless condition of the schizoid who is alienated from the world, reverts to the use of religious metaphor to drive home his point. He concludes, "Since the joy of loving seems hopelessly barred to him, he may as well deliver himself over to the joy of hating and obtain what satisfaction he can out of that. He thus makes a pact with the Devil and says, 'Evil be thou my good'" (p. 27). For Fairbairn as for Calvin, the endpoint of humanity's fall from grace is the fall from relationship.

Nature of the child: Winnicott

"In his poised, dignified, idiosyncratic, and playful manner [Winnicott] was, fundamentally, what could be called a believer in 'grace'" (Goldman, 1993, p. 28), a grace reflected in his abiding hopefulness, "the fuel by which life may advance" (Rodman, 2003, p. 244). Whereas Fairbairn depicted the declension of humankind, Winnicott's work is a study in humanity's capacity for ascendance. In his theoretical focus on development—its facets and its sequelae—Winnicott portrayed an upward directionality based on a belief in innate goodness.

In parallel fashion, John Wesley favored discourse regarding the development of a child of God from spiritual birth to maturity. Based on this preference for a developmental emphasis, the resultant sequence in Wesleyanism, in contrast to Calvinism, is a focus on being in the image of God, potentially inclined toward both maturation and connection to God and to others.

Winnicott unflinchingly held to a belief in human goodness, reconstituting the Wesleyan emphasis on being made in the image of God to the extent of rejecting any notion of original sin. In a direct reference to religions that emphasize depravity, Winnicott (1963c) comments, "Religions have made much of original sin, but have not all come round to the idea of original goodness" (p. 94). He viewed even the most antisocial of behaviors as a positive response, believing that "the child knows in his bones that it is hope that is locked up in the wicked behaviour" (p. 104). In dismantling the concept of original sin, Winnicott (1971a) also challenged its cousin, the death instinct, which he felt "could be described as a reassertion of the principle of original sin" (p. 70). In a continued deviation from Klein, he held that human goodness included an innate moral sensibility, admonishing, "We need to abandon absolutely, the theory that children can be born innately amoral" (1966, p. 111). Goldman (1993) observes, "Winnicott believed—and he seemed to differ on this point from Klein—that individuals are born with an innate morality that expresses itself in a powerful urge to ensure the survival of personal integrity" (p. 203).

Though there is still debate over the exact nature of Winnicott's secret, "true self," Winnicott appeared to maneuver strikingly close to a Biblical description of the "soul" in postulating that "at the centre of each person is an incommunicado element, and this is sacred and most worthy of preservation" (1963b, p. 187), a core self that Rodman (2003) interpreted as "the surviving unscathed inmost aspect of the individual" (p. 146). This notion, a radical departure from Freud's "'seething cauldron' of instincts" (Phillips, 1988, p. 136) and Fairbairn's endopsychic structure, presents the "true self" as lying at the foundation of Winnicott's internal world, a silent wellspring of creative and authentic living, a source of goodness not entirely unlike the human soul made in the image of God.

"A muted sacramental current runs through Winnicott's work. One senses the sanctity of individual personality, reverence for the vital spark" (Eigen, 1998, p. 15), a spark that Winnicott asserted produces an innate inclination toward maturation. In a 1949 radio talk, Winnicott observed,

> In each baby is a vital spark, and this urge towards life and growth and development is a part of the baby, something the child is born with and which is carried forward in a way that we do not have to understand. For instance, if you have just put a bulb in the window-box you know perfectly well that you do not have to make the bulb grow into a daffodil. You supply the right kind of earth or fibre and you keep the bulb watered just the right amount, and the rest comes naturally, because the bulb has life in it. (Goldman, 1993, p. 112)

Winnicott here is seen not only articulating but also amending Darwinian thought by implying that maturation toward goodness can be expected if a child is given adequate nurture. The notion of an innate teleological thrust toward wholeness and maturity is a theological concept heavily borrowed by other disciplines as Kirschner (1996) explains, discussing the work of William Kessen:

> Kessen argues that Darwin's evolutionary theory was taken up by early child psychologists ... [who] adopted a 19th-century positivistic (Spencerian) reading of Darwin, borrowing the idea of an "end" (eschatology) from the moral sciences which ultimately, were derived from Biblical history. ... Kessen points out that in the case of child psychology, the welding of Darwin's non-teleological evolutionary theory to the teleological idea of development and "progress" borrowed from the moral sciences harkens back to a much older concept, that of Salvationist history. (pp. 104–105)

Winnicott saw humans as starting from a core of goodness and as inclined toward maturity if a sufficient "facilitating environment" could be provided, detailing practical methods for ensuring such a growth-promoting atmosphere. Radically dissimilar to Fairbairn and Calvin, who were theory builders, Winnicott was indeed a Methodist, that Wesleyan term referring to the practical methods one might employ to aid in spiritual maturation. Winnicott was, in essence, the John Wesley of psychoanalysis:

He described the need and detailed the practical methodology for an ever-increasing maturational experience. With Wesley, it was the spiritual self; with Winnicott, it was the psychological, "true self." With Wesley, a means of maturation occurred through experiencing God in prayer; with Winnicott, maturation occurred via experiencing the mother in the "holding environment." With Wesley, maturation was promoted through the Eucharist; with Winnicott, via the breast. With Wesley, music provided a means of connectedness; with Winnicott, the teddy bear and the blanket served that purpose.

The theoretical sequence of inner goodness, followed by the subsequent inclination to mature, culminates in a capacity for connection. For Winnicott and Wesley, connection within and without was a repeated emphasis. Painting a canvas of brilliant hues of maternal–infant interaction, Winnicott depicted the loving bond that forms, his work exploring and defining the infant's initial connection with mother. This connection becomes the basis of a connected self and a loving connection to others; Winnicott believed that if the child did not feel "godlike" as a result of his or her early interactions, future relationships would be impaired.

Wesleyans, as well, see this "godlike" beginning as the basis for loving ourselves, and for our resultant and mandated connection to "godlike" others (Strawn, 2004). The Biblical admonition "Thou shalt love the Lord thy God ... [and] Thou shalt love thy neighbor as thyself" (Mark 12:30–31) was a teaching to which Winnicott had been amply exposed and had personally experienced through his family's involvement in civic concerns. Acting on the belief that connectedness to their fellow humans flows from a godlike common identity, Wesleyans became responsible for a virtual shift in English social topography in the wake of Wesley's ministry. Himmelfarb (2001) observes,

> The Methodists distributed food, clothing, and money to the needy, paid "visitations" to the sick and to prisoners in jail, set up loan funds and work projects for the unemployed, founded hospitals, orphanages, friendly societies, schools, libraries, and other philanthropic enterprises, and took a prominent part in the movements for prison reform and the abolition of the slave trade. Wesley himself was especially passionate on the subject of "that execrable villainy," slavery. "An African," he wrote, was "in no respect inferior to the European"; if he seemed so, it was because the European had kept him in a condition of inferiority. (p. 3)

Winnicott expanded his ideas on connectedness to encompass the culture at large. "Potential space," that interface of the subjective and objective that lies between the reliable mother and the infant, was for him the foundation of a connection to culture through the experience of transitional phenomena such as music, art, theater, and play (Ulanov, 2001). He placed religious experience in this space, reminding the analyst that it cannot be understood unless one is "willing to peddle in the intermediate area whose ancestor is the infant's transitional object" (1963b, p. 184).

Winnicott well understood the transitional character of religious experience, for Wesleyan worship celebrated creativity and spontaneity, particularly through music. That worship experience had served as an early tutorial for him on transitional phenomena, a relational experience in which one parishioner was connected to the other and all were connected to their unseen God.

This aspect of Winnicott's early religious narrative provides a final and curious correspondence between him and his Wesleyan upbringing. Charles Wesley has been acclaimed as one of the most prolific and creative of Protestant hymn writers. It was Wesley's hymns that meandered through the mind of the theorizing Winnicott and that he murmured fondly until his death. And it was, not coincidentally, from such a childhood surrounded by the works of the creative genius Wesley that one of the most prolific bards and creative theorists of psychoanalysis, D. W. Winnicott, emerged.

In conclusion, the study of "persons in relationship" that emerged in object relations theory, and even earlier in the greater British academic culture, was undoubtedly influenced by the prevailing Judaic and Christian narratives, narratives that made it particularly probable that the personal would make its entry into psychoanalysis by way of that culture. While psychoanalysis owes a debt to its object relations theorists for this emphasis, the shift from energy to humanity, from drive to love, and from instinct to relationship all bear the imprint of a narrative whose roots lie not in the last century but at the dawn of Jewish history.

ENDNOTE

1. Total depravity is not to be confused with total "badness" or evil. Its meaning should be viewed as more akin to a chronic, systemic infection with sin, affecting every part of human nature.

Part III

Gratitude/Resurrection

In Part III, I am working with gratitude in psychoanalysis (the third movement toward mutual recognition) and its analogue in resurrection (the third movement of Hegel's system).

In Chapter 8, I seek to demonstrate how, having addressed the complementarity that existed between religion and psychoanalysis, a mutual recognition of religious and psychoanalytic narratives might creatively illuminate psychoanalytic theory. Hegel's first two movements, incarnation and crucifixion, were ready analogues to identification and surrender in relational psychoanalytic literature. I propose that Hegel's third movement, resurrection, is an analogue to gratitude, though the body of literature is sparse.

I explore Hegel's movement of "resurrection," which includes the consummation of the work of Spirit, and develop its latent links as an analogue of "gratitude." I extend psychoanalytic theory on mutual recognition to include the third movement of gratitude, through reliance upon Ricoeur's hermeneutic model and a review of gratitude as it has occurred in psychoanalytic literature. Borrowing from Ricoeur, I then conduct an abbreviated lexicographic study of the word *gratitude*.

I interrogate Hegel's ideas through incorporating the reformulations of Paul Ricoeur[1] and rely upon Ricoeur's contributions on "the economy of the gift" as I develop gratitude as a third movement toward mutual recognition. In that this chapter advances new theory regarding gratitude, I will not be employing the format of previous theoretical chapters, which utilized the categories of infancy and treatment.

In Chapter 9, I review the last 5 years of treatment with Mandy, during which the traumata of earlier times have given way to some manifestations of resurrection. I explore the chronic effects of devastating trauma, which are consonant with Ricoeur's assertions regarding radical evil. We negotiate the possibility of Mandy bearing children, which reflects her giant surrender in faith to a vision of normal living. I describe the process of her pregnancy and the joy and mourning that attended the birth of her child as she recalled her own infancy. Mandy and I also approach her need for corroboration of her sexual abuse through prayer during this period, and in this integration of faith and therapy Mandy experiences some resolution. Gratitude for her renewed life and hope for the future prompts Mandy's desire to pass the gift of hope to others.

In Chapter 10, I consider the resurrection of Sándor Ferenczi and draw correlations with the resurrection of the Christian narrative in psychoanalysis. I examine Hungarian religious pluralism and especially the impact of Calvinism in that culture and upon Ferenczi's education, as well as other religious influences throughout Ferenczi's life. I then offer comparisons between the writings of Sándor Ferenczi and Christian philosopher Søren Kierkegaard, whose works were influential in Budapest during Ferenczi's lifetime. Upon this background of Hungarian pluralism, Ferenczi developed a fresh perspective on Freud's craft, one that placed in the foreground and in bold relief the preeminence of relationship. Ferenczi revived Freud's emphasis on truth but sought healing for his patients not through the containment of drives, but through the fostering of love. Though Ferenczi embraced no religious creed, he lived one. In Ferenczi's life and work, I trace the mutual influence of a resurrected subtextual Judaism and Christianity; sensing his resonance with these narratives, Christians were drawn to him. Ferenczi died, but his love and ideas survived destruction through their transmission by grateful analysts and theorists who resurrected Freud's original vision and transformed it by the work and life of Sándor Ferenczi.

ENDNOTE

1. Ricoeur, in keeping with a post-Hegelean, Kantian perspective, doubted the potential of teleologically motivated reason alone to secure a just world. For Ricoeur, resurrection is a promise that a just world can be realized, a promise held in the balance of a hermeneutic of hope in dialectical tension with a hermeneutic of suspicion that will not deny the presence and action of evil in the world.

Chapter 8

The third movement toward mutual recognition

Theoretical perspectives

> The capacity to enjoy fully what has been received, and the experience of gratitude towards the person who gives it, influence strongly both the character and the relations with other people. It is not for nothing that in saying grace before meals, Christians use the words, "For what we are about to receive may the Lord make us truly thankful." The words imply that one asks for the one quality—gratitude—which will make one free from resentment and envy.
>
> —Klein (1957/1975, p. 254)

Since Melanie Klein's magisterial *Envy and Gratitude* (1957), and Winnicott's theoretical challenges to her, gratitude disappeared from psychoanalytic literature.[1] I will review that literature focusing primarily on the contributions of Klein and Winnicott. It is my purpose in this chapter to establish gratitude as the third and final movement of recognition, linking it to Hegel's work on resurrection. In order to accomplish this, I will supplement Hegel's ideas with Paul Ricoeur's phenomenological hermeneutic approach and his post-Hegelean Kantian reformulations.

GRATITUDE IN EARLY PSYCHOANALYSIS

Freud, along with Nietzsche and Marx, was described by Ricoeur as a master of the "hermeneutic of suspicion." The infrequently found references to gratitude in Freud's early writings are often paired with a meaning that renders its positive valency questionable.

Two examples will illustrate Freud's enigmatic relationship to the concept of "gratitude." In his discussion of male object choice, Freud (1910a) describes the son's incestuous wishes toward his mother this way: *The son shows his gratitude by wishing to have by his mother a son who is like himself* (p. 173, emphasis added). In this reference to gratitude, Freud's keenly suspicious eye renders gratitude a vehicle for misdeed. Again, in correspondence to Ernest Jones regarding Otto Rank, Freud reflects this skeptical view. Regarding Rank, Freud (1926) alleges: "As it was, his gift sprang from a mixture of different motives, the oppressing feeling of owing so much to me, even in money, *a reaction of gratitude or rather against gratitude*" (p. 606, emphasis added).

In personal communication, however, Freud regularly and lavishly expressed heartfelt gratitude to colleagues and friends across his career. His personal expressions of gratitude and appreciation are in fact the most notable occurrences of the word *gratitude* in early psychoanalytic literature.

Two other occurrences of *gratitude* in the literature prior to Klein are found in Reik and Abraham. Theodore Reik (1930), in his study of religious belief and obsessional neuroses, summed his views on gratitude in religion this way:

> Psycho-analysis is now in a position to explain all these various forms of sacrifice as differentiations of a single form. Offerings of homage, *gratitude*, atonement, etc., are developments and transformations of the precautionary offering which is intended to ward off a threatening evil or an expected punishment, to assuage the anger of the god. (p. 269, emphasis added)

In Reik's 1924 paper "Some Remarks on the Study of Resistances," he mentions gratitude in this way: "Gratitude prevents the patient from manifesting his resistance in the same form and with the same intensity as do other patients" (p. 146).

Abraham was acknowledged by Klein, who credited him with paving the path to her own explorations of gratitude. Though Abraham used the word in several articles, it was not intended as a theoretical term. In his (1925) article "The Influence of Oral Eroticism on Character-Formation," he did not specifically utilize the term *gratitude*, though he spoke of generosity, linking it to oral character traits.

Melanie Klein

Klein's seminal work, *Envy and Gratitude* (1957), details the trajectory of the death instinct with its manifestation in envy and aggression as contributing to the development of gratitude. Specifically, the infant whose envy of the breast is both a reaction to environmental failure, and an expression of its innate capacity for destructiveness, attacks the breast and the goodness of the object. Klein defines *envy* as "the angry feeling that another person possesses and enjoys something desirable—the envious impulse being to take it away or to spoil it" (p. 181). Klein believed the infant feels threatened from without by the withholding and persecutory breast, and from within by its own destructive impulses. An antecedent to the development of what Klein referred to as the "paranoid position"[2] is the defensive maneuver of the ego, which projects the persecutory, destructive feelings outside the self. Fearing the persecutory breast and its own persecutory anxieties, the infant splits the breast into a "good breast," which is the breast of the infant's satiated and nurtured state and one for which the infant is grateful, and the "bad breast" of its experiences of hunger and pain. Depending on the strength of envious attack (which according to Klein is innately determined) against the goodness of the mother, the capacity for gratitude will vary as Klein explains: "I am referring to the effects of envy on the development of the capacity for gratitude and happiness. Envy contributes to the infant's difficulties in building up his good object" (p. 180).

As the infant learns to bring together the experiences of good breast and bad breast into a complex but whole object, the infant achieves what Klein termed the "depressive position." In this position the infant's omnipotence has been surrendered in return for a relationship with mother that can now allow for good and bad in mother and in self, and enjoy the gratitude for what is good in both. Concurrently, the infant's aggression inflicted upon the object that frustrates and gives is replaced by a sense of guilt for that damage, and a desire for reparation.

Klein (1957) affirmed that "the more often gratification at the breast is experienced and fully accepted, the more often enjoyment and gratitude and accordingly the wish to return pleasure are felt" (p. 189), thus emphasizing the necessary competent availability of the mother. However, Klein focused even more on a complementary aspect of development: the infant's contribution to the development or thwarting of good experiences such as gratitude, a contribution deriving from the innate virility of the infant's destructiveness toward the good object (see Fonagy, 2008, p. 208).

Klein contrasted with Winnicott

There is almost no mention of gratitude in a conceptual fashion in Winnicott's work, though one can discern the outlines of his views in excerpts from case examples in which the word is used in passing. One example is in his case study "The Piggle." We read that the little girl (Piggle) asked her mother to give presents to Winnicott. Winnicott jotted in his notes: "gratitude implies acceptance of separateness, of the reality principle, a 'fruit of disillusionment'" (James, 1979, p. 139). Thus, in accord with Klein, Winnicott appears to see gratitude as evidence of separateness, of surrender of omnipotence, much akin to Klein's depressive position. However, gratitude is not the focus of Winnicott's exploration of infant development, for reasons that I will explore shortly. Winnicott presented a divergent view on Klein's infant in its destructiveness, its greed, and its striving to mature, in a manner that turned Klein's death-instinct–informed pessimistic view of development on its head.

In contrast to Klein's emphasis on the innate destructiveness of the infant, and in keeping with his own predilections based on early upbringing (see Chapter 7), Winnicott emphasized a positive and optimistic view of human development and tilted his focus of study to the positive strivings of the infant, who would develop optimally if parental care was "good enough." In his theoretical shift away from Klein, Winnicott disposed of the death instinct and reversed Klein's emphasis on the benevolence of the providing mother through his preoccupation with the innate goodness and entitlement of the infant. Winnicott both privileged a focus upon the myriad maternal/parental failures experienced by the infant and minimized consideration of the envious attacks perpetrated by the infant toward the mother. In Winnicott's theory, the infant's destructiveness is reframed positively and is reinterpreted as "ruthlessness," and its former guilt (in Klein's view) is relabeled "a capacity for concern." Even when Winnicott spoke of hate, he viewed hate as part of a life force that he referred to as "love-strife."

In the gap between Klein's destructive infant whose aggression and demands might evoke retaliation from the mother were it not for her goodness, and Winnicott's good and entitled infant who deserves the mother's preoccupation, the concept of gratitude evaporates. With the infant's entitlement as the starting point and on-going focus, gratitude for goodness received, often through the mother's sacrifice, became superfluous (Kraemer, 1996). Klein's infant's gratitude represented a capacity for separateness from the mother (a perspective acknowledged by Winnicott) *and* the infant's appreciation of the mother's *unmerited* goodness for not retaliating to its undeserved destructiveness. For Winnicott, since there was no death instinct, there was no innate destructiveness of the infant. In Winnicott's model, if the infant is entitled to receive all of the goodness a parent might be capable of giving, there is theoretically no need for gratitude: There is simply expectation and potential frustration.[3] I believe that neither Klein nor Winnicott achieved a theoretical depressive position in which the "goodness" and "badness" of both mother and infant were reconciled.

GRATITUDE IN THE ENGLISH LEXICON

I begin by exploring definitions of the word *gratitude* in both *Merriam-Webster's Third New International Dictionary* (2002) and *The Oxford English Dictionary, Second Edition. Merriam-Webster* offers this definition:

> Gratitude: Etymology: Middle English (Scots dialect), Middle French or Medieval Latin; Middle French, from Medieval Latin *gratitudo*, from Latin *gratus* pleasing, thankful + *tudo*
>
> - tude – *More at* GRACE.
>
> 1. (Obsolete) : Favor, Gift, Gratuity.
> 2. The state of being grateful: warm and friendly feeling toward a benefactor prompting one to repay a favor: Thankfulness.

The Oxford English Dictionary (2002) offers little variation to what *Merriam-Webster* has presented. Its entry reads as such:

> Gratitude: Etymology: F. gratitude (15th c. in Godef . Comp) or ad. late L. *gratitudo*, - *inem*, f. *gratus* pleasing, thankful.
>
> 1. The quality or condition of being grateful: a warm sense of appreciation of kindness received, involving a feeling of goodwill towards the benefactor and a desire to do something in return; gratefulness.
> 2. (obsolete) Grace, favour, a favour. Chiefly Sc.
> 3. (obsolete) A free gift; a gratuity, reward; esp. Sc. A grant or contribution of money made to the sovereign

A collation of *Merriam-Webster*'s and the *The Oxford English Dictionary* definitions renders the following meanings for gratitude:

1. The quality of being grateful
2. Good will toward a benefactor
3. Desire to do something in return

Moving into a deeper analysis of the dictionary entries, I look at the etymology of the word as presented in both dictionaries. *Merriam-Webster* and *The Oxford English Dictionary* trace the etymology of *gratitude* to its early roots in Latin. There, *gratus*,[4] meaning pleasing, or thankful, is offered. *Merriam-Webster* directs us to the parallel development of the root *gratus* into *grace*, while the *Oxford English Dictionary* presents *grace* as one of the obsolete definitions of *gratitude*. Thus *grace* appears historically and linguistically connected with the root of *gratitude*.

In combination, the lexicons define *grace* (as it relates to gratitude) as an unmerited beneficence or free gift of God to humans, and of humans (usually having a superior status) to other humans. *Grace* appears to reflect the benevolent gift of the giver for whom gratitude is the appropriate response. *Grace* carries both a religiously infused definition and, analogically, an anthropological one as well. Thus, addressing both the giver's act of grace and receiver's response of gratitude, one may intersubjectively define *gratitude* as "the quality of being grateful to a benefactor (often superior) whose unmerited beneficence or gift (grace) prompts a desire to do something in return."

RESURRECTION AS ANALOGUE TO GRATITUDE IN HEGEL

> God has died, God is dead—this is the most appalling thought, that everything eternal and true is not, and that negation itself is in God; bound up with this is the supreme pain, the feeling of the utter absence of deliverance, the surrender of all that is higher. However, the course of events does not grind to a halt here; rather a reversal now comes about, to wit, God maintains himself in this process. The latter is but the death of death. God arises again to life.
>
> —Hegel (Kung, 1987, p. 1)

> Through death God has reconciled the world and reconciles himself eternally with himself. This coming back again is his return to himself, and through it he is spirit. So this third moment is that Christ has risen. Negation is thereby overcome, and the negation of negation is thus a moment of the divine nature.
>
> —Hegel (Hodgson, 2005, p. 172)

This final movement of Hegel's system has given pause to many philosophers. There are those who see it as absolutizing and leading to a collapse of recognition through domination. Other philosophers take the point of view that God maintains intersubjectivity through the final movement. I will present this movement from the second position. Following this exposition, I rely upon Ricoeur to read and extend Hegel with a postmodern sensibility of the movements from crucifixion to resurrection and from surrender to gratitude.

God the transcendent Other incarnated into human form, becoming finite and vulnerable to all the frailties of the human condition. God in the incarnated form of Christ endured our destructiveness and died—this is the essence of negation—God is dead. That God in his divine/human existence in Christ survived destruction and resurrected is the negation of negation: The impossible occurred—death itself has been negated. God in Christ demonstrated that he is "Other" by surviving death, and he accomplished something else as well: He is no longer only "Other." We can now recognize our own godlikeness in his risen, human form, and he can recognize our humanity in himself. "The infinite love that arises from infinite anguish creates a unique and unsurpassable intersubjectivity ... " (Hodgson, 2005, p. 182). The resurrection of Christ becomes the generative moment of Hegel's epic journey of "*Geist*" (i.e., of Spirit). What was first individual and particular in the Trinitarian transcendent God, through Christ the incarnate God—is now universal. The particular and individual is now communal; the Spirit of the Trinitarian God is a gift, available to all people across geographic, ethnic, and temporal boundaries: Human intersubjectivity with divinity has been achieved. The consummation of Hegel's philosophic vision of the coming of Spirit is now. St. Patrick (9th c.) reflects on his experience of this resurrected Christ, the universal Spirit, in yet another stanza of the poem introduced in Chapter 5:

> Christ be with me,
> Christ within me,
> Christ behind me,
> Christ before me,
> Christ beside me,
> Christ to win me,
> Christ to comfort and restore me,
> Christ beneath me,
> Christ above me,
> Christ in quiet,
> Christ in danger,
> Christ in hearts of all that love me,
> Christ in mouth of friend and stranger.

In his elaboration of Spirit, Hegel returned to the concept of Trinity—Father, Son, and Holy Spirit—of God as multiplicity of presentation and communal essence. This concept formed a crucial link for the rest of Hegel's thinking and was the culmination of divine subjectivity as an essential subjectivity for the reconciliation of a broken world. Each human was now able to experience his or her godlikeness and God's human-likeness through reconciliation with God accomplished by the death of the God-man, Jesus. For Hegel, the commissioning or sending of the Spirit, the third person of the Trinity, potentiated through Jesus' resurrection, augmented the human capacity to experience God within oneself and in the other. This experience was not limited by place or era of birth or other limiting parameters. God is now available to all people everywhere through the presence of the third, the Spirit. Hegel writes:

> Subjectivity has given up all external distinctions in this infinite value, distinctions of mastery, power, position, even of sex and wealth. Before God all human beings are equal. ... Herein lies the possibility and the root of truly universal justice and of the actualization of freedom [Hegel, 1821 manuscript, 3:138]. (Hodgson, 2005, p. 182–183)

The kingdom of the Spirit of which Hegel wrote is one "of infinite love in which the individual subject knows itself to have infinite worth and absolute freedom" (Hodgson, 2005, p. 182). For Hegel, the subject simultaneously "surrenders this [its] stability and maintains itself in what is utterly other. Love equalizes all things even absolute opposition" (p. 182).

This coming of the Spirit provides an intersubjective connection to the infinite God, and to one's neighbor who is intersubjectively related to both God and neighbor in the matrix of the life of the Spirit. This connection is sustained by surrender to the crucified one whose suffering provides a model of "shared suffering, creat[ing] a new kind of human relationship in which one finds oneself only by losing oneself for the sake of the other. ... Love in the fullest sense is compassion, suffering with and on behalf of another. It is grounded in the divine compassion" (Hodgson, 2005, p. 183).

Hegel goes on in *Philosophy of Religion* (2006) to detail the ways in which the self-giving Spirit is experienced in community. He describes the *cultus*, or "worship" function: "'for me to unite myself to God *in myself*, to know myself in God and God in me, this concrete unity,' (XII, 227f), and this is to be achieved both in the inward conversion of heart and mind and in the outward deed" (Kung, 1987, p. 355). The intersubjective relationship with God and with one's neighbor is thus to be demonstrated through a renewed heart that actualizes the life of Spirit through grateful giving to others of the love that was freely received from God, not on the basis of any entitlement, but because of grace. Kung concludes:

> The practical realization of faith in worship involves an act of God: God wills to dwell in man by grace! And at the same time it involves an act on man's part also: man wills by sacrifice to surrender his particularity into God! It is therefore a "two-sided act: God's *grace* and man's *sacrifice*. ... This double activity is worship, and its purpose is God's existence in man. This reconciliation is absolute, hence *accomplished* in God himself. I am to pattern myself on God; this work is mine, and it is human. Looked at from his side, the same work is God's; he moves towards man and exists through the sublation of man; what appears as my act is in fact God's act and, conversely, God appears only through my activity." (pp. 355–356)

Hegel's *tour de force* has come to its climax. God the infinite negated himself in becoming incarnate in the form of Christ. That negation reached its apex in Christ's crucifixion, when God, in his divinity and humanity, died. In Christ's resurrection, the negation of the negation allowed for the third and consummate movement in God's interaction with humanity to come into being: the giving of the Spirit. With Christ's resurrection,[5] the presence of God was no longer limited to one person in one place: The

Spirit, heralding a new birth of universal *agape* and hope over the forces of death, is available to all and becomes the intersubjective liaison (or conjunctive third) between the divinity and humanity of the transcendent God and the divinity and humanity of one's neighbor and oneself wherein all can experience the very immanent presence of God with humankind. The giving of the Spirit provides the possibility of mutual recognition with God at the individual level to mutual recognition with God at the communal level. The coming of Spirit infuses in humanity the ultimate hope of mutual recognition for all.

GRATITUDE AND RESURRECTION: THE PHILOSOPHICAL AND THEOLOGICAL CONTRIBUTIONS OF PAUL RICOEUR

My lexicographic study of *recognition* (following Ricoeur's method) revealed a third level of recognition in the expression of appreciation (i.e., gratitude). A further lexicographic study of *gratitude* clarified its intersubjective nature as being a response to a benefactor. Investigating further, I discovered that the origins of the word *gratitude* in the Latin word *grace* provided an association with a "free gift," or "unmerited beneficence"; thus, an act of grace by a benefactor is met with a response of gratitude. Consequently, I proposed that the intersubjective, operational definition of *gratitude* is "the quality of being grateful to a benefactor (often superior) whose unmerited beneficence or gift ("grace") prompts a desire to do something in return."

How might the path of recognition that leads from identification to surrender consummate in gratitude with its associated qualities of grace, gift, and the desire to do something in return? How also might the notion of *gift* correspond both with Hegel's theological/philosophical narrative of the gift of "Spirit" and the psychoanalytic trajectory of mutual recognition? The psychoanalytic lacuna for gratitude after Winnicott beckons the relational analyst concerned with mutual recognition to look for a middle or third way between Klein and Winnicott, an alternative that holds both emphases in a generative dialectic. I will look to the work of Paul Ricoeur to probe for such possibilities.

Paul Ricoeur: An introduction

Paul Ricoeur's thought has been subtextual throughout this book. This humble man would want the work of others who preceded him to have primary focus. I wish to honor Paul Ricoeur's life before I explore his considerable contributions in the area of gratitude.[6]

It seems ironic that a study of *grace* and *gift* would begin with reflections on the work of Paul Ricoeur, for he more than many was touched by early grief. Ricoeur was born in France in 1913. His mother died when he was 7 months old, and his father was killed in the Battle of the Marne when Paul was 2. He and his sister were then raised by their grandparents. Paul's intellectual prowess was energized by a devout Protestant family that encouraged Bible study, and he was admitted to study philosophy at the Sorbonne. In 1935 he married Simone, to whom he remained married for 63 years until her death in 1998. Five years into their marriage, Ricoeur, who had been drafted into the French Army in World War II, became a German prisoner of war. He spent the next 5 years in German prison camps.

The irony increases as one analyzes the body of literature that Ricoeur produced during the years he rose to preeminence as one of France's leading hermeneutic philosophers. Ricoeur's affirmation of life, of hope and faith held in tension with the tragic, permeates his philosophical corpus. Ricoeur's work echoes aspects of Hegel, though Ricoeur rejected a "totalizing" that he believed German idealism promoted. For Ricoeur, there is hope, but hope is always held on the backdrop of the tragedy of human existence, the incomprehensible mystery of good and evil that resists any attempt to codify. What Ricoeur held in common with Hegel is the hope that springs from its source in the divine, a source that Ricoeur, as others, saw evidenced in symbol, language, and human narrative and myth (Orfanos, 2006; Spero, 1996) across the history of human existence.

Perhaps the impact of war on Ricoeur's life, the loss of his father and mother, and his years as a prisoner of war contributed to his distancing from a view of recognition that simply emphasizes destructiveness as in the more Kojèvian interpretations of Hegel. Ricoeur does not dismiss struggle, but holds it in tension with a parallel reality of a recognition borne out of appreciation of the other.

RICOEUR, KLEIN, AND WINNICOTT: A STUDY IN CONTRASTS

For Melanie Klein, the giving mother who encounters the destructive attacks of the infant emerges as an object of appreciation. For Winnicott, the magnificent infant supported by loving parents evokes our appreciative gaze, particularly in its endurance of the failings of the mother. For Ricoeur, both infant and mother are far more touched by radical evil and extravagantly more abundant in their goodness than either Klein or Winnicott have envisioned. This contrast between radical brokenness and superabundant goodness leads Ricoeur (1986) to the hope-giving exultation: "Man is the Joy of Yes in the sadness of the finite" (p. 140).

Winnicott's dismissal of the death instinct (based in part on its proximity to the idea of original sin) and emphasis on maternal impact on the developing infant foreclosed upon a continuing study of infant constitutional factors that were more compatible with Klein's ideas (Carter, 1994). Psychoanalysis has since taken its lead from Winnicott and has been hesitant to directly revisit the complex, morally riddled dilemma of the origins and transmission of evil. When Klein's seminal theories on paranoid/schizoid and depressive positions are currently invoked, her contributions on destructive, constitutional factors in the infant are usually diminished or excised (i.e., the death instinct is rarely engaged).

Some recent literature recovered a vestige of Klein's death instinct. Grand (2000), in her path-breaking work *The Reproduction of Evil*, is representative of a genre of psychoanalytic literature (e.g., Boulanger, 2007; Howell, 2005) that is addressing the effects of trauma not only upon the victim but as it is passed intersubjectively and transgenerationally. While these newer contributions have gone far in cataloging evil's contagion, effects, and healing, they have not returned to examining evil's potential constitutional source in the agentic, human subject. Ricoeur (1966), referencing philosopher Jean Nabert, pointed toward Klein's destructive infant when he observed that there is an "evil self at the roots of an evil act" (p. 58). Ricoeur would maintain that this constitutionally determined condition is ubiquitous and its effects profound. Ricoeur's methodology involved an application of the hermeneutic approach to symbols and language pertaining to evil such as stain, defilement, guilt, "missing the mark." I will attempt to concisely distill his conclusions, adding scientific and psychoanalytic validation to support them.

Radical evil defined

Ricoeur's concept of evil is inseparable from his view that humans are "oriented toward realizing human freedom in concrete intentional projects [Ricoeur, 1950/1966; 1985, 647; 1995f, 569]" (Wall, 2001, p. 241). Each person's choices are intentional (Brentano, 1874/1995) and have a *telos* toward meaningful purposes (e.g., in relational psychoanalysis, orientation toward relationship is understood as an organizing, human orientation). This capacity to orient, Ricoeur describes as the "will." However, for Ricoeur, "Despite being capable of achieving many aims and goods in the world, the human being remains, at bottom, a fallen creature wracked by a fundamental incapacity to fully realize his or her *teloi*" (Wall, 2001, p. 241). Ricoeur (1995) would define evil as "*the incapacity belonging to the capable man*, the incapacity that does not abolish capability but presupposes it as the very thing that has ceased to be available to man as we know him historically" (p. 569, emphasis added). For Ricoeur, the gap between achieving a meaningful destiny and the incapacity to do so is the fountainhead of evil.

Evil causality

Humans as agents and sufferers

While humans choose to do evil, they are also the victims of it. This "thrownness" into evil is inescapable because we belong "to a history of evil, which is always already there for everyone" (Ricoeur, 1985, pp. 636–637). The infant born into the world is enmeshed in the web of incapacity before it has even parted from the womb. It is intersubjectively constructed through forces beyond its control, and it will make choices in its future based on these forces. Thus, Klein's destructive infant has before birth been stained by a biological, psychological, cultural surround.

In support of Ricoeur's view of evil, I will resource the recent findings from the field of epigenetics. The term *epigenetics* was first coined by C. H. Waddington in 1942 and refers to the genetic changes that can take place at the cellular level, with no change in DNA structure. Environmental factors have been shown to impact genetic constitution that can contradict inherited DNA endowment. Lipton (1998) observes:

> The malleable aspect of gene expression is an extremely important point in terms of fetal development. In the uterus, the fetus is in a constant state of "downloading" genetic information required for human development, growth and protection responses. ... As with every living system, the selection of growth or protection programs by the fetus is based upon its perception of its environment. The environment perceived by the fetus is the maternal blood from which it receives nourishment and "information". ... It is important to note that the environmental information observed by the fetus was not primarily intended for the fetus. The blood-borne information signals were deployed by the maternal nervous system in response to her perception of her environment. ... These blood-borne information signals not only affect the maternal system, for the same signals cross the placenta and profoundly impact the genetics and behavior of the developing fetus. (p. 8)

While impact on the developing fetus is now certain, some researchers believe that current studies will soon validate that human epigenetic changes are able to be passed to future generations based on studies that have established transgenerational transmission in mice (Jablonka & Lamb, 2005; Jablonka & Raz, 2009). Areas of research have included the effects of nutrition, posttraumatic stress disorder, and stress, and have already established first-generation non-DNA genetic mutations as a result of these environmental factors. While this research substantiates the necessity of a depth psychology that can positively impact constitutional factors in patients and their offspring (Gibbs, 2007), it also substantiates my current consideration of the potential for a radical brokenness that envelopes the human being entering the world.

Winnicott's good-enough mother may make every attempt to avoid perturbations for the unborn infant, but her finiteness will not permit her to eradicate every potentially damaging factor in the fetus's development. A host of genetic, epigenetic, nutritional, psychological, cultural, political, and other variables intersubjectively construct the forming life that is yet to be born.

Humans as fallible

Ricoeur uses the term *fallible* to describe the state of fracture and resultant conflict within all humans. Dual and sometimes oppositional motivations such as freedom and finiteness, pleasure and responsibility, reason and feeling, draw the person in disparate directions, much as Freud had depicted. Ricoeur (1986) clarifies:

> It may be said that man's specific limitation makes evil merely possible; in this case fallibility designates the *occasion*, the point of least resistance through which evil can enter into man; the fragile mediation appears then as the mere space of the appearance of evil. Man, center of reality, man, reconciler of the extreme poles of the real, man, microcosm, is also the weak link of the real. But between this possibility and the reality of evil, there is a gap, a leap: it is the whole riddle of fault. (pp. 141–142)

Humans as passive and active

Acting into the gap that fallibility endows is the "servile will." Ricoeur's observations parallel those of Fairbairn (1952), who described the bondage to internal objects, though Ricoeur privileges the agentic nature of a person capable of choice, an agency hobbled by a gravitation to what is evil. Thus, according to Ricoeur (1995):

> If evil resides somewhere, it is surely in the maxims of our actions, by means of which we hierarchize our preferences, placing duty above desire, or desire above duty. Evil, in fact, consists in a reversal of priority, an inversion or subversion on the plane of the maxims of action. (p. 77)

Waterstradt (2002) expounds Ricoeur's focus on agency: "Thus there is a passive and active; the always-already-there-ness of evil is outside of me, before me, after me, and yet my choice makes me responsible for it. Guilt is specifically *my guilt*" (p. 6). Ricoeur (1967) concludes: "The evil for which I assume responsibility makes manifest a source of evil for which I cannot assume responsibility, but which I participate in every time that through me evil enters into the world as if for the first time" (pp. 313–314).

Ricoeur's hermeneutic approach to evil becomes the means by which evil can be juxtaposed against the even more originary goodness of human beings. For though there is radical evil, stain, defilement, bondage, Ricoeur (1967) assures:

> To infect is not to destroy, to tarnish is not to ruin. The symbol here points toward the relation of radical evil to the very being of man, to the primordial destination of man; it suggests that evil, however positive, however seductive, however affective and infective it may be, cannot make a man something other than a man; infection cannot be a defection, in the sense that the dispositions and functions that make the humanity of man might be unmade, undone, to the point where a reality other than human reality would be produced. ... Evil is not symmetrical with the good, wickedness is not something that replaces the goodness of a man; it is the staining, the darkening, the disfiguring of an innocence, a light, and a beauty that remain. However *radical* evil may be, it cannot be as *primordial* as goodness. The symbol of defilement already says this about the servile will, and it says it through the symbol of captivity; for when a country falls intact into the hands of the enemy, it continues to work, to produce, to create, to exist, but for the enemy. (p. 156)

Originary goodness

Ricoeur (1970) utilized symbols and myths to achieve an understanding of evil, and with the same methodology arrived at his conception of human *originary goodness*. He writes: "More profoundly still, these myths recount, after the manner of a transhistorical event, the irrational break, the absurd leap, which separates two views, one concerned with the innocence of coming-to-be, the other with the guilt of history" (p. 39). Ricoeur asserts that human goodness predates, that is, is more primordial, than human evil.

Ricoeur illuminates the meaning of goodness through his hermeneutic method that presupposes either pole of a dialectic may aid in interpreting the other pole. As Wall (2005) suggests, "The admission—the confession—of radical evil is already, in a way an implicit affirmation of some still more radical capability for goodness" (p. 89). For Ricoeur, radical evil is understood as such only in contrast to its polar opposite, superabundant goodness.

Operating on this hermeneutic presupposition, he tests his hypothesis on myths and narratives of human creation and fall, lighting upon the Adamic myth as exemplary of originary good, upon which evil was superimposed. In that narrative, humans were created in the image of God and capable of relationship with the transcendent and one another, capable of creativity and choices for good (Ricoeur, 1967).

Human capability

Combining myth and hermeneutic linguistic analysis, Ricoeur suggests that to the extent that human freedom turned against itself in the actualization of evil, a more profound and radical capacity for human moral good remains and can be traced to the primordial gift of existence given by the Creator. Thus, Ricoeur attests that existence is ultimately meaningful. "'I can speak', 'I can act', 'I can narrate' and 'I can designate myself as imputable'" states Ricoeur. "What all these instances of 'I am able to ... ' articulate is the basic capacity of a human being to act and suffer" (Kearney, 2004, p. 168). Goodness has been defiled; original goodness of creation in the image of God remains.

Ricoeur teaches us that Klein's destructive infant and the impinging, neglectful, absent mother of Winnicott are not symmetrical with the infant whose very being is a celebration of existence and a mother who going beyond the bounds of evil choices makes the infant her "primary maternal preoccupation." Ricoeur might say that Klein's infant who will one day be a parent itself is more radically tainted than at first appears, and that both infant and parent are more superabundantly good than "good-enough" (Winnicott, 1960). The dynamic that bridges the gap between radical evil and superabundant goodness, according to Ricoeur, can only be explained through a gift of faith—faith in the originary goodness of infant and mother, analysand and analyst—faith is goodness's response to radical evil. Ricoeur's treatment of faith is a part of his larger project, "the economy of the gift."

THE ECONOMY OF THE GIFT: PSYCHOANALYTIC APPLICATIONS

Ricoeur perceives the acts of goodness shared between humans as proceeding from an "economy of the gift." Collating Ricoeur's views, Wall (2001, 2005) delineates a progression of three gifts—faith, love, and hope—which I will posit as correlating with and facilitating Hegel's progression of incarnation, crucifixion, and resurrection, and a psychoanalytic path of recognition—identification, surrender, and gratitude. Resourcing Ricoeur's "economy of the gift," I would like to interpolate the first two movements of recognition, identification and surrender, in light of Ricoeur's categories. I will then consider the third movement of gratitude.

The gift of faith: The empowering third in identification and incarnation

Faith is the gift offered that affirms one's potential, one's capability, in the face of seeming incapacity. Faith, according to Ricoeur, is a gift one has received and in turn—in the economy of the gift—gives to others. For the mother celebrating the gift of life in her newborn infant, her faith in the infant's capacity to live a meaningful life, fulfilling its potential, is a gift that she gives. This gift she received as well from people—parents, teachers, friends—who offered it to her in the cycle, the economy, of the gift. The analyst offers the gift to the patient who can see no possibilities, a gift based on faith gifted to the analyst. Gift is beyond mere technique. Transcending the law of equivalence, faith's surplus can only come from an abundance once received. This gift when received energizes both the infant and the patient to continue in their respective agentic struggles to develop. This same gift is to greater and greater extents reciprocally offered back to the mother and the analyst as basic trust develops.

Faith is the first response to evil and is seen in the psychoanalyst's courage to *incarnate* into the life of a patient, not only to *identify* with the patient's suffering, but to *identify* with potentials in the patient yet to be realized (Loewald, 1960). McWilliams (2004) offers this apt description: "What I mean by faith is a gut-level confidence in a process, despite inevitable moments of skepticism, confusion, doubt, and even despair" (p. 42). Faith is the gift the psychoanalyst offers based on his own experience of personal growth. With the faith that this can be our patient's experience as well, we are willing to suffer alongside her in order to see that potential realized.

The gift of love: The empowering third in surrender and crucifixion

Love is the gift that is offered when as mother or as analyst we are surviving destruction. It was a gift once given to us as our parents and analysts *surrendered* to the difficult process of receiving our destructiveness, and survived our destructiveness through love and its corollary, forgiveness. Love is the capacity to respect the infant or analysand as other while they are not yet able to respond in kind, surviving their destruction—or *crucifixion* in Hegel's terms. Love is heard in the echo of the words of Jesus on the cross, "Father, forgive them, for they know not what they do," a plea that offers recognition when mutuality is made impossible due to projective processes that blind. This second movement of a love that survives introduces into the world of the infant and the patient the possibility of seeing parent and analyst as other, as surrender to the process brings about a relinquishing of omnipotent control and an openness to the gift of love that is being offered.

Klein's infant was construed as performing reparative tasks to recompense the mother for her suffering. The mother and analyst in Ricoeur's economy of the gift extend full forgiveness for destructiveness suffered, for it was a gift freely given to them first.[7] Not only is there no retaliation, but there is no expectation of compensation, for that would render the gift void. The economy of the gift supersedes the logic of equivalent justice with the logic of superabundant love.

The gift of hope: The empowering third in gratitude and resurrection

Hope is the third gift in Ricoeur's economy, and it facilitates experiencing the third movement of recognition: resurrection and gratitude. Emerging from the chaos of destructiveness, a new birth of sight occurs in which mother and analyst are no more mere projections of the infant and the patient, but are separate and in this sense, new. There is a resurrection experience in which the patient does not recognize the analyst as the person previously seen.[8] The gifts of faith and love create a passage for the arrival of the gift of hope, of things radically new, of goodness rebirthed. These gifts have time after time resonated in the lives of both mother and analyst, and now hope rekindles as it is gifted to another.

Apprehending the mother and the analyst as separate people provides the new experience of the highest form of recognition: gratitude. At this apex of the recognition process, there is the experience and acknowledgment of the receipt of "other than me substance" (Winnicott, 1968); until this point both infant and analysand have been being sustained by the faith and love of the mother and analyst. As Benjamin (2006) observes:

> Within the paradigm of the analytic dyad, what the patient initially finds beneficial in opening to the analyst's independent mind is the possibility that there really can be an Other mind that tunes into his own. When the analyst is empathic, for instance, the empathy is coming from an Outside Other. As Winnicott put it in the nursing metaphor in "The Use of an Object and Relating through Identifications," such understanding is "not me" nutriment, it is real—the milk is coming from an outside breast, not from something that is under my omnipotent control. By the same token, this relinquishing of omnipotent control is what makes it valuable to the patient because it means that there is somebody out there from whom I can receive and learn something that is not auto generated.

> There is somebody, an Other, out there whom I might connect to. In short, since the outside can be a source of goodness, it becomes safe and even desirable to go outside. Otherness is not simply inherently threatening. (p. 140)

Gratitude and the economy of the gift

Ricoeur positions *gratitude* at the height of the path of mutual recognition. Neither in identification nor in surrender could acknowledgment of dependence upon the giver be achieved, even while the giver's gifts of faith and love facilitated the moves to identification and surrender. Gratitude goes beyond a recognition that merely comprehends roles of mother and infant, analyst and patient; gratitude also goes beyond a recognition of the alterity of mother and infant, of analyst and patient: Gratitude surrenders to their asymmetrical positions. Gratitude acknowledges dependency upon another whose grace has been received. Gratitude is the first moment of the gift being accepted as such. Gratitude follows in the wake of resurrection and is always at risk of running amok on the shoals of obligation and reciprocity, risks that would pervert gratitude into a submissive act of coercion. Gratitude for a gift given poses a dilemma: How may gratitude be expressed if a reciprocal gift invalidates the first gift? As Derrida (1992) has commented: "For there to be a gift, *it is necessary [il faut]* that the *donne* not give back, amortize, reimburse, acquit himself, enter into a contract, and that he never have contracted a debt" (p. 13).

In his attempt to address the conundrum of receiving the gift, Ricoeur invokes Mauss's (1989) work on gifting practices among tribal groups. In groups such as the Maori, the gift itself carries a magical power that binds the community together, a power that demands to be passed on. Ricoeur (2005) demystifies these practices and establishes that, in fact, the Maori practice points to a universal desire to pass on the gift as part of the action of gratitude. This notion is apparent in the lexicographic definition of gratitude.

A ready illustration of Ricoeur's observation occurs in the parent/child relationship. The early smiles and coos of the infant bring delight to the parents, the earliest responses of an infant to the good it is receiving. As the child matures, it finds little in its power to give beyond verbal expressions of gratitude that might adequately compensate the parents for their efforts. A child's greatest expression of gratitude occurs in time when the good gifts of faith and love which the child has received are in turn given to another. This resurrection and replication of the now-internalized good parent is the indirect gift of hope, which the parent in turn receives. The parent's hope is fortified as the economy of the gift recycles through the lives of their children. It is further instantiated as this new birth of transformative faith and love is transmitted by their children into their own communities of relationships, gifts which will sustain them and those they love in this good world stained with moral tragedy.

The resurrection I describe eclipses mere resuscitation of the originary good. In a reformulated, yet distinct echo of Hegel, Devin Singh offers a riveting explication of Ricoeur's use of the metaphor of Christ's resurrection, envisioning its symbolic potential in this way:

> The possibility opened up through the resurrection is the future of history. It portrays the *novum*, the radically new, which comes to transform history, not merely to interrupt it. ... The surplus of meaning in the resurrection contributes to new possible meanings for reality. ... The ordinary of existence is ruptured, and God's new possibilities have entered our realm. As a historian discovers hope in the mode of memory, so the prophet shapes memory in the mode of hope. Our past and present must be viewed in light of the future. They are the past and present of things future. ... The resurrection as metaphor has a surplus of meaning. It is a poetic redescription of reality, projecting new possibilities for existence. (Singh, 2008, p. 6)

The gifts given by both parents and analyst evolve into far more than justice would require and supersede the logic of recompensed equivalence. Good-enough parents and analysts are not merely good enough. Their love becomes superabundant as it transforms the trajectory of a person's life, an evidence of the "surplus" of the economy of the gift grounded in a grateful recognition of the other. This is the economy of the gift: a circular economy of mutual recognition and awe for the abundance, the surplus, the essential affirmatory goodness of other and of life, the "yes" in the sadness of the finite.

ENDNOTES

1. Four notable exceptions exist. Nancy McWilliams & Stanley Lependorf (1990) and Glen Gabbard (2000) wrote articles that engaged the construct. A book entitled *Envy and Gratitude Revisited* (Roth & Lemma, 2008) reviewed and elaborated on Klein's basic ideas. Peter Shabad's *Despair and the Return of Hope* (2001) addresses *gratitude* directly and beautifully, though only briefly, for it is not the main focus of his book. Shabad's work, however, remains the sole substantive theoretical contribution on the topic since Klein.
2. In agreement with Fairbairn's amendation, Klein eventually referred to the "paranoid-schizoid" position.
3. Lewis Aron (personal communication) linked the desire for gratitude with the day-to-day experience of the analyst, a topic meriting further attention. Who of us has not experienced the patient who says, "You only do this because I pay you," implying that our care and survival of destruction is an entitlement.

4. An interesting consideration arises here. The Greek word for Latin *gratus* is *charis* meaning grace as well, and forming the basis of *eucharistos*, which is the sacramental meal of Eucharist. It is noteworthy that this meal represents the survival of destruction, the ongoing gratitude for this survival, and the communion of believers around this survival.
5. "Under the motif of 'resurrection,' Hegel offers images of the raising up, ascent, return, and consummation of the whole divine process" (Hodgson, 2005, p. 175). Resurrection and ascension are treated as one movement in Christ's exaltation.
6. Biographical material is based on Charles Reagan's book, *Paul Ricoeur: His Life and His Work* (1996).
7. "Forgiveness" is examined by Ricoeur in great detail, especially in *Memory, History, Forgetting* (2004). To venture into that topic more fully departs from the central project of this book. However, his ideas regarding justice, amnesty, reparation, political guilt, moral guilt, and so forth are nuanced and thought provoking, offering no facile equation to apply unilaterally.
8. This reference is to the apparent unrecognizability of Jesus by his disciples after the resurrection.

Chapter 9

From mourning to resurrection with Mandy

Clinical perspectives

This final section chronicling Mandy's journey covers the past 5 years of our work together. In the last 2 years, Mandy has reduced her sessions to once weekly and continues to utilize the therapy productively. I would characterize the most striking aspect of this period as an experience of resurrection. For both Mandy and me, things that we had only hoped would come true have begun to materialize.

CLINICAL NOTES: 2004–2005

Fall 2004

Mandy is experiencing her marriage as strengthening and has celebrated their 9th wedding anniversary. She is much more able to withstand conflict without resorting to compliance or dissociation.

Mandy is beginning to talk about wanting a child. This is terrifying for her. Can she have a normal infant? Can she love the child enough? Is she too damaged? Can her husband enter into the role of father?

Mandy expresses hope that Trudy will someday be willing to enter therapy.

There is excitement in Mandy at fulfilling her potential. "I want to own all aspects of my life that I used to just feel ashamed about."

December 2004

There is news from the district attorney. Father wants another hearing and has hired a new attorney. There is a new judge, and all bets are off now. Mandy and Trudy are being required to attend the hearing in person. Mandy will see her father for the first time since the murder. We prepare for the inevitable. Mandy and her sister visit the courtroom. I speak with my new relational supervisor about my desire to attend the hearing. He strongly encourages me.

January 2005

Mandy sees the psychiatric notes, as well as the medical records from the time of the murder for the first time. She feels intense pain at what she went through. The hearing is next week.

February 2005

At the last minute the hearing was canceled and postponed until March. Mandy feels like "cocooning" after the events of the last few weeks. Father is putting her through more pain. Mandy has resorted to turning off feelings in order to cope, with a subsequent increase in obsessive thoughts.

We spent much time processing memories of the murders. Mandy feels fearful of experiencing too much compassion for Father when she sees him.

March 2005

I attend the hearing with Mandy. She reads a prepared letter to the judge describing the pain that she has endured since the murder. She is congruent and articulate. The audience is spellbound by her story.

Mandy sees her father, as did I. He appears dapper and in no way reflecting the insanity that hides within him. The newest woman in his life was in attendance. (His second wife, a nurse he had married at the hospital, had committed suicide.) His psychiatrist attempts to portray him as fully cured. The state has a forensic psychiatrist who was brilliant and capably refuted each assertion.

Mandy retires to an antechamber, overcome with feelings. I hug her and she lays her head on my shoulder and weeps like a child for quite a while. It is a moment I will never forget.

April 2005

The defendant's request to leave the hospital is denied. The judge decrees that he have absolutely no contact with his daughters.

Mandy begins to contemplate the possibility of writing her story someday.

This has been an amazing period in Mandy's life. The opportunity to accompany her to the hearing was important for her and for me. I only hope that Mandy will continue to feel that she can rely on me to support her in this more engaged fashion.

Clinical commentary: Destruction—survival, sequelae, potential

Mandy had physically survived her father's attack, but as trauma literature indicates, the psychological effects are devastating. Evil—brutal, alienating, and demolishing—imprints its stain for the rest of life's journey and lingers as a historic injunction of the fragility of any hope. Relationally based psychoanalytic therapy offers no romantic "magic bullets" to do battle with such evil. Yet we can utter with Ricoeur that there is a "Yes" to life that can emerge from the shattered remains of destruction, though it be uttered with a survivor's eternal vigilance.

For Mandy, affective hyperarousal as a result of her trauma was countered by affective numbing and obsessive thoughts, remnants of the embedded nature of such trauma. This became a long-standing oscillation in the treatment (Davies & Frawley, 2004; van der Kolk & Greenberg, 1987), though Mandy preferred to remain most often in her dissociated, feeling-free state. Only gradually, and within the safety of loving relationship, did she begin to rediscover any states of aliveness and resultant hope. Initially, hope was unconsciously an enemy, as Primo Levi (1993) observed: "Hope ... is harmful because it keeps alive a sensitivity which is a source of pain, and which some providential natural law dulls when suffering passes a certain point. Like joy, fear and pain itself, even expectancy can be tiring" (p. 171). As hope tentatively sprouted its tender shoots in Mandy's life, the specter of a father, both within and without, perpetually cast its menacing shadow on her path. When these shadows of evil darkened our work, I could do nothing but witness (Oliver, 2001), relinquishing the benign omnipotence that I had fantasied, and internally murmuring for us both, "Yea though I walk through the valley of the shadow of death, I will fear no evil: for Thou art with me" (Psalm 23:4, KJV).

The mutual survival of destruction that occurs in a vital psychotherapy can build a resilience that bolsters the patient for the even more intense affects that life outside of the consultation room will bring. Such was the case with Mandy. Had Mandy not been helped to tolerate the intense feelings and the pain that we encountered in our work, she might have been unable to confront and emerge successfully from the encounter with her father.

Mandy was able to confront Father fortified by many sessions of experiencing a balance of reason and experience that allowed her to feel, but also to mentalize her unformulated (Donnel Stern, 2003) feelings. Experiencing both the hermeneutic of suspicion that focused on her father's evil deeds, and also the hermeneutic of faith that recognized the woundedness that had led him to his evil, she looked at what he had perpetrated upon her in the past with the hope that someday her story might be of help to others. For years, she and I oscillated through our attempts to hold these central dialectics in order to promote the force for growth within.

Mandy's feelings about Mother remained secondary, emerging only infrequently, but now emerging with affect. Though Mandy could feel love for her father, in spite of his many crimes against her, love for her mother languished under her dissociation of memories following the trauma. It would take the birth of her own child in combination with the death of my father to resurrect our respective mothers, so they could be both mourned and transformed.

CLINICAL NOTES: 2006–2007

Winter 2006

Mandy continues to debate whether to have children. She states, "I feel so defective. Any child of mine is going to be the same." I encourage her to contemplate a portrait of her and her husband with children. She has a hard time looking at the portrait because she cannot believe that could be her life. Through several sessions Mandy discusses what that portrait of her future might look like.

Mandy is starting to contemplate changing churches. She is feeling at home in her old church where she grew up as a child, but is finding a greater and greater disparity between how she perceives her faith and what she is being taught. If she should have children someday, she would want them to be in a church where she feels comfortable.

Spring 2006

Plans are underway for Mandy and her husband to buy land to build a house. Many sessions are spent on wrestling with her lack of worthiness for something so nice. She fears what relatives would think, what God would think. Mandy wants to set her roots down.

Mandy has a dream that she and her husband received a coveted award. She feels it is a sign that she is able to start receiving good things.

Father has hired another attorney. He asserts his right for an annual review, and another hearing is scheduled, which she attends. The outcome is the same.

Fall 2006

Mandy sees more clearly how her dissociation of affect is linked to an increase in her intrusive thoughts. Such thoughts only emerge at times of great stress or fatigue at this point. We return to processing the sexual implications of the thoughts and have concluded that there is no doubt that there was sexual abuse before the murder that she cannot remember. These thoughts are invoked, however, as "chatter" when the even more threatening feelings of loss arise.

November 2006

Mandy is pregnant.

Winter 2007

Mandy and I oscillate between discussing what mothering will be like in the future and imagining what her mother had experienced with her. Was Mother excited about her birth? What was her pregnancy like? Many questions sadly have to remain unanswered.

Mandy and Ken have built a new home. Mandy struggles with enjoying the successes of her life.

February 2007

My father passes away. Sessions are cancelled the week of his funeral.

Clinical commentary: Between crucifixion and resurrection

Pregnancy

After several years of processing her capacity for both bearing and raising a child, Mandy had come to the conclusion that she was capable. Her fears, however, manifested in her voracious reading of books on pregnancy and child-rearing to fortify herself for the task. Mandy had arrived at a point of faith in life and in God and was relinquishing some of her omnipotent control. Though her feelings of defectiveness continued, she could now risk having a child and committing to such an attachment, with the knowledge that in life there are no guarantees.

Pregnancy is a developmental milestone, the pregnant mother encountering her own mother (Freud, 1931) in the process. It has also been understood as a time for potential restructuring of the pregnant mother's internal world (Benedek, 1959; Kestenberg, 1976). Current neuroscience findings confirm that

> during pregnancy and in the first year of the baby, striking changes occur in mothers' brains (Panksepp, 1998). ... Neuroscientific research indicates, additionally, that the intense hormonal fluctuations that occur during pregnancy, birth, and lactation may remodel the female brain, increasing the size of neurons in some regions and producing structural changes in others. (Ammaniti & Trentini, 2009, p. 548)

For Mandy, becoming a mother meant navigating fears of her own death, of her child's death, as well as her fears of her possible incapacity to be a mother. As Mandy began to experience the new life within her, she was plagued by ruminations about whether she should continue teaching at the college or whether she should be at home with her child. In her own childhood, Mandy's mother worked outside of the home and Mandy remembers feelings that Mother did not have enough time to know her. Mandy realized that relinquishment of her tenure, educational community, and financial stability might feel like becoming trapped by circumstances (i.e., becoming like her mother).

Mourning

Memories of Mother began to surface with more frequency during Mandy's pregnancy. During this time as well, the death of my father had stirred memories of Mother for me, memories that for both of us took on a new cast. For Mandy, there was a reactivation of a mourning that had never fully occurred (Wright & Strawn, 2010). This was to increase until sometime after her baby's birth. While there was still mourning for me as I stood at the grave of my parents, I had already completed much of that work with respect to my mother. What emerged in me was a sense of rediscovery, of a *resurrection* of aspects of my mother that had previously been obscured by my anger and sadness at her absence. I began to recognize her creativity, her beauty, her giftedness; and I began to recognize and be grateful for those aspects of myself that were my mother. My ability to transcend the shroud of my own dead mother and experience a resurrection of a new experience of Mother would be a foretaste of what Mandy would ultimately experience, though after a very difficult period of her own mourning.

CLINICAL NOTES: 2007

June 2007

Mandy refound her baby book and talked about her mother's care. She went on to discuss the death of her brother. Mandy cried as she imagined the terror that he must have felt.

Mandy discussed the relationship of her mother to her own sisters. Her mother was the most attractive and held the most promise. We discussed the possibility that her mother was envied for this.

Mandy feels guilty for being so blessed in her life now.

July 2007

Mandy is experiencing increased sadness as she approaches the birth of the baby. We processed her feelings about being called "Mom."

Mandy has a dream in which she sees Christ, and he tells her that she is a wise person and that she has insight. Mandy feels very supported by this dream.

August 2007

Alicia is born.

Clinical commentary: Days of darkness—In the tomb of mourning

Postpartum

The days that followed the birth of Alicia were very difficult for Mandy. Realizing the extent of Mandy's abandonment by Mother, I decided to make home visits to her periodically over the next 2 months, supplementing the phone sessions we were having. In these early months of Alicia's life, Mandy was more in touch with depressive affect than ever before. This time proved to be a period of deep mourning, a time when I simply needed to be a participant/observer of her pain. What had been successfully dissociated before was being catapulted into consciousness in the presence of her more volatile hormonal state, her lack of distractions, and the work that we had done to allow the mourning to recommence.

Mandy began to experience feelings of anger at the difficulties she was experiencing in the postpartum period. For the first time in years, Mandy did not feel that she had control of her life. We discussed how it would have been for her to have her mother there for her. The dissociation of mourning for Mother having been breached, and the spontaneous enactment of a "death-filled analyst with a death-filled patient" having been survived, I was in position to provide a more responsive, therapeutic enactment in her life. During this time I worked with Mandy much as a mother would have, helping her to schedule her life, encouraging her to ask for my help when she needed it, and insisting that she attend to her rest. At one point, Mandy, in an assertive style that I had not seen before, disagreed with my perspective on parenting her daughter and chose a different path. We processed this as a developmental milestone. Mandy was no longer the compliant, fearful child. She and I discussed her feeling "a bit rebellious" toward me as a sort of adolescent step toward autonomy and celebrated this rite of passage.

During these months of a continuing mix of mourning and celebration, Mandy's bond with her daughter deepened, and she became convinced of her ability to adequately mother. Picture after picture of Alicia, shared during appointments, would bring me delight. At times, Alicia would come, and I appreciated the privilege of seeing transitions in her development.

Mourning and internalization

This period of mourning was a necessary aspect of Mandy's healing, for it would allow Mandy's mother to move from being a dissociated "ghost" to "an ancestor" (Mitchell, 1998). The stage was now set for Mandy's recognition of repressed goodnesses in her mother as well, which would lead to her internalization[1] of mother with its potential for resurrection in a transformed fashion. Loewald (1962) spoke to this process in his paper "Internalization, Separation, Mourning, and the Superego." He writes:

> Loss of a love object does not necessarily lead to mourning and internalization. The object lost by separation or death may not be mourned, but either the existence or the loss of the object may be denied. Such denial is the opposite of mourning. Instead of internalizing the relationship,

> external substitutions may be sought. One patient, for instance, used all available figures in the environment as substitutes for the lost parents, clinging forever to relatives and friends of his parents and from his own childhood, appealing to them, often successfully, for care and love. But he was unable to establish lasting new relationships and lasting and effective sublimations; his capacity for productive work was severely limited; his superego development was rudimentary. Both the ability to form lasting new external relationships and the capacity for stable sublimations appear to be based on, among other things, firmly established internalizations. (p. 487)

In the Christian narrative, internalization is the coming of the Spirit. For Hegel, this was the negation of the negation. This internalization in Mandy's life included the coming to life of the image of God that was in her mother, a negation of the stranglehold of death in Mandy's history (see Brokaw, 2008). Mother remained dead, but she was no longer twice dead for Mandy—physically and intrapsychically.

SEXUAL TRAUMA AND THE RECOGNITION OF THE SACRED

These initial months of Alicia's life were also the first time in years that Mandy was not occupied with teaching, and she had time to ruminate. Her concerns regarding sexual abuse resurfaced but did not occlude the good feelings about Mother. Mandy simply wanted to remember her own sexual abuse. Vague memories of being drugged with alcohol, being taken to a doctor far away, and of having someone walk into her bedroom at night plagued her mind, though she could not corroborate the veracity of these memories.

Mandy's faith had dramatically changed over the course of our work. No longer did she experience God as a celestial taskmaster who would care for her only if she were perfect. To greater and greater extents Mandy allowed God to be caring but mysterious, and beyond her capacity to control through prayer or good deeds (Hall & Brokaw, 1995; McDargh, 1983).

Mandy and I both shared a belief that God was involved in her treatment and that we could share our concerns with him about any difficulties that arose. Mandy and I agreed one day in mid-October to pray that God would give her some clarification of her intuitions about what had been done to her sexually. My class at New York University's Postdoctoral Program in Psychotherapy and Psychoanalysis was on a Wednesday night, and I typically read my articles earlier in the day, which was the day after our prayer. As I went to class that night and we discussed an article by Sándor Ferenczi (1949), the very kinds of abuses that Mandy had described were referenced by Ferenczi, including the implication of substances as a contributing variable to the abuse of children. I was startled by the similarity between Ferenczi's accounts and Mandy's description of what she may have endured.

At her next session, Mandy began by wanting to talk of a dream that she had had right after our last session. Mandy described being in a house in which very young children were being drugged and molested and were unable to escape. I listened with amazement and then shared the article, which I had brought with me to show her. In that article, Ferenczi (1949) recounts the plight of such young children: "These children feel physically and morally helpless, their personalities are not sufficiently consolidated in order to be able to protest, even if only in thought, for the overpowering force and authority of the adult makes them dumb ... " (p. 228). Although Mandy to this point had no direct corroboration of her abuse, in the coalescing of the prayer, the class, and the dream, Mandy felt with some certainty that her intuitions had been correct.

CLINICAL NOTES: 2008

Alicia is growing into a lively and enchanting infant. Mandy expresses periodic concern over her ability to attach and over her handling of maternal responsibilities.

Mandy is remembering her mother as she interacts with Alicia. She reports that looking at her baby's hand reminds her of the feel of her mother's hand. She begins to cry as she remembers the last time she saw her mother's hand on that day of the murder. Could Mother, who no longer could see and who no longer had a mouth with which to speak, have wanted to protect her in those final moments? Mandy begins to ponder Mother's feelings from the vantage point of being a mother herself.

Mandy continues to recall memories about Mother. She remembers how her mother dressed, feeling saddened that there was no clothing of Mother's left to her as a keepsake.

Alicia is maturing nicely and Mandy has decided to return to teaching. Her sister Trudy will be watching Alicia on the days Mandy is teaching. Trudy has been married several years at this point and has begun therapy with my husband. Mandy and Trudy are experiencing a sense of family connectedness that had not existed since they were young children.

Mandy's college is delighted that she has returned. They are fashioning a schedule that will allow her to be at school only 3 days a week. Mandy's husband is supportive of her staying home if she desires. Mandy feels it is important to resume her career.

Mandy talked again about the possibility of writing a book about her life. She and her sister are considering collaborating in this venture.

I begin to discuss with Mandy the possibility of using her story for this book and she seems interested and very willing.

Mandy and Ken have decided to attend a new church. Mandy seems very pleased to have settled on a church near home. This change marks the leaving of the church that she had attended since childhood.

CLINICAL NOTES: 2009

Mandy and Trudy are both expecting. Irony would have it that Mandy's due date is the anniversary of her mother's death.

Clinical commentary: Resurrection and gratitude

Understanding some of the neuroscientific substratum of our work, I was better able to comprehend the resurrection of good mother that occurred as Mandy interacted with her child. Memories long dissociated of being with Mother, along with painful memories recollected after Mother's death, were reencountered via the neural pathways that seeing, hearing, touching, and smelling her infant provided. Once, Mandy was the infant of her mother, and stored in her preverbal memories were smiles and gentle touches. For Mandy, resurrection meant a lifting of the "dissociation of goodness" both in herself and in the memories of her mother. The kaleidoscope of life had shifted.

Perhaps, in the terms of Mandy's faith, this shift can be described as a new birth. For Mandy, the mother she has in recent times experienced is far different from the mother of earlier years of her therapy. Mother is not just a victim dimly remembered; she is her mother. As I walked through this period in Mandy's life, I too came to love my parents in a way that I never before would have thought possible. Even as I write, my eyes moisten for the gift of new birth.

Mandy's desire to make a difference as a result of her struggles is growing stronger, a desire primarily focused on speaking to people locked in her previous fundamentalist ways of thinking. Mandy hopes to someday also help children of abuse, children who never had the opportunity to receive the even meager support that as a child she received. From a psychodynamic standpoint, Mandy's dissociated affect that had been avoided is becoming understood and "mentalized" and is a source of greatest sensitivity and empathy. The gift of hope is reigniting the cycle that starts with identification and incarnation as Mandy looks for opportunities to give. As I have been writing her story, she has been my consultant and trusts that her journey will give hope to others.

In the terms of Mandy's faith, her psychotherapeutic resurrection is a new birth, and her experience of gratitude accompanied by the superabundant good is, in reality, "conversion." The psychic energy that was once consumed by dissociation and repression is beginning to be available for creative purposes, a veritable conversion to a generative life from the purposelessness of death. Many psychoanalysts might say that Mandy has achieved the "depressive position." I would like to suggest that Mandy can at times surpass the "depressive position" and experience "the transcendent position" (Grotstein, 1993).[2] The transcendent position is one in which life's negations are not only survived but are themselves transcended through the transformation of redemption. A new creation rises from the ashes of trauma, subverting evil's designs and orienting toward an altruistic, other-centered *telos*.[3]

CLINICAL NOTES: 2010

Seth Matthew is born on the eve of the anniversary of the death of Mandy's mother and brother.

ENDNOTES

1. Loewald, in his seminal paper on internalization, references the incarnation and death of Christ as the event par excellence in Western history that facilitated a culturalwide internalization. He writes: "The death of a love object, or the more or less permanent separation from a love object, is the occasion for mourning and for internalization. The unconscious and conscious experiences of threats to one's own existence as an individual, heightened by the increasing awareness of one's own eventual death, is, I believe, intimately connected with the phenomenon of internalization. It seems significant that with the advent of Christianity, initiating the greatest intensification of internalization in Western civilization, the death of God as incarnated in Christ moves into the center of religious experience. Christ is not only the ultimate love object which the believer loses as an external object and regains by identification with Him as an ego ideal, He is, in His passion and sacrificial death, the exemplification of complete internalization and sublimation of all earthly relationships and needs. But to pursue these thoughts would lead us far afield into unexplored psychological country" (1962, pp. 486–487).
2. Though I use the same term as Grotstein, his usage differs from mine. For Grotstein, this position is a mediating one between a coupled paranoid/schizoid and depressive position, and does not refer to a state of altruism borne out of gratitude and redemption.
3. There are several concluding thoughts. As a result of the research that I have done for Mandy's case, I have been able to utilize the lens of psychoanalysis to understand and demythologize certain aspects of Christian faith that had been difficult for me to understand. Specifically, Mandy's early Christian faith gave

her something that went far deeper than I was able to describe. In my discovery with Mandy of what was previously hidden from me, a fuller import of this book is now apparent to me.

How can the crucifixion of Christ 2,000 years ago have such a profound effect on the lives of so many people, and why do Christians believe that this was a necessary aspect of his story? And how does this relate to Mandy's journey?

Rereading the neuroscience literature was helpful in offering some potential clarity for my questions. If we understand with Ricoeur that the "symbol gives rise to the thought," and that strong affect and particularly painful affect is stored in the right brain, then the figure of the dying Christ vivified by visual representations of his life and redounded by auditory communal worship such as nativity reenactments accompanied by sacred music, forever enshrine love and belief in the minds of those who see and hear. Should other emotions be paired with these same images as has been the case with anti-Semitic co-opting of the passion story, these love-imbued symbols can and have conjured love-dystonic feelings of anger, pain, and exclusion. Perverse treacheries such as the pairing of anti-Semitic slogans with the Christ story are the very antithesis of the sacrificial and accepting love of Christ.

For Mandy and others who have faith in this Christ, the visual and auditory symbols of the cross, the Eucharist, baptism, hymns, and so forth, become transitional objects across the expanse of the centuries that attach Christians to one another and to this Christ. The death of one has become a superabundance of life for many. But this life is not given for the individual quiescence of oneself. It is an internalization of a life that embraces surrender, self-sacrifice, and suffering love in order to consummate God's covenant of love with humankind.

Chapter 10

In grateful memory—

The resurrection of Sándor Ferenczi and the renewal of the relational covenant

Historical perspectives

Spanning the legendary Danube, at the point where the now-united cities of Buda on the west bank and Pest on the east exchange gazes, is a bridge whose existence symbolizes the extraordinary cultural heritage of the Hungarian, or Magyar, people. At the time of its opening in 1849, the Chain Bridge was one of the world's largest. Count Istvan Széchényi of Hungary had seen London's Hammersmith Bridge and ultimately secured the services of English designer William Clark and an engineer, Scotsman Adam Clark, to erect a bridge across the Danube. Széchényi, a Catholic, was impressed by that Protestant country's democracy, emulating it as a role model for his initiatives in Hungary. Széchényi eagerly encouraged other English and Scottish people to bring their skills to Hungary, including engineers, professionals, skilled workers, and shipbuilders such as the English shipwright Fowles, who collaborated with the Danube Steamship Company (Kovács, 2006, p. 9). Though these mercantile associations may appear inconsequential, in the political climate of Eastern Europe they reflected a burgeoning struggle for freedom. The Chain Bridge stands not simply as a bridge between Buda and Pest but as a heroic link with Protestant Great Britain in a land dominated by the Hapsburgs.

Such associations fostered a religious and ethnic pluralism that reached its apex in Budapest in the late 1800s to early 1900s and synthesized a unique climate of brilliance rarely paralleled in modern times. A short list of luminaries from this era reflects Hungary's far-reaching impact: Karl Mannheim, sociologist; Lipót Fejér, mathematician; Todor Kármán, physicist and pioneer of aerodynamics; Dezsö Kosztolányi, novelist; Georg Lukács, philosopher; Karl Polanyi, economist; Michael Polanyi, chemist and philosopher; George Polya, mathematician; Edward Teller, physicist, father of the hydrogen bomb; Leo Szilard, physicist, developer of the concept of "nuclear chain reaction"; Eugene Wigner, physicist, Nobel Prize winner.

Most Hungarian academics were bilingual or polylingual, sometimes writing in German, sometimes in Hungarian (Haynal, 2002, p. 2). There has always been a "traditional contrast in intellectual history between 'contemplative Austrians' and 'activist Hungarians'" (Demeter, 2008, p. 4). Demeter explains: "Due to the fact that verbs play a more important role in Hungarian, it is more natural to express ideas by images rather than abstractions. And this creates a less hospitable environment for philosophical reasoning" (p. 3). Thus, the Hungarian language supported a more experientially based orientation to life than its academic neighbor Vienna might have. The compact Hungarian greenhouse of active erudition supported the emergence of the passionate genius of Sándor Ferenczi, who would impact psychoanalysis and, in turn, the world.

Quite sadly, Ferenczi, like earlier European reformers, was crucified by the psychoanalytic community and died in 1933 without experiencing recognition for the monumental impact of his contributions. Yet his work did survive his destruction through the activity of those whose lives he had touched. Apart from the few brave sages who publicly acknowledged his genius, it was not until the publication of his *Collected Papers*: *First Contributions to Psychoanalysis* (1952a), *Further Contributions to the Theory and Technique of Psycho-Analysis* (1952b), *Final Contributions to the Problems and Methods of Psycho-Analysis* (1955), and *Clinical Diary* (1985) that Ferenczi's breathtaking corpus was resurrected. Scholars principally in the stream of relational psychoanalysis (i.e., Lewis Aron, Jessica Benjamin, Emmanuel Berman, Jay Frankel, Adrienne Harris, Jeremy Safran), for reasons that I will later interrogate, have been at the forefront of the renewed interest in Ferenczi (Aron & Harris, 1993).

In *Reading Psychoanalysis* (2002), Peter Rudnytsky offers an assessment, relevant to our study, of Ferenczi's ethos: "Despite his endorsement of Freud's atheism, however, Ferenczi's version of psychoanalysis recognizes the existential truth of Christianity" (p. 140). Thus, while the contributions to Ferenczi's giftedness are undoubtedly multidetermined, in this chapter I would like to explore and recognize the role that religious narratives played in his life. I will survey Ferenczi's personal life and his Hungarian culture for evidence of religious influences, and I will then investigate Ferenczi's works in order to recognize those influences. In a concluding chapter I will present the implications of my findings for relational psychoanalysis.

RELIGIOUS INFLUENCES FROM HUNGARIAN CULTURE

Religious and ethnic pluralism

Ferenczi's Budapest and Freud's Vienna lie slightly more than 150 miles apart, but their cultural trajectories, each as luminous as the other, developed in profoundly disparate ways (Congdon, 1991; Haynal, 2009, personal communication; Kovács, 2006). In stark relief to Vienna, religious pluralism and its ethnic substrate flourished in Hungary due to an atmosphere of exemplary cooperation and tolerance. Kovács (2006) elaborates:

> In the nineteenth century religion and ethnicity overlapped to a great extent. [Magyarized] Hungarians[1] were mainly Calvinist and some were Roman Catholic. Croats were Roman Catholic, Slovaks either Catholic or Lutheran, Swabian Roman Catholic, the *Zipsers* of northern Hungary and Transylvanian Saxons were Lutheran, Rumanians were Orthodox and finally there was an increasing number of Jews from the 1830's onwards. As the Hungarian Kingdom was ruled by the absolutist power of the Habsburgs, the Hungarian response to it was a rise of nationalism. (pp. 14–15)

The heterogeneity of Hungarian society facilitated

> that readiness to express themselves in diverse tongues and take over, or share, alien idioms and other cultural paradigms, [and] has had a big hand in keeping them relatively open to the outside world, encouraging an engagement with other cultures and the evolution of cultural pluralism which has been a hallmark of the Hungarian tradition. (Frank, 2007, p. 10)

Not only were Hungarians tolerant of the diversity within their borders, but they were enriched by "an astonishing range of influences, showing considerable ability to adapt many of the features of what constitutes 'Hungarianness' to the ebb and flow of those impacts" (Frank, 2007, p. 10).

Calvinism: Political implications

Held in common by many Protestant and Jewish Hungarians, as well as emigrated Scots, was the memory of persecution for their faith principally by ruling Catholic monarchies. The influx of Reformation teaching into Hungary since the 1500s landed on fertile soil. In the hands of Hungarian liberators, these Protestant teachings became a political force that propelled Hungarian nationalism. It was Calvinism that prevailed as the dominant Protestant faith in Hungary, particularly in the northeast part of the country, the Hungarian scholar Botond Gaal (2007) observing that "The life of the Calvinist Church merged with the destiny of the Hungarian nation" (p. 2).[2]

Debrecen, in Hungary's northeast, and only 55 miles from Ferenczi's hometown of Miskolc, became known as *Calvinist Rome* (Gaal, 2007; Kovács, 2006). Of even greater significance, Debrecen served as the nation's capital during the 1848–49 War of Independence. There, from the halls of Debrecen College, a Calvinist institution founded in 1538, the strains of the

French revolution's "Liberty, Equality, and Fraternity" were heard. From the Calvinist perspective, these virtues were filled with the emphasis on a Providence who gifts people with innate rights, in contrast to the French revolution's sundering from that Providence. Calvinist Lajos Kossuth led the Hungarian revolution of 1848, becoming briefly governor-president of Hungary. His spiritual advisor, Mihály Könyves Tóth, invoked this Calvinist perspective on rights in a final injunction to the Hungarian nation: "And you, dear, sweet Homeland! Sublime Hungarian Home! Hear the divine propagator of the real felicific equality, real felicific freedom, real felicific brotherhood, Christ Jesus" (Gaal, 2007, p. 7).

Though the 1848 War of Independence failed, Calvinism continued to leave its imprint on all phases of Hungarian life. Calvin streets and squares cropped up across the kingdom and are even today found throughout Hungary—Budapest, Gyula, Miskolc, Pécs, Makó—except for those sectors where Catholicism regained dominance.

Calvinism: Religious implications

In Chapter 6, I elaborated the distinctives of Calvinism as they emerged in Scotland. These major distinctives appeared as well in the Calvinism of Hungary: A privileging of understanding based on the Scriptures, and favor with God as the result of grace, not works or indulgences. Both of these remained central to the refutation of certain Catholic doctrines, ones that had fortified that Church in its climb to political empire. In Calvinism, both understanding and pleasing God no longer were the purview of the priest: Each person made in the image of God was equal before God and needful of His grace, a grace received first and foremost through the Scriptures.

Emancipation

The values of egalitarianism and respect for each individual made in the image of God led to a short-lived attempt by the Calvinist-led government in 1848 to emancipate Jews. With the return to Hapsburg dominance, it was not until 1867, when Hungary became a dual monarchy, that emancipation for Jews became a reality. On November 25 of 1867, both houses of parliament declared one of the fundamental laws of Hungary: "the Israelite inhabitants are equal to the Christian inhabitants in their civic and political rights" (art. 1); "all the laws, usages, and decrees which are in contradiction with these are hereby abrogated" (art. 2) (Parliamentary Archives, 1867–1944).

From 1867 until the so-called White Terror (1919–1920), anti-Semitism receded and Christians and Jews for the most part peacefully coexisted in Hungary (Congdon, 2009, personal communication; Gaal, 2007; Haynal, 2008, personal communication). Many Jews assimilated, assuming Hungarian names, not because of fear of persecution but because of pride in Hungarian nationalism. Jews and Christians together fought for the liberation and growth of that country. Though many Jews left the faith entirely, there were those who affiliated with the Unitarian Church that was birthed in Hungary. In this Christian denomination, the doctrine of the Trinity is rejected in favor of a view of God similar to Judaic beliefs (Haynal, 2009, personal communication). It is to this denomination that Michael Balint converted.

Education

Wherever Calvinism flourished, education flourished. As with the Calvinist founding of the American Harvard, Princeton, and Yale,[3] Hungarian Calvinists established a network of schools emphasizing classical training and advanced their particular emphases in contrast to the Lutheran and Catholic institutions that existed. Professor H. H. Meeter (1930) offers one explanation for Calvinism's prioritizing of education:

> Science and art were the gifts of God's common grace, and were to be used and developed as such. Nature was looked upon as God's handiwork, the embodiment of His ideas, in its pure form *the reflection of His virtues. God was the unifying thought* of all science, since all was the unfolding of His plan. But along with such theoretical reasons there are very practical reasons why the Calvinist has always been intensely interested in education, and why grade schools for children as well as schools of higher learning sprang up side by side with Calvinistic churches, and why Calvinists were in so large measure the vanguard of the modern universal education movement. These practical reasons are closely associated with their religion. The Roman Catholics might conveniently do without the education of the masses. For them the clergy—in distinction from the laity—were the ones who were to decide upon matters of church government and doctrine. Hence these interests did not require the training of the masses. For salvation, all that the layman needed was an implied faith in what the church believed. It was not necessary to be able to give an intelligent account of the tenets of his faith. At the services not the sermon but the sacrament was the important conveyor of the blessings of salvation, the sermon was less needed. And this sacrament again did not require intelligence, since it operated *ex opere operato*.
>
> For the Calvinist, matters were just reversed. The government of the church was placed in the hands of the elders, laymen, and these had to decide upon the matters of church policy and the weighty matters of doctrine. Furthermore, the layman himself had the grave duty, without the intermediation of a sacerdotal order, to work out his own salvation, and could not suffice with an implied faith in what the church

believed. He must read his Bible. He must know his creed. And it was a highly intellectual creed at that. Even for the Lutheran, education of the masses was not as urgent as for the Calvinist. It is true, the Lutheran also placed every man before the personal responsibility to work out his own salvation. But the laity were in the Lutheran circles excluded from the office of church government and hence also from the duty of deciding upon matters of doctrine. From these considerations it is evident why the Calvinist must be a staunch advocate of education. If on the one hand God was to be owned as sovereign in the field of science, and if the *Calvinist's* very religious system required the education of the masses for its existence, it need not surprise us that the Calvinist pressed learning to the limit. Education is a question of to be or not to be for the Calvinist. (pp. 96–99)

Calvinism: Pietistic influences

Hungary engaged in a form of Calvinism that differed from its Swiss and Scottish versions in ways that would prove relevant for Ferenczi's formation. Rather than the Calvinist/Wesleyan tilts of reason versus experience that existed in Great Britain, Hungarian Calvinism evolved in a fashion that emphasized both mind and heart, orienting both toward God's calling to service in the world and to examination of the self. Hungarian Calvinism was influenced by the pietism of the Hutterites (ancestors of Mennonites) and Moravians who lived within its borders. An example of such Pietist sentiments is the admonition of Ludwig Von Zinzendorf, founder of the Moravian movement: "Talk to the heart. And the heart to whom you are talking will understand you" (Van Lieburg & Lindmark, 2008, p. 16). For the Calvinists in Hungary, emotions were more central in the relationship with God and with each other. Unlike Weber's characterization of a Calvinism that assured its salvation through outward successes, Hungarian Calvinist literature emphasized inward reflection and outward goodness: "repentance, perception of sin, need for Christ, and love as the signs of predestination" (Molnar, 1997, p. 157). This was the ethos and pathos of the cultural milieu in which the young Sándor Ferenczi developed.

RELIGIOUS INFLUENCES FROM FAMILY

Sándor Ferenczi was born in Miskolc, Hungary, in 1873. His father, Bernat, had earlier emigrated from Poland, more than likely to escape anti-Semitic pogroms; and his mother, Roza, also born in Poland, had lived in Vienna before marrying Bernat and settling in Miskolc. When Sándor was

6 years old, his father, who was fully engaged in the nationalist movement, Magyarized their name to Ferenczi from Fraenkel.

So involved in the national struggle was the elder Ferenczi that in 1848, before his marriage, he joined the patriotic forces under Calvinist leader Kossuth in the War of Independence from the domination of the Hapsburg Empire (Stanton, 1991, p. 5). Following the return of Hapsburg rule in Hungary, Bernat became manager of a Miskolc bookstore owned by Michael Heilprin, a Hasidic Jew and distinguished Hebrew scholar who spoke 13 languages, and also an ardent supporter of Kossuth during the attempted revolution. Heilprin's bookshop was in the center of Miskolc and published and sold "patriotic and radical literature" (Stanton, 1991, p. 6). In 1856, Heilprin[4] decided to leave Hungary for the United States, and Ferenczi's father inherited the bookstore (Kapusi, 2007). Radical literature was often paired with the Protestant faith, and Haynal notes that Ferenczi's father "became the printer for an entire vein of Hungarian progressive literature. Interestingly, the works issuing from his press included those of a Protestant pastor from a nearby village, Mihály Tompa" (Haynal, 2002, pp. 1–2). Tompa's collection of sermons "have been favorably compared with those of major western contemporaries such as Robertson, Monod, and Parker" (Makkai, 1996, p. 289).[5] Kapusi (2007) notes that Bernat sold the books of prominent Protestant theologians and was always interested in purchasing the newest works that were authored.

The Ferenczis lived in an apartment above the bookstore, and Rachman notes that intellectually stimulating conversations on art, literature, political theories, and so forth were normative in the Ferenczi household (Rachman, 1997a, p. 3). Sándor's insatiable desire for knowledge was additionally nourished in his regular forays to his father's bookstore. Clara Thompson (1988), former analysand of Ferenczi, adds this detail:

> [Ferenczi] sought always to master the secret of people—why they did what they did, what they really felt. He sought in his father's bookshop for the answer. No bookshelf was too high for him, and he often read while still sitting on the top of the ladder. So quiet and lost to his surroundings would he become that once the clerk actually started to carry the ladder away, not realizing that he was perched there. In this way he very early became acquainted with the greatest writers and philosophers. (p. 182)

The intermarriage of religion and politics was most natural in the life of the Ferenczi family, an intermarriage that remained robust due to the ideals that were dear to them. According to Haynal (2002), "During the years of repression pending the reconciliation between the House of Hapsburg and the Hungarian nation in 1867, Ferenczi the elder was one of those who kept these cultural ideals aloft" (p. 2).

RELIGIOUS INFLUENCES FROM EDUCATION

From age nine until his graduation at 17, Sándor was educated at the Miskolc Calvinist *Gymnasium* (Stanton, 1991, p. 8; Karády, 2009, personal communication). Three of his older brothers had already graduated from there, and the family maintained a very congenial relationship with the *gymnasium*, donating books, providing coupons for shopping, and giving financial support (Kapusi, 2007).

Ferenczi had ample exposure to Christian stories and doctrines at the *gymnasium*, but Calvinist proselytism was minimal. Historian Victor Karády[6] observes: "Classes of religion, an obligatory subject at all levels of secondary schooling, were separately organized for each denominational cluster of students. Calvinists were not particularly insistent to convert, let alone discriminate against Jews, unlike some Catholic teaching congregations" (Karády, personal communication, October 18, 2009). Thus, Ferenczi was educated in an atmosphere that reflected Calvinist values, but he was also expected to study his Jewish faith. Viktor Karády graciously offered to retrieve Sándor Ferenczi's final report card at the Miskolc Calvinist *Gymnasium* from the national archives (1/26/2010):

> Ferenczi completed his 8th class of the Miskolc Calvinist *Gymnasium* in 1889/90, apparently at the early age of 17. His marks are all excellent (the best available on a scale of 4 with 1 as the best and 4 as the fail mark). He was exempted from sports. His mark "good" for behavior (conduct) is the normal one.
>
> Here with his marks jeles [excellent]
>
> vallástan (religion): jeles,
> magyar (Hungarian language and literature): jeles,
> latin: jeles,
> görög (Greek): jeles,
> német (German): jeles,
> történelem (history): jeles,
> természettan (physics): jeles,
> mennyiségtan (math): jeles,
> bölcsészeti előtan (philosophy): jeles,
> torna (sports): f.M. [exempted]
> írásbeli dolgozat külső alakja (formal aspect of written essays): szép [beautiful]
> magaviselet (conduct): jó [good]

RELIGIOUS INFLUENCES FROM PERSONAL RELATIONSHIPS

Though Ferenczi professed no kinship with religion, several of his strongest documented relationships are with people of genuine faith, whether Jewish[7] or Christian. Since Ferenczi's professional work was intermingled with his personal relationships, I will without distinction list the names of people whose biographical material suggests an association with religion.

Miksa Schachter

> Today I am writing only to ameliorate somewhat the mood into which the death of my friend Schachter put me. After my natural father, he was actually the one whom I loved and revered as a model. He was an Old Testament character, also a fighter by nature, very conservative and religious ... (Ferenczi to Freud, April 30, 1917)

Ferenczi's connection with Schachter begins in a most mystical fashion. Experimenting with automatic writing during his off hours in Budapest's Rokus Hospital junior physician's room, he found his hand unexpectedly penciling, "Write an article on spiritualism for *Gyogyaszat*, the editor will be interested" (Ferenczi, 1993, p. 430). With that, Ferenczi wrote his first medical paper, "On Spiritualism," and began a lifelong friendship with the journal's editor, Miksa Schachter. Schachter was a crusader for justice and ethics in the field of medicine, and he was a devout Jew, whose religion was lived out in love and kindness. Ferenczi relates that "at the beginning of our relationship, we worked together on moral issues" (p. 431), so much so that Ferenczi was dubbed "Schachter-boy" (p. 431). Ferenczi's ideas on issues of morality and religion moved away from Schachter's as the Ferenczi/Freud dialogue matured.[8] Nonetheless, Ferenczi found "in Miksa Schachter: friendliness, warmth, a hospitable family which became my second home, and—above all—an example. While I was fully aware that his example was unmatchable, for years my main inspiration was to emulate him" (p. 431).

Ian and Jane Suttie

The lines of communication between Scotland and Hungary were well-established; Scottish/Hungarian industrial and church ventures were commonplace. Hungary's kinship with Scotland existed particularly because of the persecution both countries had suffered from a state Catholicism bereft of its historic Christian narrative anchored in loving relationship. This ideal of loving relationship was shared most profoundly between Christians Ian and Jane Suttie (see Chapter 3 on Suttie's faith) and Sándor Ferenczi. As a result, John Bowlby, in the foreword to Suttie's book, *The Origins of Love and Hate*, linked Suttie and Ferenczi in a mutual struggle against the mechanization of the mind espoused by Freud. "That was the model," Bowlby observed, "that both Suttie in London and Sándor Ferenczi ... were criticizing during the 1930s" (Suttie, 1935, p. xvi). British psychoanalyst Dorothy Heard, Suttie's niece, confirms their mutual views: "It is likely that Sándor Ferenczi influenced the way that Suttie developed his ideas. Suttie acknowledges Ferenczi in *The Origins of Love and Hate*, stating explicitly that he agrees with Ferenczi's dictum, 'It is the physician's love that heals the patient'" (p. xxii).[9] Suttie, drawing his perspectives from a Christian narrative, elaborates: "In the study of religion, then, we have found the main concern of the Christian teachings to be the cultivation of 'love' as the basis of happiness, mental stability and social harmony" (p. 154).

Evidence suggests that a warm relationship had developed between the Sutties and Sándor Ferenczi (Suttie, 1935, xxii), Jane Suttie having translated most of the papers in Ferenczi's *Further Contributions to the Theory and Technique of Psycho-Analysis* (1952b). Ferenczi (1952b) acknowledges her contributions, adding in the preface to his work:

> It gives me great pleasure to lay my work once more before Anglo-Saxon readers, particularly because I have found that with their broad-mindedness they often strive to view such opinions as mine without prejudice, whereas elsewhere these are turned down *a limine* on account of their novelty or their boldness. (pp. 8–9)

Bowlby muses that Ferenczi's reference to the "Anglo-Saxons" could not have meant Ernest Jones and other members of the establishment (with the exception of Rickman), but must have referred "to people outside the psychoanalytic movement, like the Sutties, then in Scotland, and others associated with the then 6-year-old Tavistock Clinic in London" (Suttie, 1935, p. xxiii), which Jones had placed on interdict.

Izette de Forest

Raised Episcopalian, "lay" psychoanalyst Izette de Forest practiced the Quaker faith in her adult life and published spiritually and psychoanalytically relevant articles in pastoral counseling journals such as the *Journal of Pastoral Care* and *Pastoral Psychology*. Though her activities are now somewhat obscure, she was both an analysand and trainee of Ferenczi, and her translation of Ferenczi's ideas to the psychoanalytic community in the United States (1942) predated the work of Clara Thompson. Her most known work, *The Leaven of Love: A Development of the Psychoanalytic*

Theory and Technique of Sándor Ferenczi (1954), is a book-length exposition of psychoanalytic practice based on her experience with Ferenczi. The last chapter of the book clearly articulates her Christian faith.

Izette de Forest was tightly connected to the psychoanalytic movement through her marriage to Alfred de Forest, cousin of Dorothy Tiffany Burlingham. Dorothy and Anna Freud were closest of friends, and the de Forests socialized with the Freud family and the psychoanalytic community in Vienna (Brennan, 2010).

As analysand, supervisee, friend, and champion of Ferenczi's work, de Forest was responsible for the translation and publishing of *Thalassa: A Theory of Genitality* in English in 1933, paved the way for Ferenczi's lectureship at the New School in 1926, and worked fervently with Fromm in constructing his refutation of Jones' attacks against Ferenczi (Bonomi, 1999). More personally, during the 8-month 1926 lectureship of Ferenczi at the New School for Social Research in New York, the Ferenczis stayed at the de Forest's Connecticut home most weekends (Brennan, 2010). Following his visit to the United States, Ferenczi began to assert his own ideas and to develop greater independence from Freud.

RELIGIOUS INFLUENCES FROM PROFESSIONAL AFFILIATIONS

Michelle Moreau-Ricaud (1996) indicates that Ferenczi was deeply involved in interaction with the literary community of Budapest, and was a contributing author to *Nyugat*, the premier literary journal in Hungary during the years that Ferenczi practiced psychoanalysis in Budapest. Ferenczi was personal friend to *Nyugat*'s editor, Hugo Ignotus (see correspondences with Freud), and numerous other writers, some of whom became his analysands. Ferenczi's correspondence with Freud (May 5, 1909) reveals that he lived for a period of time directly above the writers' gathering place, the Café Royal at the Royal Hotel, and later he maintained a residence directly across the street. Moreau-Ricaud (1996) writes:

> In Budapest, more than Vienna, the relationship between psychoanalysis and literature was like that of two "communicating vessels" to use an image dear to the surrealists. This symbiotic relationship was typified by Ferenczi. Warm and open to new ideas in every field, he was not afraid to mix with the *avant-garde literati*. He attended their meetings and passed his reluctantly bachelor evenings with writers gathered around specially reserved café tables. As he lived in the Royal Hotel (where he had a room on the third floor), he was easily able to join his friends from the review *Nyugat* (*Occident*) at the Café Royal or elsewhere. (pp. 43–44)

Who were these literary friends that coalesced around the *Nyugat*? Haynal (1992) provides a summary list that "included the writer Dezsö Kosztolányi, Georg Lukács (at that time closely associated with thinkers such as Søren Kierkegaard, Georg Simmel, and Stefan George), the great Hungarian poet Endre Ady, the composers Béla Bartók and Zoltán Kodály—*and Sándor Ferenczi*" (p. xix, emphasis added). Lukács was the founder of the Sunday Circle, which included yet more *literati*, and Ferenczi was member of the Galileo Circle,[10] which focused on scientific endeavors; in the culture of early 1900s Budapest, philosophy, science, and literature—like the pluralism of the nation—were generatively intermixed (Congdon, 1991; personal communication, 2009). For this reason, the respective disciplinary emphases of the Sunday Circle and the Galileo Circle would coalesce during incessant discussions at the Café Royal and anywhere groups of forward-thinking writers and scientists would gather.

Georg Lukács

Philosopher Georg Lukács stands as a towering figure even among the intellectual elite of Budapest. Born in 1885, his insatiable desire for learning led him in 1902, at the age of 17, to meet the playwright Henrik Ibsen in Oslo, Norway (Congdon, 2008). The Scandinavian Kierkegaard's writings had, in the view of many scholars, for example, Edna Hong, Howard Hong (Elbrond-Bek, 1996), left an indelible impression on the works of Ibsen. Kierkegaard and Ibsen were of utmost interest to Lukács in his early years. In combination with the Protestant milieu of Budapest and the Christianity of Kierkegaard, Lendvai asserts that Lukács even converted briefly to Protestantism (Lendvai, 1997, p. 160).

The influence of Lukács was augmented by his founding of the Thalia Society. With his colleagues (Balàzs, Kodály, Homan, Benedek, etc.), Lukács staged dramatic productions at the Thalia Theater, which was active from 1904 to 1908 and "introduced the Hungarian public to works of the founders of the modern drama: Hebbel, Ibsen, Strindberg, and Hauptmann. Thus it had written an important chapter in the history of Hungary's emerging counterculture" (Congdon, 1983, p. 19).

Ibsen's works particularly captured the Budapest society, and Ferenczi himself was taken by Ibsen's plays, which commonly enacted Kierkegaardian themes. Ferenczi excitedly writes to Freud on July 17, 1908:

> My next project will be a commentary on Ibsen's works in the light of their psychology. It is astounding how much he has anticipated. The Lady from the Sea, for example, could be compared with the psychoanalytic treatment of an obsessional idea. The other works are also full of apt presentiments and allusions. Before I became acquainted with

> your work I never fully understood Ibsen, and I don't completely understand his previous commentators even now.

On February 16, 1910, Ferenczi (1910a) writes again to Freud concerning Ibsen:

> It is with difficulty that I venture to take up a literary theme, although a case just recently totally illuminated Ibsen's *Peer Gynt.* It is the patient to whom I owe our connection with the treasure hunter. The identity with the liar-hero Peer Gynt is astonishing—it coincides with minute details of his fantastic plans. ... But what Ibsen and my patient were able to make out of this terrible complex is worthy of admiration. After the breakdown (in Peer Gynt as well as in the patient), comes the fear of death and the flight to the old mother. ... So there I have the second Ibsen theme; the first, already partially set down in notes is the "Lady from the Sea."

At the time that he wrote *Peer Gynt*, Ibsen had read Kierkegaard and was involved with a group that discussed his works (Shapiro, 1990, p. 8). Shapiro offers a striking comparison of themes in "Peer Gynt" and Kierkegaard. He writes:

> The drama of Peer Gynt is about its title character's experience of the three existential spheres: the esthetic, the ethical, and the religious. During this experience Peer Gynt confronts all the foes and self-negating figures described by Kierkegaard: despair, anxiety, inclosing reserve, the absurd paradox, offense, and so forth. (p. 209)

Shapiro further elaborates:

> Henrik Ibsen, the greatest dramatist since Shakespeare, effectively changed Western civilization's dramatic conception of the common individual—what it means to live as a human being—via the philosophy of Søren Kierkegaard. Thus, Ibsen was a great artist not simply by virtue of his eloquent poetry and skill as a dramatist, but because he was ethically willing to recognize the profound philosophical notions which lay just in front of him, notions which were elucidated before Ibsen by Kierkegaard. Accordingly, Peer Gynt, the *fons et origo* of modern drama, is a brilliant representation of Kierkegaardian philosophy. (pp. 209–210)

It is noteworthy that Georg Groddeck,[11] who would later become a close friend to Ferenczi, expressed intense interest in Ibsen's plays. Specifically, Lore Schacht, in the introduction to Groddeck's (1977) selected writings, averred that Groddeck articulated at great length his ideas on the human attitude toward the self in his "Peer Gynt" essay (p. 25). These ideas mirror those that would become expressed by Martin Buber, who was greatly influenced by Kierkegaard. Groddeck states:

> Peer Gynt can regard his "self" as an object, he can "*vaere dig selv*"; he can also "*vaere sig selvnok.*" If we try to translate the "*vaerl dig selv*" we must not say: "Man, be thyself!" but "Man, be a thou, a thou to thyself, or, by all means, be a self to yourself. Stop being an 'I.'" Try to confront yourself the way a child does. Make yourself a part of the great whole, the universe. Deal with yourself on the basis of the knowledge that you are not an "I," but a "thou." (p. 25)

Ferenczi never published an article about Ibsen's plays, nor did he reveal the commentators who may have linked Ibsen's works with Kierkegaard. And though there is no direct record that Ferenczi studied Kierkegaard, I will present further evidence to support a contention that he knew of that philosopher's writings and intermediately was influenced by him.

RELIGIOUS INFLUENCES FROM KIERKEGAARD

Kierkegaard and Christianity

Crucial to a relational study of Ferenczi are the social contexts of his life. Thus, a review of biographical material about Søren Kierkegaard, whose works were hugely influential in Budapest, is relevant for understanding the passions of Sándor Ferenczi. Kierkegaard was born into a staunch Danish Lutheran home, but one that was deeply touched by Moravian (Brethren) Pietism, an emphasis that challenged a Lutheran religion principally focused on doctrine, with a "religion of the heart" and the affect as well. Though Michael Kierkegaard, Søren's father, attended the state Lutheran church, Alastair Hannay (2001) remarks:

> He himself, however, felt closer ties with the Congregation of Moravian Brothers, the *Herrnhuters* (*Herrnhut*, literally, "the Lord's keeping") which with its hold among the peasant community he would have known from his childhood. Moravian teaching was almost diametrically opposed to the liberal-rationalist Lutheranism prevailing at the time. It spoke to the feelings rather than to the intellect, was anticlerical and preached inner rebirth and indifference to the trappings of bourgeois life. (p. 37)[12]

Exposure to Moravian Pietism decisively contributed not only to Kierkegaard's outcry against hypocrisy and dogma but also to his existential and experiential orientation (Barnett, 2008). Kierkegaard's existential orientation, of such interest to intellectuals in Copenhagen and Budapest, was according to Maurice Friedman (1955) "one of the most important single influences on [Martin] Buber's thought" (p. 2). Vernard Eller (1968) confirms the link of Pietism between Buber and Kierkegaard, stating: "It probably is no accident that the two great contemporary theologians who best understood Kierkegaard and best appropriated his contributions in their own work were Martin Buber, with his strong background in Hasidism, i.e. Jewish pietism, and [the Christian] Emil Brunner, schooled by the Pietist Blumhardt of Boll" (p. 183). This Kierkegaardian influence on Martin Buber[13] is salient, for it provides additional substantiation of the influence of religious narratives in Ferenczi's relationality. According to Lewis Aron (1996), "Among all 20th century philosophers, Martin Buber elaborated a philosophy of dialogue that most closely resonates with the relational psychoanalytic approach and its emphasis on mutuality" (p. 154).

Kierkegaard and love

Kierkegaard, the philosopher, was a devout Christian, as evidenced in this opening prayer to *Works of Love* (1847):

> How could love properly be discussed if You were forgotten, You who made manifest what love is ... You who take nothing for your own but remind us of that sacrifice of love, remind the believer to love as he is loved, and his neighbor as himself. (p. 20)

It is most likely Kierkegaard's book, *Works of Love* (1847/1962), that sustained love as an ongoing topic for Lukác's Sunday Circle, an emphasis that is of particular significance in light of Sándor Ferenczi. Lee Congdon (1991) elaborates:

> As the acknowledged leader of the circle, Lukács always chose the subject for discussion. Anna Lesznai remembered that members touched upon a variety of themes—"painting, folklore, history. Most often the conversations turned to love, the philosophy of love." Perhaps it would be more accurate to say that the conversations revolved around religion in the broadest sense of the word. ... All of the members of the circle respected Kierkegaard's indifference to dogma and emphasis on the importance of belief. (p. 10)

Lukács, better known for his later Marxist philosophy, had immersed himself in the writings of Kierkegaard and no doubt made Kierkegaard's ideas the topic of discussion not only in his group, but wherever he would congregate with the intellectuals of Budapest. Kierkegaard's love is extolled by Lukács (2010): "Such was the ideal of love of the ascetic medieval knights, but it was never to be romantic again. ... This, I believe, was the root of Kierkegaard's religiosity. God can be loved thus, and no one else but God." (pp. 50–51).

In 1908 when Ferenczi first spoke of Ibsen's plays to Freud, Lukács had sponsored Ibsen's plays and had begun to lecture and write on Kierkegaard. According to Congdon, "Karl Polanyi, the [Galileo] circle's first president, often invited Lukács to attend meetings." At a 1910 meeting, the year of Ferenczi's second Ibsen reference to Freud, Lukács delivered a Galileo Circle address and "expounded upon the toxic cocktail of positivism, determinism and liberal individualism, how these acted to dissolve social bonds and attenuate the intellectual basis for conscious human action" (Dale, 2009, pp. 111–112). This address was printed in the journal *Nyugat* shortly after it was given. *Nyugat* was edited by Ferenczi's close friend, Hugo Ignotus, who also published Ferenczi's articles, and was without doubt read by Ferenczi. On pages 190–193 of the 1910 volume, Lukács' article "The Ways Have Parted" was published. On pages 378–387 of the same volume, another Lukács article, "Søren Kierkegaard and Regine Olsen," explicates love and loss in Kierkegaard's life, and its philosophical ramifications. Kierkegaard permeated the air that Ferenczi breathed.

KIERKEGAARDIAN EVIDENCES IN THE THINKING OF SÁNDOR FERENCZI

Of the salient aspects of Ferenczi's thinking that I might examine, I have chosen three[14] that correlate most closely with religious influences through Kierkegaard: love, truth, and intersubjectivity. Kierkegaard's anti-establishmentarian spirit emanating from his Pietistic leanings made his writings of interest to the Budapest *literati*, and I believe that in this milieu Ferenczi's prior religious influences were confirmed and extended through Kierkegaardian understandings of love, truth, and intersubjectivity.

In the segments to follow I will present each of these three emphases in Ferenczi's works. I will then offer correlations between writing excerpts from Ferenczi and from Kierkegaard, relying most heavily on *Works of Love* (1847).

Love in Ferenczi and Kierkegaard

It can be said that the dazzling array of innovations that emanated from Ferenczi's mind, when traced to their point of origin, lead to his abiding capacity for, and belief in, love. Izette de Forest (1954) recalls Ferenczi's words to her as they discussed his approach in Budapest: "Psychoanalytic 'cure' is in direct proportion to the cherishing love given by the psychoanalyst to the patient; the love which the psychoneurotic patient *needs*, not necessarily the love which he thinks he needs and therefore demands" (p. 15).

The topic of love had interested Ferenczi from the beginning of his professional career. One of his early papers, entitled "Love in the Sciences" (1901), "deals with love, which is, according to Ferenczi, disregarded with no reason in scientific research. Ferenczi minutely describes the fluctuations of mood and thought related to falling in love, proposing a 'cognitive' vision of affectivity and an invitation to develop a semiotics of love" (Casonato, 1993, p. 740).

Belief in people

Clara Thompson (1988) illuminates Ferenczi's devotion to people in a tribute she wrote, portraying him as "possessed of a genuine sympathy for all human suffering. ... His efforts were tireless and his patience inexhaustible (p. 182). Thompson suggests that he was never willing to give up on a patient but always stated, "Perhaps it is simply that we have not yet discovered the right method."

Izette de Forest (1954) reflects on Ferenczi's love as well, musing, "[I] have outlined what I believe to be the similarity between the love given to the patient in psychotherapy and divine love ..." (p. xii). She then refers to Ferenczi's method as "redemption by love," an attribution used in appreciation of Ferenczi by a patient (Eleanor M. Burnet) who experienced his transformative belief in her (p. 179).

This unfailing belief was earlier conceived by Kierkegaard (1847):

> "Love believes all things," for to believe all things means precisely, even though love is not apparent, even though the opposite is seen, to presuppose that love is nevertheless present fundamentally, even in the misguided, even in the corrupt, even in the hateful. ... Remember that the prodigal son's father was perhaps the only one who did not know that he had a prodigal son, for the father's love hoped all things. ... In spite of the son's misguided conduct there was no break on the father's side (a break is just the opposite of building up); he hoped all things ... (p. 209)
>
> If you have seen a physician going around among the sick, you have noticed that he brings the best gift, better than all medicines, even better than all his care, when he brings hope, when it is said, "The physician has hope." (p. 242)

Forgiveness

In his *Clinical Diary* (1985), Ferenczi writes of the need for forgiveness between patient and analyst. The analyst must recognize complicity in treatment impasses. When the analyst falls into some of the same attitudes as the traumatizing parents, he must confess to the offense at hand, and also vicariously for the patient's parents' offenses, and be forgiven by the patient. He writes:

> It does not seem to suffice to make a general confession ... patients want to see all the sufferings that we caused them corrected one by one ... and then to wait until we no longer react with defiance or by taking offense, but with insight, regret, indeed with loving sympathy. (p. 209)
>
> *Analyst* after receiving catalogue of sins, and after overcoming his defiant reaction: breakdown—"wanted the best and this is what happened!" *Patient:* in a position to *forgive*. That the first step could be taken toward forgiveness for causing trauma indicates that they had attained insight. ... Finally, it is also possible to view and *remember* the trauma with *feelings of forgiveness* and consequently *understanding*. (p. 201)
>
> I released R.N. from her torment by repeating the sins of her father, which then I confessed and for which I obtained forgiveness. (p. 214)
>
> *The analyst who is forgiven*: enjoys in the analysis what was denied him in life and hardened his heart. Mutual Forgiveness!!—Final success. (p. 202)

Kierkegaard's (1847) perspectives on forgiveness anticipate those of Ferenczi:

> Only love is handy enough to take the sin away by forgiving it ... when love forgives, the miracle of faith occurs ... that which is seen nevertheless by being forgiven is not seen. (p. 274)
>
> When a sin is not forgiven, it requires punishment, it cries to God or men for punishment; but when a sin cries for punishment, it appears quite different, far greater than when this same sin is forgiven. (p. 275)
>
> Now, then, if you wish to pretend to be completely outside the matter in hand and wish privately before God to complain of your enemies, God makes short work of it and opens a case against you, because before God you yourself are a guilty person—to complain against another is to complain against oneself. (p. 349)
>
> But why, I wonder, is forgiveness so rare? Is it not, I wonder, because faith in the power of forgiveness is so small and so rare? ... If you yourself have ever needed forgiveness, then you know what forgiveness accomplishes ... (p. 274)

Egalitarianism[15]

Arnold Rachman's (1997a) biography of Ferenczi underscores his egalitarian, therapeutic manner in his title *Sándor Ferenczi: The Psychotherapist of Tenderness and Passion*. Ferenczi discloses his humble approach in these words:

> Should it even occur, and it does occasionally to me, that experiencing another's and my own suffering brings a tear to my eye (and one should not conceal this emotion from the patient), then the tears of doctor and of patient mingle in a sublimated communion, which perhaps finds its analogy only in the mother-child relationship. And this is the healing agent, which, like a kind of glue, binds together permanently the intellectually assembled fragments, surrounding even the personality thus repaired with a new aura of vitality and optimism. (Ferenczi, 1985, p. 65)

"Ferenczi allowed no artificial distance to intervene between him and his patients, for he thought of them as friends. ... He freely voiced his affectionate regard and beneficent hopes" writes Izette de Forest (1954, p. 8) of Ferenczi's egalitarian stance. For Ferenczi, hierarchy gave way to mutual respect and affection.

Clara Thompson (1988) described Ferenczi as void of pretense and "the pompous important air and authoritative manner so common to many physicians" (p. 183). However, Ferenczi's demeanor was not reserved for the consulting room. Thompson relates this poignant story:

> During the war a soldier who was a personal acquaintance was being disciplined for some serious misdemeanor. Under the strain of the disgrace the man developed an acute mental illness in which he became very slovenly, neglecting all care of his body. On hearing of this, Ferenczi hastened to the man and, completely disregarding his appearance, embraced him in genuine concern. Intuitively, without a word from the man, he had seen his need of being reassured that a friend could like him no matter how great his disgrace. The man's recovery began in that hour. (pp. 183–184)

In a passage from his 1926 paper "The Problem of Acceptance of Unpleasant Ideas," Ferenczi depicts the necessity of relinquishing omnipotent control of the external world in the painful process of accepting reality.[16] He takes occasion to link this idea to the wisdom of the Christian notion of "loving one's enemies," for the external world not under one's control is both an enemy and a precondition for true relationship. He writes:

> Since, as we know now, a quota of Eros, i.e. of "love," is necessary for this recognition, and since this addition is inconceivable without introjection, i.e. identification, we are forced to say that recognition of

> the surrounding world is actually a partial realization of the Christian imperative "Love your enemies." (p. 319)

Kierkegaard's (1847) egalitarian ideas resonate with Ferenczi's writing:

> One's neighbor is one's equal. One's neighbor is not the beloved, for whom you have passionate preference, nor your friend, for whom you have passionate preference. Nor is your neighbor, if you are well educated, the well-educated person with whom you have cultural equality—for with your neighbor you have before God the equality of humanity. Nor is your neighbor one who is of higher social status than you, that is, insofar as he is of higher social status he is not your neighbor, for to love him because he is of higher status than you can very easily be preference and to that extent self-love. Nor is your neighbor one who is inferior to you, that is insofar as he is inferior he is not your neighbor, for to love one because he is inferior to you can very easily be partiality's condescension and to that extent self-love. No, to love one's neighbor means equality. (p. 72)
>
> Therefore he who in truth loves his neighbor loves also his enemy. The distinction *friend or enemy* is a distinction in the object of love, but the object of love to one's neighbor is without distinction. One's neighbor is the absolutely unrecognizable distinction between man and man; it is eternal equality before God—enemies, too, have this equality. (p. 79)

Truth in Ferenczi and Kierkegaard

In examining Ferenczi's emphasis on "truth," and its connections to the Jewish and Christian narratives, I am contrasting truth as integrity over against hypocrisy, falsehood, and dishonesty. Ferenczi admitted to his meager grasp of objective truth in nearly postmodern terms. But what Ferenczi would militate against was a wanton promulgation of falsehood whether at the personal, cultural, or theoretical level.

Honesty

Ferenczi's authentic personhood emerged even more clearly in the final years of his life. His allegiance to Freud became less important than his allegiance to truth as he wrote in ever more emphatic tones of the perils of hypocrisy: "A great part of the repressed criticism felt by our patients is directed towards what might be called *professional hypocrisy*" (1949, p. 226). In his *Clinical Diary* (1985) he returns repeatedly to this emphasis:

> Patients *feel* the hypocritical element in the analyst's behavior; they detect it from hundreds of tiny signs. ... These far too seldom become the object of analysis (and too seldom are acknowledged by the analyst). (p. 200)
>
> I may remind you that patients do not react to theatrical phrases, but only to real sincere sympathy. Whether they recognize the truth by the intonation or colour of our voice or by the words we use or in some other way, I cannot tell. In any case, they show a remarkable, almost clairvoyant knowledge about the thoughts and emotions that go on in their analyst's mind. (1949, p. 227)[17]

Ferenczi's value of honesty is resonant with Kierkegaard (1847):

> What more loathsome combination is possible than love—and falsity! Yet this combination is impossible, for to love falsely is to hate. ... As soon as there is a lack of honesty, there is also something concealed. In this concealment hides selfish self-love, and inasmuch as this is present in a man he does not love. (p. 150)
>
> The best defense against hypocrisy is love; yes, it is not only a defense but a yawning abyss; in all eternity it has nothing to do with hypocrisy. This also is a fruit whereby love is known—it secures the lover against falling into the snare of the hypocrite. (p. 32)
>
> If the mother's love is not manifest, you will vainly seek in her face and manner for evidence of mother-love's joy in the child and concern for it, and you will see only inertia and indifference which is glad to be free of the child for a time ... (p. 203)
>
> For human beings, however, there is the possibility in freedom of becoming a self, an authentic individual, by willing before God to be oneself. The ethical-religious implication of this authentic individuality is to esteem the individuality of others as they are ... (p. 372)

Integrity

Ferenczi chose a life of integrity rather than to compromise his ideals and became more vocal concerning his differences with Freud toward the end of his life. He writes this of his relationship with Freud:

> This was the point where I refused to follow him [Freud]. Against his will I began to deal openly with questions of technique. I refused to abuse the patients' trust in this way, and neither did I share his idea that therapy was worthless. I believed rather that therapy was good, but perhaps we were still deficient, and I began to look for our errors (1985, p. 186)

As a clinician, Ferenczi never privileged truth above loving relationship, and saw them as inseparable. This view is reflected in an excerpt concerning his wife:

> Mrs. F[erenczi] felt, and rightly so, attracted by the essence of psychoanalysis—trauma and reconstruction—but repelled by all analysts for the way they make use of it. ... She longs for an analyst who will be analytically as gifted as she is, who will be concerned above all with truth, but who will not only be scientifically true but also truthful regarding people. (p. 186)

Again, the correlation with Kierkegaard (1848) is noticeable:

> And therefore, Christianly understood, truth is obviously not to know the truth but to be the truth. Despite all modern philosophy, there is an infinite difference here. ... And that is why it becomes untruth when knowing the truth is separated from being the truth. (p. 205)
>
> There is no deed, not a single one, not even the best, of which we dare to say unconditionally: he who does this thereby unconditionally demonstrates love. It depends upon *how* the deed is done. There are, indeed, acts which in a special sense are called works of love. But, in truth, because one makes charitable contributions, because he visits the widow and clothes the naked—his love is not necessarily demonstrated or made recognizable by such deeds, for one can perform works of love in an unloving, yes, even in a self-loving way, and when this is so, the works of love are nevertheless not the work of love. (1847, p. 30)

Intersubjectivity in Ferenczi and Kierkegaard

Ferenczi's resurrection in relational psychoanalysis is due in large part to his recognition of intersubjective realities of the analytic dyad. Haynal (1997) observes:

> Ferenczi's research made it possible to conceive of a field of interactions and finally of intersubjectivity (though, to my knowledge, he never used the term). ... His various experiments with changing the analyst's role ... ended up by *centering* his interest on countertransference ... wanting to create a transparency in this respect, opening up a whole line of psychoanalytical thinking as it appears in the works of Winnicott, Little, Heimann, Bion, and the contemporary literature on countertransference (Coltart, Bollas, etc.), on the emotional experiences of the analyst and their value for a better understanding of the "dark spots" of his/her analysand. The emphasis put on projective identification as

> a means of communication has also in Ferenczi his forebear (see his *Clinical Diary*, passim). (pp. 449–50)

Relational psychoanalysis is developing the concepts that Ferenczi enacted, though some were not yet formulated by him. Intersubjective concepts include a variety of related terms that have been formulated in relational literature: mutual influence (Aron, 1996; Stolorow & Atwood, 1996), mutual recognition (Benjamin, 1990), mutual regulation (Beebe & Lachmann, 1988a). Deriving from an application of these intersubjective concepts in the clinical situation is the notion of "thirdness" elaborated in relational literature principally, though variously, by Aron (2006), Benjamin (2004a), and Ogden (1994). In the following paragraphs, I offer evidences of the religious influences on Ferenczi's recognition of intersubjective dimensions of psychoanalytic work. I will focus on the constructs of mutual influence and thirdness.

Mutual influence

In her book *Leaven of Love* (1954), Izette de Forest extends Ferenczi's method of psychotherapy, interweaving it in the last chapter with religious concepts. Drawing on Ferenczi's model she writes:

> That the psychotherapeutic relationship is in essence a replica of the mother-child relationship need arouse no surprise nor questioning. God in His plan of creation has given an initial situation which lays the basis for the child's growth. ... In the success of this remedial accomplishment ... he [the patient] has learned, through the therapeutic study of his self-betrayal, to recapture his wholeness and thus to give to himself the hope and the healing of love. This recovery ensures gratification of his basic need as a child of God: the need to be ... a creator of loving mutuality, a giver of love. (pp. 188–189)

Ferenczi ventured into unexplored, even forbidden territory in the practice of psychoanalysis.[18] To him, the barriers of anonymity and aloofness, cool rationalism and superiority only served to retraumatize the patient. Mutuality as a value and acknowledgment of the unavoidability of mutual influence were precociously practiced by Ferenczi. He writes:

> The analytical situation—i.e. the restrained coolness, the professional hypocrisy and—hidden behind it but never revealed—a dislike of the patient which, nevertheless, he felt in all his being—such a situation was not essentially different from that which in his childhood had led to the illness. When, in addition to the strain caused by this analytical situation, we imposed on the patient the further burden of reproducing

> the original trauma, we created a situation that was indeed unbearable. (1949, p. 226)
>
> In the third session after the termination of material help and mutuality, sudden about-face: I was received with a radiant face and a conciliatory gesture; numerous apologies for having provoked and infuriated me. ... I did not suppress my satisfaction, and praised her ability to get the better of herself. She returned the compliment: *I* have shown myself stronger than my actual tendency to let myself be terrorized by suffering. I did not conceal the fact that this cost me a considerable expenditure of effort. The session was spent mainly in discussing the analytic event, yet I also succeeded in steering her into the depths, and into the past. (1985, pp. 48–49)

Similar conceptions of mutual influence are found in these excerpts from Kierkegaard (1847):

> When before God you accuse another man, there straightway are two cases; simply because you come and report another man, God happens to think of how it involves you. (p. 350)
>
> When you praise him [a person] as a loving person, you mean that love is a characteristic which he possesses, which it is, too, and you feel yourself built up by him, simply because he is loving, but you do not detect the true explanation, *that his love means he presupposes love in you and that you are built up precisely by this*, that precisely by this is love built up in you. (p. 211, emphasis added)

Thirdness

Jessica Benjamin has enriched relational psychoanalysis through her concept of the "third." Benjamin acknowledges Ferenczi's technical innovations as modeling the work of the "moral third." Through awareness of a therapist's contribution to impasses by means of the moral third and a subsequent acknowledgment of the therapist's contribution, asymmetry in mutuality is demonstrated, and transformation occurs. Benjamin (2009) observes:

> The part I am calling the moral third relating to the asymmetry is that, as Ferenczi says, in enactments we repeat old injuries, and if we do not acknowledge them we also become failed witnesses. Acknowledgment becomes the way in which we transform the repetition into a new experience in which the "new object" communicates and receives communication about the "old object." (p. 461)

A striking example of Ferenczi's deployment of the moral third involves his personal rejection of Freud's privileging of male interests, a singular response based on his egalitarian values in a professional culture loyal to Freud. Ferenczi wrestles with his previous views and muses about the creation of a new model:

> The ease with which Freud sacrifices the interests of women in favor of male patients is striking. This is consistent with the unilaterally androphile orientation of his theory of sexuality. In this he was followed by almost all of his pupils, myself not excluded. My theory of genitality may have many good points, yet in its mode of presentation and its historical reconstruction it clings too closely to the words of the master; a new edition would mean complete rewriting. (1985, p. 187)

Kierkegaard's (1847) precocious writings anticipate an intersubjective sensibility:

> When there is no third in the relationship between man and man, every such relationship becomes unsound, either too ardent or embittered. The third, which thinkers would call the idea, is the true, the good, or more accurately, the God-relationship. ... With the help of the third, which the lover gets placed between them, both are humbled: for the lover humbles himself before the good, whose needy servant he is, and, as he himself admits, in frailty; and the vanquished one humbles himself not before the lover but before the good. (p. 313)
>
> When a relationship is only between two, one always has the upper hand in the relationship by being able to break it, for as soon as one has broken, *the relationship* is broken. But when there are three, one person cannot do this. The third, as mentioned, is love itself, which the innocent sufferer can hold to in the break, and then the break has no power over him. (p. 283)

SUMMARY

Ferenczi was not unique in his exposure to Christian thought. Within the egalitarian atmosphere of Hungary marked by a burgeoning nationalism, Jews and Christians alike shed many distinctives, blending their ideologies and mental capital to become, more importantly, *Magyars*. Jews trained in Christian schools; Christians dialogued with Jews about science and literature. The Unitarian Church became the symbol of Christianity's deep affinity with Jewish monotheism. The paternal aspects of Judaism were infused with the Christian emphasis on the maternal. When Ibsen obliquely introduced the population of Budapest to the works of Kierkegaard, there was little objection to his Christian ideals.[19] Thus, through Ferenczi, Budapest not only became the locus where the covenantal Judaic narrative of truth and loving relationship became renewed in psychoanalysis, but it also became the incubator for Jewish and Christian dialogue. This dialogue, though unrecognized, would be registered in the theory and practice of psychoanalysis and would be nurtured through the emergence of a moral third: a yearning for redemption for the individual and for the culture.

ENDNOTES

1. This quotation may be misleading. In the 16th and 17th centuries up to 95% of Hungarians were Calvinist. During the 19th century, a majority of Hungarians (about 65%) had become Roman Catholic as a result of the Hapsburg monarchy, and the severe persecution of Protestants. The majority of those who "Magyarized," that is, became by nationality Hungarian, were Calvinists, the move toward Hungarian nationalism being strongly supported by the Calvinists. This impetus toward nationalism was most dominant in the northeastern sector of Hungary, where there was a continuous and majority Calvinist presence—the area that included Ferenczi's childhood home.
2. For those interested, a historic anecdote on the establishment of Calvinism in Budapest is worth mentioning. The news had been carried to Archduchess Maria Dorothea of Hungary by English author Julia Pardoe, who was passing through Pest (Pardoe wrote books on travel and had met Maria Dorothea during a previous visit; Kovács, 2006, pp. 50–53). Pardoe reported to her highness that two Scottish Presbyterian ministers visiting the city took ill, one manifesting cholera symptoms. They were desperately in need of care. The archduchess—third Protestant wife of the Palatine Josef—was a woman of courage and resourcefulness, having survived with the Palatine the hostility of the Catholic Hapsburgs after defying their preferences, and procuring a Papal decree permitting their marriage. She quickly ordered that every possible means of care be mustered for the visitors. The ministers, Alexander Black and Alexander Keith, recovered, and found in Archduchess Maria Dorothea a fervent Christian supporter. She had been waiting for the possibility of fellow Protestants of devout faith like hers to unite with her in Pest's largely Catholic environment. As they parted she entreated, "Send out missionaries here, and I will protect them" (p. 52).

   That Black and Keith had landed in Budapest was, in itself, a mishap. On April 12, 1839, Robert Murray McCheyne, Andrew Bonar, Alexander Black, and Alexander Keith had set sail for Palestine upon the behest of the Church of Scotland, with the firm conviction that "the moment a man begins to take the statements of the Word of God as literally true, that moment he begins to care for Israel" (Kovács, 2006, p. 49). While travelling by camel, Black drifted to sleep, fell, and suffered injury necessitating that the group split: McCheyne and Bonar would continue to Palestine, and Alexander and Black would return to Scotland. Originally planning to go by steamer from Beirut, they decided to return via the Danube. They stopped in Pest and found that if it was Jewish people they were seeking, they needed to look no further. When they finally returned to Scotland they recommended that a mission be started in Pest, one that would ultimately impact Hungarian culture.

Bonar and McCheyne returned to Scotland as well and distributed a widely read memorandum, "A Narrative of a Mission of Inquiry to the Jews From the Church of Scotland in 1839" (1842). This was followed by "Memorandum to Protestant Monarchs of Europe for the restoration of the Jews to Palestine" and appeared in the *London Times* (1840). Lord Shaftesbury was integrally involved in these developments, and his voice paved the way for the later crafted *Balfour Declaration*.

3. Harvard and Yale were both founded as Puritan Congregationalist schools; Princeton was founded as a Presbyterian institution.
4. An interesting bit of history involves an influential editorial written by Heilprin in the *New York Tribune*, January, 1861. In this editorial, Heilprin offers a scathing rebuttal to a rabbi's interpretation of Torah that supports slavery. He eloquently defends, on Biblical grounds, an abolitionist perspective.
5. Magyar nationalism inspired many biblical themes in literature; hence, the bookshop was a virtual library of religious influences. Ferenc Kölcsey tied patriotism to Biblical sources in *Hymnus* (1823), which was based on Jeremiah 32:21–29. It became the Hungarian national anthem. Biblical themes are seen in the works of János Arany, Imre Madách, Mór Jókai, Kálmán Mikszáth, Endre Ady, Gyula Juhász, Attila József, and Mihály Babits.
6. Victor Karády is author of more than 100 scholarly articles, as well as numerous books. Born in Budapest, he studied in Vienna and graduated from Sorbonne, France. He is a full-time research fellow at the French *Centre Nationale de la Recherche Scientifique*, as well as lecturer in universities across Europe. His areas of research include Jewish social history, education and culture, and the history of social mobility.
7. Tom Keve, in his book *Triad: The Physicists, the Analysts, the Kabbalists* (2000), which unfortunately weaves biographical material with novel, presents a fascinating case for Sándor Ferenczi's interest in Kaballah.
8. It is probable that the desire to please Freud contributed to Ferenczi's move away from the views of his previous mentor, Schachter, who allowed a place both for religion and science in his worldview. In this manner, the personal relationship with Freud was an antireligious influence on Ferenczi. This influence is intimated in their correspondence.

On one occasion, a curious interchange regarding a biblical theme that Ferenczi wanted to develop occurs. On November 22, 1914, Ferenczi (1914a) writes to Freud: "I would like to write down for the *Zeitschrift* a very interesting dream that generally explains the biblical episode of the downfall of Sodom and Gomorrah. Analysis shows that *Lot's* wife became a *pillar of salt* not only because she looked back at the burning cities, but also because salt at the same time symbolizes the perverse manner of sexual satisfaction in those cities (cunnilingus, etc.)." Freud (1914a) does not respond at first to this proposal, though he sends another note on November 25, 1914, in which he states his concerns that Ferenczi is moving toward the occult, presumably in Jung's direction. Ferenczi (1914b) replies on November 30, 1914, assuring Freud by saying,

"My 'occultism' is very distinctly separated from my other knowledge and doesn't disturb it in any way; it is completely free of *mysticism*." He then adds, "Should I publish the dream of the pillars of salt and the analytic interpretation of Lot's wife as a pillar of salt? I interpret your silence on the subject as a sign of displeasure; or am I mistaken?" Freud (1914b) responds on December 2, 1914, "What should I have against it?" The article was never published.

Numerous exchanges between Freud and Ferenczi continue to reflect the latter's concern to assure Freud that he is not interested in mysticism. He self-discloses in this note written to Freud on July 24, 1915: "My 'inclination toward occult matters' is not 'secret' but rather quite obvious—it is also not actually an inclination toward the occult, but rather an urge toward de-occultization, at the base of which there may be, in the final analysis, magic-religious strivings, which I am defending myself against by wanting to bring clarity to these matters."

9. Daniel Shaw, in a superb article "Analytic Love" (2003), draws on Suttie's connection with Ferenczi, linking it to the centrality of love in the analytic relationship.
10. The Galileo Circle was a radical student organization, whose first president and founder was Karl Polanyi, and to which Ferenczi belonged. Its express purpose was "the defense and propagation of unbiased science" (Gelwick, 2005, p. 26). In the foment of revolution in the early 1900s, the group was divided into those who saw Marxism as the answer to the gaps between rich and poor, rulers and citizens; those who supported violent revolution; and those who made no room for aggression in the pursuit of change.

Karl, his brother Michael, and sister Laura were well known to Ferenczi and referred to in his correspondence with Freud (1910b). The Polayni family was a model of liberal thought; their mother, Cecile Polayni, was the daughter of Rabbi Andreas Wahl, a leader in progressive Judaism whose essay "The Significance of the Talmud for Christianity" exemplifies this liberality (Gelwick, 2005, p. 26). In the tight-knit café society of Budapest, radical changes in any of its leading members were duly noted. Such was the case with the Polayni brothers, whose mother, Cecile, became an advocate of psychoanalysis.

Crosscurrents between Circles existed, as is evidenced by the visits of Michael Polanyi to the Sunday Circle in 1915. Though a member of the Galileo Circle that his brother Karl had founded, he was invited to take part in the discussions held at the home of Béla Balàzs, a poet, a libretto writer of the opera and ballets of Béla Bartok, and one of the first theoreticians of filmology (cf. Zsuffa, *Béla Balàzs, The Man and the Artist*, 1987). Richard Gelwick (2005) confirms that Polanyi found that the "topics discussed revolved around the philosophy of love. ... Atheism or belief in God was often on the agenda. Particularly engaging for the group were the writings of Kierkegaard and of Dostoyevsky" (p. 27).

During this time, Michael Polanyi read Dostoyevsky and Tolstoy. "He reports years later in a letter to Karl Mannheim that he had at that time a feeling of conversion to Christianity along the lines of Tolstoy" (Gelwick, 2005, p. 13fn). His brother Karl moved away from his antireligious stance so prevalent in the Galileo Society, as seen in this excerpt from a speech delivered at Endre Ady's funeral. He wrote: "There is no science that could alter, only science that will affirm the truth that the bird flies not in accordance with the laws of gravity, but in spite of them, that the tree does not spread in foliage according to the law of creative profusion, that society rises to higher spiritual levels not in accordance with material interests but in disregard of them, and that of human faith, force and self-sacrifice lead us on high, not the downwards pulling gravitational force of material interests, but by force of the hallowed laws of spirit which defy them" (Polanyi, 1919, p. 6).

11. I refer readers to the well-researched work of Peter Rudnytsky (2002) for a thorough exploration of the influence of Georg Groddeck. Though Groddeck was born into a Lutheran home, went to religious school, and avidly read Ibsen's plays, his trajectory moved into mysticism in certain ways like Jung, whom I have also chosen not to investigate. However, Rudnytsky solidly asserts Groddeck's Christian influence reflected in an excerpt from "Repression and Release" (1926) in which Groddeck characterizes psychoanalysis as: "the road open to all who wish to unlearn hatred and to learn love. It is, notwithstanding its origin, identical with the method of Him who called Himself the Son of Man, perhaps even by virtue of its origin, since however painful it may be for the world's haters, it cannot be denied that Christ was a Jew" (p. 219). Groddeck's perspectives complemented and supported Ferenczi's embracing of more relationally oriented ideas, ideas that also resonated with his early religious narratives. Groddeck was admired by many including Horney, Fromm-Reichmann, Jones, and Freud.
12. The genealogy of the Moravians winds its path back through history, through Sarospatak, Hungary, a town 25 miles from Ferenczi's Miskolc, Hungary, to its point of commencement on July 6, 1415, in Konstanz, Germany. The religious reformer Jan Hus of Prague, nurtured through the writings of the English theologian Wycliffe, and a century before Luther, was burned at the stake in Konstanz because he challenged the hypocrisy of the church nobility who cared little for the needs of the common person. His execution lit a fire in the hearts of his followers, and the "Hussite" movement was founded, calling itself the "Unity of Brethren." The last Bishop of the Brethren was Jan Comenius, who fled with survivors of the counterreformation into exile. The Brethren teachings were pre-Calvinist Calvinism, but with a deep emphasis on the heart.

    Comenius is respected as the forerunner of modern pedagogy. Piaget (1993) extolled his visionary modifications which included greater support to learning-disabled children and the following comment on the education of girls: "They are endowed with equal sharpness of mind and capacity for knowledge (often with more than the opposite sex) and they are able to attain the highest positions, since they have often been called by God Himself to rule over nations ... to the study of medicine and of other things which benefit the human race. ... Why, therefore, should we admit them to the alphabet, and afterwards drive them away from books" (p. 9).

    In 1550, Comenius was invited by the prince of Transylvania, Hungary, to establish the newly founded Calvinist college in the town of Sarospatak; this college would later relocate to Debrecen and become the headquarters of Hungarian Calvinism. The college that Comenius founded was attended by Mihály Tompa (an anti-Hapsburg Protestant pastor whose inspiring sermons

Bernat Ferenczi avidly published), as well as Lajos Kossuth, the leader of the 1848 revolution. The Pietistic openness of the Brethren to passion and social change would leave their mark on the Calvinist Hungarian spirit.

In the early 1700s, there would be another bishop of the "renewed" Brethren. The exiled Brethren would move to a community in Saxony called Herrnhut, where they were called the Moravians; and their leader, who bequeathed his estate for their survival, was Count Ludwig von Zinzendorf. In the spirit of Comenius, Ludwig von Zinzendorf held women in high esteem. His view of the Trinity emphasized the nurturing, maternal aspects of Christ. Childlike faith and surrender were encouraged, including imagery of resting upon Christ. Zinzendorf also emphasized the goodness of sexuality and the body, linking its blessedness with the validation of Christ's incarnation. Zinzendorf's passionate view of religion, however, later came under attack from Oskar Pfister, who had historically taken issue with Pietism. He wrote a monograph that analyzed and interpreted what he viewed as Zinzendorf's sexual pathology (Pfister, 1925). A complete rebuttal of Pfister's points was given by Reichel (1911) the following year.

Zinzendorf was of royal Austrian blood, and his duties would take him, and his Moravian beliefs, to Kierkegaard's Copenhagen: "The most important event for Herrnhutism in Denmark was Count Zinzendorf's visit to Copenhagen in 1731, on the occasion of King Christian VI's coronation. Zinzendorf was a second cousin to Queen Sofie Magdalene. During the visit Zinzendorf gained a degree of influence within the royal court. ... On both his outward journey and on his return he established links with the leading men within the duchy. One of the results was the foundation of a 'Society of Brethren'" (The Christianfeld Initiative, 2004).

13. In a letter dated December 20, 1911, Lukács "informed Buber that he had called attention to his books in Hungary: 'I have written a brief review [entitled Jewish Mysticism] of both volumes in the Hungarian philosophic journal *A Szellem*'" (Congdon, 1983, p. 78).
14. Each of the evidences that I propose are multidetermined. Many have been linked to Ferenczi's psychological predispositions as well as other influences. I merely wish to suggest contributing sources of a religious nature.
15. Space does not permit an elaboration of the very intentional democratic government of Calvinist churches, an aspect of Hungarian life of which Ferenczi would have been very familiar. Presbyterian (Calvinist) churches have a representative government with elected leaders. Ferenczi went to a Calvinist school and lived in a section of Hungary that was imbued with Calvinist influences, not the least of which was the belief that each person is made in the image of God and has equal worth.
16. In this brilliantly prescient exposition, Ferenczi articulates what would become both Klein's theoretical contribution on paranoid/schizoid and depressive positions and Winnicott's views on destruction and survival of the object.
17. This quotation is taken from Ferenczi's last major paper, one which marked a final theoretical parting with Freud. The original title of this paper, delivered at the Twelfth International Psycho-Analytical Congress, Wiesbaden, September 1932, was "The Passions of Adults and Their Influence on the Sexual and Character Development of Children." It is interesting to note that its final title became "Confusion of the Tongues Between the Adults and the

Child—*(The Language of Tenderness and of Passion).*" Peter Hoffer (1995) clarifies the very specific biblical meaning of this title: "The German equivalent, *Sprachverwirrung* (stemming from the story of the Tower of Babel in the Old Testament) literally means 'confusion of speech'" (p. 1047).

18. It must be acknowledged that during his career, Ferenczi was also justly confronted about the serious ethical transgression that occurred with a patient who became his wife. Though boundary violations were more common in the early days of psychoanalysis, this was disapproved of by Freud, and is a blemish on his history.
19. The religious and ethnic pluralism of Hungary encouraged the influence of Great Britain within its populace, and welcomed Scottish Calvinists with their messianic ideals, to establish their enterprises and build elite Hungarian *gymnasiums*. Hungary had welcomed Moravians, Hutterites, Anabaptists, and Pietists, and these peoples influenced the culture toward an affective engagement with life. Moravians and Hutterites also provided a long-standing model of communal living, a Christian precursor to the socialist vision. Jewish mysticism and orthodoxy were debated and encouraged to flourish. Even the occult practices of the gypsy population and tolerance toward theosophy were accorded a place in the culture.

Chapter 11

Conclusion

Continuing paths toward mutual recognition

> We are, whether we acknowledge it or not, what the past has made us and we cannot eradicate from ourselves ... those parts of ourselves which are formed by our relationship to each formative stage in our history.
>
> —MacIntyre (1984, p. 130)

> The development of psychoanalytic theory and practice in the 60 years since Ferenczi's death, encompass[es] object relations, the "widening scope" of psychoanalysis, direct infant observation and research, general recognition of the reality of widespread childhood sexual abuse, contemporary theories of self psychology and intersubjectivity, and relational and social constructivist models of the psychoanalytic situation, the upshot of which is that psychoanalysis has finally caught up with where Ferenczi had been all along.
>
> —Vida (1997, p. 406)

Three orientation streams converge to form what is now called *relational psychoanalysis*: object relations, interpersonal analysis, and self psychology. Each of these streams are tributaries, which trace to their source in Sándor Ferenczi. Many of the analysts who entered these streams were affected, for better or worse, by the Christian narrative. I believe that Ferenczi's hope-filled perspective toward life and the resonance of his subtextual Jewish and Christian narrative influences drew these analysts to him.

OBJECT RELATIONS

> Even in the early history of psychoanalysis, Freud's followers in Vienna and in Budapest took different directions. ... All of them [Hungarians], long before object-relations theory was born, held that life begins with a *relationship* between infant and mother. ... This is in contrast to

> Freud's and the Viennese school's contention that the newborn's need to reduce pain is caused by the accumulation of instinctual tension in the libidinously charged organs. For the Hungarians ... It is the *whole* infant's striving for contact with, or "primary love" for mother. ... The infant was seen as an active as well as reactive organism whose character develops in response to the constant interplay between himself/herself and the caretaking environment. (Deri, 1990, p. 491)

In Chapter 4, I referred to many object relations theorists who had been influenced by the Christian narrative. Of those who contributed to the object relations shift from drive to relationship, John Rickman, Ian Suttie, Jane Suttie, and Michael Balint were intimately connected with Ferenczi, Balint being the principal voice for Ferenczi's ideas in the British Isles. Ferenczi's ideas matured in the works of Fairbairn, Winnicott, Bowlby, and Guntrip. John Rickman was closely associated with Hugh Crichton-Miller of Tavistock, whose work mirrors Ferenczi's approaches to war-neuroses (Gunther & Trosman, 1974); Rickman in turn analyzed Wilfred Bion.

Object relations cannot be described without the seminal work of Melanie Klein. She had been analyzed by Ferenczi, and her work became central to the development of object relations in Great Britain. Her elaboration of projective identification became a bridge to relational theory and, when wed with a two-person perspective, contributed to the understanding of intersubjectivity.

AMERICAN INTERPERSONAL

> There is now a long and rich interpersonal tradition, one that can be traced back to Ferenczi, that emphasizes a much freer, although still disciplined, use of the self, forms of interaction that highlight spontaneity, mutuality, affective responsiveness, the experientially immediate, and the analyst's actively bringing into the work a much wider range and a great variety of forms of interaction. (Aron, 2005, p. 27)

The principal carriers of Ferenczi's ideas to the United States were Clara Thompson and Izette de Forest, both influenced by Christianity. De Forest was analyst to Andras Angyal, better known in humanistic psychological circles. Through Thompson's widespread influence, Ferenczi's work was embraced by American psychoanalysis, Bergmann and Hartman (1976) crediting Ferenczi as the ultimate originator of the interpersonal approach.

Thompson was the Washington Psychoanalytic Society's first president, and Ferenczi addressed this society during his trip to the United States in 1927 (Silver, 1993). Following her analysis by Ferenczi and upon returning from Budapest, Thompson moved to New York City "but continued collaboration with Sullivan as well as with Fromm-Reichmann and their associates, who taught in the Washington School of Psychiatry and what would become The William Alanson White Institute of New York, commuting between Washington and New York weekly" (p. 647). During her time at the White Institute, she was analyst/mentor to a generation of key figures who extended interpersonal theory.

Fromm-Reichmann, who came to the Chestnut Lodge in 1935 (Silver, 1993), was impacted both by Ferenczi through Thompson and also by Ferenczi's friend Groddeck, with whom she had developed a close relationship in Baden-Baden. Silver notes:

> I believe that Fromm-Reichmann had brought the spirit of Groddeck's and Ferenczi's and certainly her own work to the United States through her work at Chestnut Lodge; however she, like Sullivan, did not reminisce about the specific contributions of colleagues who had shaped her views. During those years, Ferenczi's and Groddeck's names had become anathemas; the psychoanalytic applications to treating severely ill patients were often heavily attacked. (p. 649)

Another Washington, D.C., clinician influenced by Ferenczi was psychiatrist Lewis Hill, who traveled to Budapest for consultations. Lewis Hill was analyst to Hans Loewald, who became a prominent figure in the Yale education of Stephen Mitchell and undoubtedly contributed to Mitchell's seminal role in the development of relational psychoanalysis.

SELF PSYCHOLOGY

> The major aim of the present discussion is to outline the pioneering clinical and theoretical work of Sándor Ferenczi and demonstrate its relevance as a precursor to self psychology. ... In an earlier discussion, I introduced the notion that Ferenczi was the originator of the empathic method in psychoanalysis (Rachman, 1988). It is necessary at this juncture to expand this perspective to add Ferenczi to the list of psychoanalytic thinkers who pioneered an alternate form of psychoanalysis that anticipated many aspects of the self psychology framework. In this regard, there are several basic concepts that bear comparison between Ferenczi and Kohut: (1) The role of empathy in psychoanalysis; (2) The self object transference; (3) Reintroduction of the trauma theory; (4) Revision of the resistance model. (Rachman, 1997b, p. 342)

Heinz Kohut, born Jewish, had converted to Christianity. Both he and his wife had been analyzed by the Catholic August Aichhorn, an analyst whose techniques and passion resembled Ferenczi's. Ferenczi offers his opinion of Aichhorn: "I had a discussion with Aichhorn, whose special talent I admired. Nevertheless, I called his attention to a certain bias in his psychoanalytic conception of youthful boasting, etc. He acknowledged my statement with a willingness, indeed, gratitude which is rare in authors. He is a very nice person" (December 30, 1929). In another place he describes "the masterly skill of Aichhorn's devices for making even the most difficult children tractable in analysis" (1931, p. 469). Moreau-Ricaud (1996) notes that Aichhorn, along with Groddeck, Reich, and Anna Freud, were specifically invited to attend meetings of the Hungarian Psychoanalytic Association. In light of these facts, Aichhorn was most likely a conduit of Ferenczi's sensibilities to the Kohuts.

Kohut's biographer, Charles Strozier, noted John Gedo's assertion that Kohut was very familiar with Ferenczi's writings. Gedo offered this comment:

> I received the commission for my 1967 Ferenczi article for *Psyche* through Heinz. He was my first reader and commented specifically about how odd he found it that candidates at that time no longer studied Ferenczi in detail. He was clearly thoroughly familiar with SF's contributions and esteemed them very highly. (He wrote me that Abraham was Ferenczi's only equal among Freud's early adherents.) (Strozier, 2001, p. 353)

Ferenczi's influence on self psychology comes in part through John Gedo himself, who was closely allied with Kohut in his work. Gedo was born in Hungary and was analyzed by Therese Benedek, an analysand of Ferenczi, before moving to Chicago. While Gedo's religious beliefs are unknown, there is a striking excerpt from his 1972 paper in which he interrogates some prevalent ideas expounded by Eissler. He responds:

> It is his [Eissler's] fervent conviction that the etiology of this sea of troubles is the Rise of the West and the consequent spread of the corrupting influence of Christianity that deserves some discussion—and provokes disagreement.
>
> Savagery, destructiveness, and exploitation are, as far as I can see, not Western monopolies; on the contrary, what seems to be unique in the Western tradition is the steady and growing counter-current of altruism, perhaps epitomized in the figure of Jesus. "This is my commandment, That ye love one another, as I have loved you. Greater love hath no man than this, that a man lay down his life for his friends." (p. 312)

The Jewish Hungarian Benedek (1977) also revealed her ease with Christian religious concepts:

> It is no accident that sexual passion is not the first in the dictionary's definitions of passion. The word originates from the Latin verb *patior* (*pati, passus*) and has the primary meaning to suffer—sufferance, tolerance. It implies a tendency to be forbearing. It was used by Christian theologists in the narration of the sufferings of Christ in the Gospels. This is the most telling example of the psychodynamic process of passion. Jesus' love for all mankind is proven by his self-sacrifice, and his awareness of suffering is revealed in his anguish that he felt abandoned by God, the Father. But one aspect of human passion is not recognizable in his suffering. His passion does not show the human characteristic of narcissism. (p. 56)

Finally, there is the contribution of Paul and Anna Ornstein, who were Jewish and were mentored by Michael and Enid Balint (Rachman, 1997b). The Ornsteins became another rivulet for the self psychology stream that originated in Ferenczi and passed through Michael Balint.

REDEMPTION: THE HOPE OF ETERNAL RETURN

The robust convergence of cultural, scientific, and religious assets that flourished in Budapest and manifested in Ferenczi's work were disseminated into the three streams that united to form relational psychoanalysis, broadly defined. Flowing from their shared, originary source, each stream transmitted the substance of the original Judaic narrative of truth, loving relationship, and redemption with their distinctive enhancements, into the basin of relational psychoanalysis. I will conclude my project on mutual recognition by tracing the journey of these originary Judaic values into relational psychoanalysis in yet one more fashion: pairing the movements in psychoanalysis with parallel developments in the larger culture. In so doing, I will for one last time assert that a loving force for life, Hegel's *Geist*, God's grace, is operative in the evolution of culture and the transformation of individual lives in the consultation room.

Emphasis on truth

"Human beings live, develop, maintain, and sustain themselves in cycles of eternal return" states Fogel (1991), as interlocutor of Loewald's perspective. He continues, "This is not 'theory' for Loewald in the abstract sense, or a consciously chosen 'philosophy of life' in the superficial sense. It is the nature of human life as he sees it" (p. 174).

Incarnation, crucifixion, and resurrection as a cycle of "eternal return" are reflected in a psychoanalysis matured by a plurality of narratives including the ones that Freud contemplated but rejected. Freud, who embraced his

University of Vienna professor Brentano's seminal construct of intentionality (every mental act is oriented toward an object), developed Brentano's idea along objectivist lines, which Brentano would define as "genetic psychology." Brentano, in contrast, developed "intentionality" toward a "descriptive psychology" (1874/1995) which focused on the more experientially oriented inner perception of the subject.[1]

Brentano is acknowledged as the father/grandfather of phenomenology, but until recently has remained an obscure figure in philosophy. Those he mentored went on to reorient philosophy and psychology in the direction of hermeneutics. Edmund Husserl, Brentano's closest protégé, first developed Brentano's shift toward phenomenology. Among the people influenced by Husserl were philosophers such as Heidegger and Lukács. Heidegger would become mentor to Hans Loewald, who would exert an influence on Stephen Mitchell during his years at Yale and in turn upon Mitchell's conception of relational psychoanalysis. The shift from understanding truth in Freud's objectivist terms to a phenomenological/hermeneutic approach would provide a more comprehensive and impassioned deconstructive approach to falsehood unrecognized by positivist thought and replicate an earlier approach to truth found in Judaic *midrash*. Relational psychoanalysis, in much the same fashion as dissenting rabbis of old, labors to maintain the dialectic between hermeneutics and scientific empiricism, a balance observable in the earlier work of Sándor Ferenczi.

Emphasis on loving relationship

The psychoanalytic shift from drives to relationship emerged powerfully in the British Isles. This shift was abetted by a philosophical evolution concurrently emerging in Great Britain, which cultivated a soil exceptionally receptive to Ferenczi's ideas.

Ferenczi was not solely responsible for the burgeoning of British objects relations theory. Truth, loving relationship, and redemption had been central to the teachings of John Knox of Scotland and John Wesley of England. They saw their faith as one that placed them as humans in "the bundle of life" (I Samuel 25:29, KJV). For Calvinist John Knox, the emphasis on the "Word" and reason led him to establish an egalitarian vision of education and equality as a national priority. For John Wesley, the experience of loving community was the heart of meaningful living and led to redemptive social action.

Also, concurrent with the influence of Ferenczi's ideas, an interdisciplinary group of Oxford scholars had begun meeting in 1924 for the express purpose of examining the "relationship of faith and science" (Costello, 2002, p. 137). Members of this group included Martin Buber and his friend, Oxford scholar John Macmurray, whose later books were found in Fairbairn's library (M. Hoffman, 2004, p. 797). As a Quaker interested in social transformation, Macmurray would collaborate on a book with Karl Polanyi entitled *Christianity and the Social Revolution* (Kitchin, Lewis, & Polanyi, 1936). He would serve as well as mentor and thesis supervisor to Harold Guntrip. Also in this Oxford group was the Christian philosopher Seth Pringle-Pattison, a mentor to Fairbairn.

From this Oxford "think tank," the Christian John Macmurray emerged as a preeminent philosopher and was appreciated by the Jewish Martin Buber, for his specific philosophical project— "to conceptualize the form of the personal" (Costello, 2002, p. 14). Costello elaborates:

> This project had two dimensions to it: first, the recovery of a recognition of the fully personal from the reductionism imposed by mechanical and organic categories of thinking on human persons and social institutions ... second, to achieve a coherent and consistent articulation of the unique logic of personal existence ... Martin Buber, whom Macmurray knew even more personally, considered himself to be the poet of this project; and he saw Macmurray as its metaphysician and told him so. (pp. 14–15)

Macmurray, like Buber, detailed the necessity of understanding personhood as existing within the matrix of relationship.

In his Gifford lectures, British Broadcasting Corporation (BBC) talks, and books (including the later *Persons in Relation*, 1961), Macmurray linked the Christian narrative to relationality and to social action. Regarding Macmurray's messianic emphasis, Costello writes:

> Is there, then, something unique to Christianity? He says there is. He proposes that it is "the spirit of Christ" that launched the revolution impelling human beings to seek openness in truth, freedom in action, equality in relationships and full community *for all people*. For Macmurray, *this* movement to universality in the search for freedom and equality in community expresses the uniqueness of what he calls "true" Christianity. ... *Any* action or movement that advances this openness, freedom, equality and participation for all is thereby truly in and of the Christian revolution. ... Conversely, wherever religion, customs, politics or economics serve as an obstacle to this movement to freedom, equality and inclusiveness they will be overcome by this spirit for life. (p. 149)

Openness, freedom, equality, inclusiveness: This list reads like a lexicon of Ferenczi's values, the values of relational psychoanalysis, values that John Macmurray believed are the offspring of "true Christianity," a Christianity whose source is the covenantal God of Judaism. Ferenczi's work was interpolated into a burgeoning British movement toward relationality that anticipated relational psychoanalysis.

Emphasis on redemption

> Everything flows, but the river comes from a source every time. It takes matter with it from the regions through which it has run, this colours its waters for a long time. Equally for that new form there are remnants of an older one, there is no absolute cut between today and yesterday. There is no totally new work, least of all the revolutionary kind ... (Ernst Bloch, 2005, p. 35)

Ferenczi's Budapest harbored a generation of geniuses with utopian dreams, dreams that had once been part of the Judaic narrative of redemption. According to Congdon (2001), "Their detachment from religious values left behind a spiritual vacuum to be filled by a new religion, mysticism, or communism" (p. 151fn). In the wake of having reached the limits of "reason" in the political realities of *fin de siècle* Hungary, Lukács became the figurehead for intellectuals seeking an alternative hope.

Between 1910 and 1912 Lukács moved away from *Nyugat*, forming his own journal, *Szellem*. He became interested in philosophical idealism and also in religious mysticism. This turn to mysticism was abetted by his reading of Meister Eckhart and his reading and corresponding with Martin Buber in 1911. Béla Balàzs, literary contemporary of Lukács, notes the following regarding Lukács in his journal: "Gyuri's (Georg) new philosophy. Messianism. The homogenous world ... as the redemptive goal ... Gyuri discovered and acknowledges the *Jew* in himself!" (Congdon, 1983, p. 78).

Lukács moved in a more Marxist direction with his messianic hopes. He became close friends with Max Weber, Ernst Bloch, and Georg Simmel, and his ideas ultimately influenced a young group of intellectuals who would extend Lukács' ideas in the Frankfurt School. Lukács' continued messianic yearnings are seen in his 1916 penetrating response to Nietzsche:

> But if, for all that, God exists? Perhaps only one God has died, and another, of a younger generation, of another essence, who is in different relationships with us, is yet to come. Perhaps the darkness of our aimlessness is only that of the night between the sunset of one God and the dawn of another? ... Is it certain that we have found here—in the world of tragedy, a world devoid of all the gods—our ultimate goal? Hidden in our desolateness, isn't it the cry of sorrow, the desire for a God to come? (Lendvai, 1997, pp. 161–162)

The epitome of secularized messianism emerged in the founding of the Frankfurt School in 1923, a cause to which Lukács served as intellectual benefactor. Mendiata (2005) elaborates:

> In order to appropriate the most fruitful elements of Marxism, the Frankfurt School also had to engage in a genealogical analysis of Marxism that traced its roots to Hegel, in particular, but also to German idealism in general. ... Another current of thought that converged in the critical theory of the Frankfurt School is what has been called an atheistic Jewish Messianism which was very unique and particular to assimilated central European Jews, especially those of Germany, where the Jews, paradoxically, had achieved the greatest assimilation. (pp. 5–6)

Emanating from Lukács' and Ferenczi's Budapest was a secularized longing for redemption inherited by the Frankfurt School. The Frankfurt School extended its influence to the New York community when, in 1933, its fleeing scholars found safe haven at Columbia University, founding the Institute for Social Research. Some members of that institute lectured at the New School for Social Research. And today, that institution—the New School for Social Research—safeguards the memory of psychoanalyst Sándor Ferenczi at the Sándor Ferenczi Center. Innumerable members of the relational psychoanalytic community have been inspired by professors, analysts, and supervisors influenced by this secularized redemptive *telos*. Relevant to this study as well is the redemptive desire for social action that the Frankfurt School deposited directly into the milieu of relational psychoanalysis through the work of Jessica Benjamin. Having studied at the Frankfurt School, her writings on intersubjectivity theory with its emphasis on mutual recognition have served to further egalitarian and humane treatment both in the therapeutic dyad and in the culture at large.

FINAL THOUGHTS

One may depict the ethos of relational psychoanalysis in purely secular terms, in the terms that have become normative. I hope that this book has offered a lens by which that redemptive force depicted in ancient narratives—the covenantal God of Judaism and Christianity—may be recognized as a generative source, in Bloch's sense, of our psychoanalytic ideals. And in the spirit of mutual recognition, it is my desire that both secular and believing psychoanalysts will be motivated to gratefully partner together in a shared, resurrected vision of truth, loving relationship, and redemption.

> Once there was a time when the whole of rational creation formed a single dance chorus looking upwards to the one leader of this dance. ... And the harmony of that motion which was imparted to them by

> reason of his law found its way into their dancing. ... And this victory will come [again] and thou shalt be found in the dancing ranks of the angelic spirits.
>
> —Gregory of Nyssa (335–394 CE)
> (Rahner, 1967, pp. 89fn)

ENDNOTE

1. Moving away from objectivism, Brentano (1980) was able to retain a place for spiritual experience and for his phenomenologically derived perspective that loving relationship birthed humanity, and that loving relationship is humanity's highest aim.

References

Abraham, K. (1925). The influence of oral eroticism on character-formation. *International Journal of Psychoanalysis*, *6*, 247–258.
Adorno, T. (1993). *Hegel: Three studies* (S. Nicholsen, Trans.). Cambridge, MA: MIT Press.
Akhtar, S. (2000). From schisms through synthesis to informed oscillation: An attempt at integrating some diverse aspects of psychoanalytic technique. *Psychoanalytic Quarterly*, *69*, 265–288.
Altman, N. (2002). Where is the action in the "talking cure"? *Contemporary Psychoanalysis*, *38*, 499–513.
Ammaniti, M., & Trentini, C. (2009). How new knowledge about parenting reveals the neurobiological implications of intersubjectivity: A conceptual synthesis of recent research. *Psychoanalytic Dialogues*, *19*, 537–555.
Arden, M. (1987). A concept of femininity: Sylvia Payne's 1935 paper reassessed. *The International Review of Psychoanalysis*, *14*, 237–244.
Arieti, S. (1976). *Creativity: The magic synthesis*. New York: Basic Books.
Aron, L. (1996). *A meeting of minds: Mutuality in psychoanalysis*. Hillsdale, NJ: The Analytic Press.
Aron, L. (2000). Self-reflexivity and the therapeutic action of psychoanalysis. *Psychoanalytic Psychology*, *17*, 667–689.
Aron, L. (2003). The paradoxical place of enactment in psychoanalysis: Introduction. *Psychoanalytic Dialogues*, *13*, 623–631.
Aron, L. (2004a). Empathy and authenticity. Unpublished manuscript.
Aron, L. (2004b). God's influence on my psychoanalytic vision and values. *Psychoanalytic Psychology*, *21*, 442–451.
Aron, L. (2005). On the unique contribution of the interpersonal approach to interaction: A discussion of Stephen A. Mitchell's "Ideas of interaction in psychoanalysis." *Contemporary Psychoanalysis*, *41*, 21–34.
Aron, L. (2006). Analytic impasse and the third: Clinical implications of intersubjectivity theory. *International Journal of Psychoanalysis*, *87*, 349–368.
Aron, L. (2007). Reflections on Heinz Kohut's religious identity and anti-Semitism: Discussion of Charles B. Strozier's "Heinz Kohut and the meanings of identity." *Contemporary Psychoanalysis*, *43*, 411–420.
Aron, L., & Anderson, F. (Eds.). (1998). *Relational perspectives on the body*. Hillsdale, NJ: The Analytic Press.

Aron, L., & Harris, A. (Eds.). (1993). *The legacy of Sándor Ferenczi*. Hillsdale, NJ: The Analytic Press.
Aron, L., & Mitchell, S. (Eds.). (1999). *Relational psychoanalysis: The emergence of a tradition*. Hillsdale, NJ: The Analytic Press.
Bacal, H. A. (1987). British object-relations theorists and self psychology: Some critical reflections. *International Journal of Psychoanalysis, 68*, 81–98.
Balint, M. (1968). *The basic fault: Therapeutic aspects of regression*. Chicago, IL: Northwestern University Press.
Barnett, C. (2008). Should one suffer death for the truth? Kierkegaard, *Erbauungsliteratur*, and the imitation of Christ. *Journal of the History of Modern Theology, 15*(2), 232–247.
Barsness, R. (2006). Surrender and transcendence in the analytic encounter. *Journal of Psychology and Christianity, 25*(1), 44–55.
Beebe, B., & Lachmann, F. M. (1988a). Mother–infant mutual influence and precursors of psychic structure. In A. Goldberg (Ed.), *Progress in self psychology* (vol. 3, pp. 3–25). Hillsdale, NJ: The Analytic Press.
Beebe, B., & Lachmann, F. M. (1988b). The contribution of mother–infant mutual influence to the origins of self- and object representation. *Psychoanalytic Psychology, 5*, 305–337.
Beebe, B., & Lachmann, F. M. (1998). Co-constructing inner and relational processes: Self- and mutual regulation in infant research and adult treatment. *Psychoanalytic Psychology, 15*, 480–516.
Beebe, B., & Lachmann, F. M. (2002). *Infant research and adult treatment: Co-constructing interactions*. Hillsdale, NJ: The Analytic Press.
Benedek, T. (1959). Parenthood as a developmental phase: A contribution to the libido theory. *Journal of the American Psychoanalytic Association, 7*, 389–417.
Benedek, T. (1977). Ambivalence, passion, and love. *Journal of the American Psychoanalytic Association, 25*, 53–79.
Benjamin, J. (1988). *The bonds of love*. New York: Pantheon Books.
Benjamin, J. (1990). Recognition and destruction: An outline of intersubjectivity. In L. Aron & S. Mitchell (Eds.), *Relational psychoanalysis: The emergence of a tradition* (pp. 181–210). Hillsdale, NJ: The Analytic Press.
Benjamin, J. (1995). *Like subjects, love objects*. New Haven, CT: Yale University Press.
Benjamin, J. (2000). Response to commentaries by Mitchell and by Butler. *Studies in Gender and Sexuality, 1*, 291–308.
Benjamin, J. (2004a). Beyond doer and done to: An intersubjective view of thirdness. *Psychoanalytic Quarterly, 73*, 5–46.
Benjamin, J. (2004b). Escape from the hall of mirrors: Commentary on paper by Jody Messler Davies. *Psychoanalytic Dialogues, 14*, 743–753.
Benjamin, J. (2006). Two-way streets: Recognition of difference and the intersubjective third. *Differences, 17*, 116–146.
Benjamin, J. (2009). Psychoanalytic controversies response. *International Journal of Psychoanalysis, 90*, 457–462.
Bergmann, M., & Hartman, F. (Eds.). (1976). *The evolution of psychoanalytic technique*. New York: Basic Books.
Bion, W. (1962). *Learning from experience*. London: Heineman.

Bion, W. (1970). *Attention and interpretation: A scientific approach to insight in psycho-analysis and groups*. London: Tavistock.
Bion, W. (1982). *The long weekend*. London, England: Karnac.
Blatner, H. A. (1973). *Acting-in: Practical applications of psychodrama methods*. New York: Springer Publishing.
Bléandonu, G. (1994). *Wilfred Bion: His life and his works*. New York: Other Press.
Bloch, E. (1971). *Man on his own: Essays in the philosophy of religion* (E. B. Ashton, Trans.). New York: Herder and Herder.
Bloch, E. (2005). On the original history of the Third Reich. In E. Mendieta (Ed.), *The Frankfurt School on religion* (pp. 21–40). New York: Routledge.
Bollas, C. (1979). The transformational object. *International Journal of Psychoanalysis*, *60*, 97–107.
Boettner, L. (1983). *Reformed faith*. Phillipsburg, NJ: Puritan and Reformed Publishing.
Bonar, A., & McCheyne, R. M. (1840). Memorandum to Protestant monarchs of Europe for the restoration of the Jews to Palestine. *London Times*.
Bonar, A., & McCheyne, R. M. (1842). *A narrative of a mission of inquiry to the Jews from the Church of Scotland in 1839*. Edinburgh, Scotland: Edinburgh.
Bonomi, C. (1999). Flight into sanity: Jones' allegation of Ferenczi's mental deterioration reconsidered. *International Journal of Psychoanalysis*, *80*, 507–542.
Boston Change Process Study Group. (2010). *Change in psychotherapy: A unifying paradigm* New York: Norton.
Boulanger, G. (2007). *Wounded by reality: Understanding and treating adult onset trauma*. New York: The Analytic Press.
Boyarin, D. (1997). *Unheroic conduct: The rise of heterosexuality and the invention of the Jewish man*. Berkeley, CA: University of California Press.
Boyarin, D. (2004). *Border lines: The partition of Judaeo-Christianity*. Philadelphia, PA: University of Pennsylvania Press.
Brennan, W. (2009). Ferenczi's forgotten messenger: The life and work of Izette de Forest. *American Imago*, *66*(4), 427–455.
Brentano, F. (1980). *Geschichte der mittelalterlichen Philosophie* (Klaus Hedwig, Ed.). Hamburg: Meiner Verlag.
Brentano, F. (1987). *On the existence of God*. Dordrecht, the Netherlands: Martinus Nijhoff Publishers.
Brentano, F. (1874/1995). *Psychology from an empirical standpoint* (A. Rancurello, D. Terrell & L. McAlister, Trans.). London: Routledge.
Brierley, M. (1947). Notes on psycho-analysis and integrative living. *International Journal of Psychoanalysis*, *28*, 57–105.
Brokaw, B. F. (2008). Winter meets its death. *Psychoanalytic Inquiry*, *28*(5), 599–611.
Bromberg, P. (1996). Standing in the spaces: The multiplicity of self and the psychoanalytic relationship. *Contemporary Psychoanalysis*, *32*, 509–535.
Bromberg, P. (1998). *Standing in the spaces*. Hillsdale, NJ: The Analytic Press.
Browning, D. S. (1987). *Religious thought and the modern psychologies: A critical conversation in the theology of culture*. Philadelphia, PA: Fortress.
Brustein, W. (2003). *Roots of hate: Anti-Semitism in Europe before the Holocaust*. Cambridge, UK: Cambridge University Press.
Bucci, W. (1997). *Psychoanalysis and cognitive science*. New York: Guilford Press.

Caird, E. (1893). *The evolution of religion*. Glasgow: James Maclehose and Sons.
Cantor, J. (2008). Vision and virtue in psychoanalysis and Buddhism: Anatta and its implications for social responsibility. *Psychoanalytic Inquiry*, *28*, 532–540.
Capelle, E. (1998). Clara Thompson as culturalist. *Psychoanalytic Review*, *85*, 75–93.
Capps, W. (1996). Erikson's contribution toward understanding religion. *Psychoanalysis and Contemporary Thought*, *19*, 225–236.
Carter, J. (1994). Psychopathology, sin, and the *DSM*: Convergence and divergence. *Journal of Psychology and Theology*, *22*(4), 277–285.
Carter, J., & Narramore, B. (1979). *The integration of psychology and theology*. Grand Rapids, MI: Zondervan.
Carveth, D. (2008). *Erik Erikson and the American psyche: Ego, ethics, and evolution* by Daniel Burston. *Canadian Journal of Psychoanalysis*, *16*, 108–111.
Casonato, M. (1993). Ferenczi's preanalytic writings (1899–1908): A listing. *Contemporary Psychoanalysis*, *29*, 736–745.
Chesterton, G. K. (1908). *Orthodoxy*. San Francisco: Ignatius Press, 1995.
The Christianfeld Initiative. (2004). Conference document Moravian Heritage Network Second International Conference, November 6–10, 2004.
Clarke, W. K. & Harris, C. (1932). *Liturgy and Worship: A companion to the prayer books of the Anglican Communion*. London: Society for Promoting Christian Knowledge. Rietzig. *Die Bebelirung des Paulus*.
Coles, R. (1970). *Erik H. Erikson: The growth of his work*. Boston: Little, Brown & Co.
Congdon, L. (1983). *The young Lukács*. Chapel Hill, NC: University of North Carolina Press.
Congdon, L. (1991). *Exile and social thought: Hungarian intellectuals in Germany and Austria 1919–1933*. Princeton, NJ: Princeton University Press.
Congdon, L. (2001). *Seeing red: Hungarian intellectuals in exile and the challenge of Communism*. DeKalb, IL: Northern Illinois University Press.
Congdon, L. (2008). For neoclassical tragedy: Gyorgy Lukács drama book. *Studies in East European Thought*, *60*, 45–54.
Cooper, S. (2000). *Objects of hope: Exploring possibility and limit in psychoanalysis*. Hillsdale, NJ: The Analytic Press.
Cooper-White, P. (2008). Interrogating integration, dissenting dis-integration: Multiplicity as a positive metaphor in therapy and theology. *Pastoral Psychology*, *57*, 3–15.
Costello, J. E. (2002). *John Macmurray: A biography*. Edinburgh, UK: Floris Books.
Crichton-Miller, H. (1922). *The new psychology and the teacher*. New York: Thomas Seltzer.
Crichton-Miller, H. (1923). *The new psychology and the parent*. New York: Thomas Seltzer.
Crichton-Miller, H. (1924). *The new psychology and the preacher*. London: Jarrolds.
Dale, G. (2009). Karl Polanyi in Budapest: On his political and intellectual formation. *Archives of European Sociology*, *50*(1), 97–130.
Davies, J. (1998). Repression and dissociation—Freud and Janet: Fairbairn's new model of unconscious process. In N. Skolnick and D. Scharff (Eds.), *Fairbairn, then and now* (pp. 53–69). Hillsdale, NJ: The Analytic Press.
Davies, J. M., & Frawley, M. G. (2004). *Treating the adult survivor of childhood sexual abuse: A psychoanalytic perspective*. New York: Basic Books.

Decety, J., & Chaminade, T. (2003). When the self represents the other: A new cognitive neuroscience view on psychological identification. *Consciousness and Cognition, 12*, 577–596.

De Forest, I. (1942). The leaven of love: A development of the psychoanalytic theory and technique of Sándor Ferenczi. *International Journal of Psychoanalysis, 23*, 120–139.

De Forest, I. (1954). *The leaven of love*. New York: Harper.

Demeter, T. (2008). The sociological tradition of Hungarian philosophy. *Studies in East European Thought, 60*, 1–16.

Deri, S. (1990). Great representatives of Hungarian psychiatry: Balint, Ferenczi, Hermann, and Szondi. *Psychoanalytic Review, 77*, 491–501.

Derrida, J. (1992). *Given time, I: Counterfeit money*. Chicago: University of Chicago Press.

Dicks, H. V. (1970). *50 years of the Tavistock Clinic*. London: Routledge & Kegan Paul.

Dobbs, T. (2005). *Faith, theology, and psychoanalysis: The life and thought of Harry S. Guntrip*. Eugene, OR: Pickwick Publications.

Dubose, T. (2000). Lordship, bondage, and the formation of *homo religiosus*. *Journal of Religion and Health, 39*(3), 217–226.

Dueck, A., & Goodman, D. (2007). Substitution and the trace of the other: Levinasian implications for psychotherapy. *Pastoral Psychology, 55*, 601–617.

Eckardt, M. H. (1984). Karen Horney: Her life and contribution. *The American Journal of Psychoanalysis, 44*(3), 236–241.

Editor. (1953). Karen Horney. *Pastoral Psychology, 4*(34), 8.

Edwards, J. (1852). *Charity and its fruits*. Edinburgh, UK: Banner of Truth Trust.

Eigen, M. (1981). The area of faith in Winnicott, Lacan and Bion. *International Journal of Psychoanalysis, 62*, 413–433.

Eigen, M. (1998). *The psychoanalytic mystic*. Binghamton, NY: ESF Publishers.

Elbrond-Bek, B. (1996). Kierkegaard in America: An interview with Howard and Edna Hong. *Scandinavian Studies, 683*, 76–97.

Ellenberger, H. (1970). *The discovery of the unconscious*. New York: Basic Books.

Ellens, J. H. (2007). *Radical grace: How belief in a benevolent god benefits our health*. Westport, CT: Praeger.

Ellens, J. H. (Ed.). (2009). *The healing power of spirituality: How faith helps humans thrive*. Santa Barbara, CA: Praeger Press.

Eller, V. (1968). *Kierkegaard and radical discipleship*. Princeton, NJ: Princeton University Press.

Eller, V. (1968). *Kierkegaard and radical discipleship: A new perspective*. Available from http://www.hccentral.com/eller2/part6f.html

Enckell, M. (2001). *The soul that wouldn't shrink: Essays on Jewish topics*. Helsinki: Söderströms.

Epstein, M. (1995). Thoughts without a thinker: Buddhism and psychoanalysis. *Psychoanalytic Review, 82*, 391–406.

Erikson, E. (1950). *Childhood and society*. New York: Norton.

Erikson, E. (1958). *Young man Luther: A study in psychoanalysis and history*. New York: Norton.

Erikson, E. (1969). *Gandhi's truth: On the origins of militant nonviolence*. New York: W. W. Norton.

Erikson, E. (1996). The Galilean sayings and the sense of "I." *Psychoanalysis and Contemporary Thought, 19*, 291–337.

Fairbairn, W. R. D. (1952). *Psychoanalytic studies of the personality.* London: Routledge.

Ferenczi, S. (1901). Love in the sciences. *Gyogyaszat, 41*(12), 190–192.

Ferenczi, S. (1908). Letter from Sándor Ferenczi to Sigmund Freud, July 17, 1908. *The correspondence of Sigmund Freud and Sándor Ferenczi: Volume 1, 1908–1914* (p. 16). Cambridge, MA: Harvard University Press.

Ferenczi, S. (1909). Letter from Sándor Ferenczi to Sigmund Freud, May 5, 1909. *The correspondence of Sigmund Freud and Sándor Ferenczi: Volume 1, 1908–1914* (pp. 60–62). Cambridge, MA: Harvard University Press.

Ferenczi, S. (1910a). Letter from Sándor Ferenczi to Sigmund Freud, February 16, 1910. *The correspondence of Sigmund Freud and Sándor Ferenczi: Volume 1, 1908–1914* (pp. 140–143). Cambridge, MA: Harvard University Press.

Ferenczi, S. (1910b). Letter from Sándor Ferenczi to Sigmund Freud, December 2, 1910. *The correspondence of Sigmund Freud and Sándor Ferenczi: Volume 1, 1908–1914* (pp. 236–239). Cambridge, MA: Harvard University Press.

Ferenczi, S. (1913). Laughter. In *Final contributions to the problems and methods of psycho-analysis.* London: Karnac, 1955.

Ferenczi, S. (1914a). Letter from Sándor Ferenczi to Sigmund Freud, November 22, 1914. *The correspondence of Sigmund Freud and Sándor Ferenczi: Volume 2, 1914–1919* (pp. 28–29). Cambridge, MA: Harvard University Press.

Ferenczi, S. (1914b). Letter from Sándor Ferenczi to Sigmund Freud, November 30, 1914. *The correspondence of Sigmund Freud and Sándor Ferenczi: Volume 2, 1914–1919* (pp. 31–33). Cambridge, MA: Harvard University Press.

Ferenczi, S. (1915). Letter from Sándor Ferenczi to Sigmund Freud, July 24, 1915. *The correspondence of Sigmund Freud and Sándor Ferenczi: Volume 2, 1914–1919* (pp. 70–72). Cambridge, MA: Harvard University Press.

Ferenczi, S. (1917). Letter from Sándor Ferenczi to Sigmund Freud, April 30, 1917. *The correspondence of Sigmund Freud and Sándor Ferenczi: Volume 2, 1914–1919* (pp. 199–200). Cambridge, MA: Harvard University Press.

Ferenczi, S. (1926). The problem of acceptance of unpleasant ideas: Advances in knowledge of the sense of reality. *Int. Jour. of Psycho-Anal.*, 7: 312–323.

Ferenczi, S. (1929). Letter from Sándor Ferenczi to Sigmund Freud, December 30, 1929. *The correspondence of Sigmund Freud and Sándor Ferenczi: Volume 3, 1920–1933* (p. 377). Cambridge, MA: Harvard University Press.

Ferenczi, S. (1931). Child-analysis in the analysis of adults. *International Journal of Psychoanalysis, 12*, 468–482.

Ferenczi, S. (1933). Thalassa: A theory of genitality (I. de Forest, Trans.). *Psychoanalytic Quarterly*, 2, 361–364.

Ferenczi, S. (1949). Confusion of the tongues between the adults and the child. *International Journal of Psychoanalysis, 30*, 225–230.

Ferenczi, S. (1952a). *Collected papers: First contributions to psychoanalysis.* New York: Brunner/Mazel.

Ferenczi, S. (1952b). *Further contributions to the theory and technique of psycho-analysis.* New York: Basic Books.

Ferenczi, S. (1955). *Final contributions to the problems and methods of psychoanalysis*. London: Karnac.

Ferenczi, S. (1985). *The clinical diary of Sándor Ferenczi* (J. Dupont, Ed., M. Jackson, Trans.). Cambridge, MA: Harvard University Press.

Ferenczi, S. (1993). My friendship with Miksa Schachter. *British Journal of Psychotherapy*, 9(4), 430–433.

Foakes-Jackson, F. J. (1927). *Peter: Prince of the apostles: A study in the history and tradition of Christianity*. London: Hodder & Stoughton, 1927.

Foakes-Jackson, F. J. (1927). *The life of Saint Paul: The man and the apostle*. London: Jonathan Cape.

Fogel, G. (1991). Transcending the limits of revisionism and classicism. In G. Fogel (Ed.), *The work of Hans Loewald* (pp. 153–190). Northvale, NJ: Jason Aronson.

Fonagy, P. (2008). Being envious of envy and gratitude. In P. Roth & A. Lemma (Eds.), *Envy and gratitude revisited* (pp. 201–210). London: Karnac.

Fonagy, P., & Target, M. (1998). Mentalization and the changing aims of child psychoanalysis. *Psychoanalytic Dialogues*, *8*, 87–114.

Fonagy, P., Target, M., Gergely, G., & Jurist, E. (2002). *Affect regulation, mentalization, and the development of the self*. New York: Other Press.

Frank, T. (2007). *The social construction of Hungarian genius*. Princeton, NJ: The Witherspoon Institute.

Freud, S. (1897). Abstracts of the scientific writings of Dr. Sigmund Freud, 1877–1897. In J. Strachey (Ed. & Trans.), *The standard edition of the complete psychological works of Sigmund Freud* (Vol. 3, pp. 223–257). London: Hogarth Press.

Freud, S. (1910a). A special type of choice of object made by men (Contributions to the Psychology of love). In J. Strachey (Ed. & Trans.), *The standard edition of the complete psychological works of Sigmund Freud* (Vol. 11, pp. 163–176). London: Hogarth Press.

Freud, S. (1910b). Letter from Sigmund Freud to Oskar Pfister, June 5, 1910. *The International Psycho-Analytical Library*, *59*, 38–40.

Freud, S. (1914a). Letter from Sigmund Freud to Sándor Ferenczi, November 25, 1914. *The correspondence of Sigmund Freud and Sándor Ferenczi: Volume 2, 1914–1919* (pp. 29–31). Cambridge, MA: Harvard University Press.

Freud, S. (1914b). Letter from Sigmund Freud to Sándor Ferenczi, December 2, 1914. *The correspondence of Sigmund Freud and Sándor Ferenczi: Volume 2, 1914–1919* (pp. 33–34). Cambridge, MA: Harvard University Press.

Freud, S. (1926). Letter from Sigmund Freud to Ernest Jones, September 27, 1926. *The complete correspondence of Sigmund Freud and Ernest Jones, 1908–1939* (p. 606). Cambridge, MA: Harvard University Press.

Freud, S. (1927). *The future of an illusion*. In J. Strachey (Ed. & Trans.), *The standard edition of the complete psychological works of Sigmund Freud* (Vol. 21, pp. 3–56). London: Hogarth Press.

Freud, S. (1931). Female sexuality. In J. Strachey (Ed. & Trans.), *The standard edition of the complete psychological works of Sigmund Freud* (Vol. 21, pp. 223–243). London: Hogarth Press.

Freud, S., & Silberstein, E. (1990). *The letters of Sigmund Freud to Eduard Silberstein 1871–1888* (W. Boehlich, Ed., & A. Pomerans, Trans.). Cambridge, MA: Harvard University Press.
Friedman, L. (1999). *Identity's architect: A biography of Erik H. Erikson*. London: Free Association Books.
Friedman, M. (1955). *Martin Buber: The life of dialogue*. Chicago, IL: University of Chicago Press.
Fromm, E. (1966). *You shall be as gods*. New York: Holt, Rinehart, and Winston.
Gaal, B. (2007). Calvinist features on the spiritual face of the Hungarians. Unpublished article.
Gabbard, G. O. (2000). On gratitude and gratification. *Journal of the American Psychoanalytic Association*, *48*, 697–716.
Gadamer, H. (1989). *Truth and method* (2nd ed.). New York: Crossroad.
Gallese, V. (2009). Mirror neurons, embodied simulation, and the neural basis of social identification. *Psychoanalytic Dialogues*, *19*, 519–536.
Gay, P. (1987). *A Godless Jew: Freud, atheism, and the making of psychoanalysis*. New Haven, CT: Yale University Press.
Gay, P. (1988). *Freud: A life for our time*. New York: W. W. Norton & Co.
Gedo, J. (1972). Caviare to the general. *American Imago*, *29*, 293–317.
Gelwick, R. (2005). Notes toward understanding the Hungarian roots of Polanyi's heuristic philosophy of religion. *Tradition and Discovery: The Polanyi Society Periodical*, *32*(3), 24–34.
Ghent, E. (1990). Masochism, submission, surrender: Masochism as a perversion of surrender. *Contemporary Psychoanalysis*, *26*, 108–136.
Gibbs, P. (2007). The primacy of psychoanalytic intervention in recovery from the psychoses and schizophrenias. *Journal of the American Academy of Psychoanalysis and Dynamic Psychiatry*, *35*(2), 287–312.
Ginot, E. (2009). The empathic power of enactments: The link between neuropsychological processes and an expanded definition of empathy. *Psychoanalytic Psychology*, *26*, 290–309.
Goldberg, C. (2003). A personal and professional reminiscence of Heinz Kohut. *Progress in Self Psychology*, *19*, 347–358.
Goldman, D. (1993). *In search of the real: The origins and originality of D. W. Winnicott*. Northvale, NJ: Aronson.
Grand, S. (2000). *The reproduction of evil*. New York: Routledge.
Green, A. (1974). Surface analysis, deep analysis: The role of the preconscious in psychoanalytical technique. *International Review of Psychoanalysis*, *1*, 415–423.
Green, A. (1983). The dead mother. In *On private madness*. London: Hogarth Press, 1986, pp. 142–173.
Green, A. (2004). Thirdness and psychoanalytic concepts. *Psychoanalytic Quarterly*, *73*, 99–135.
Green, M. (Ed.). (1964). *Interpersonal psychoanalysis: The selected papers of Clara M. Thompson*. New York: Basic Books Inc.
Greenberg, I. (2004). *For the sake of Heaven and Earth: The new encounter between Judaism and Christianity*. Philadelphia, PA: The Jewish Publication Society.
Greenberg, J., & Mitchell, S. (1983). *Object relations in psychoanalytic theory*. Cambridge, MA: Harvard University Press.

Grenz, S. (2001). *The social God and the relational self: A Trinitarian theology of the Imago Dei.* London: Westminster John Knox Press.

Groddeck, G. (1926). Repression and release. In Groddeck, 1949, 214–224.

Groddeck, G. (1949). *Exploring the unconscious.* (V. M. E. Collins, Trans.) London: Vision Press, 1989.

Groddeck, G. (1977). *The meaning of illness: Selected psychoanalytic writings.* The International Psycho-Analytical Library. London: The Hogarth Press.

Grossman, W. & Stewart, W. (1976). Penis-envy: From childhood wish to developmental metaphor. *Journal of the American Psychoanalytic Association, 24,* 193–212.

Grotstein, J. (1981). Wilfred R. Bion—The man, the psychoanalyst, the mystic: A perspective on his life and work. *Journal of Contemporary Psychotherapy, 17,* 501–536.

Grotstein, J. (1993). Towards the concept of the transcendent position: Reflections on some of the "unborn" in Bion's *Cogitations. Journal of Melanie Klein and Object Relations, 11,* 55–73.

Grotstein, J. (1997). Bion's "Transformation in 'O'" and the concept of the "Transcendent Position." Unpublished paper, digital edition. http://membres.multimani.frarrigo/bion/papers/grots.htm

Gunther, M., & Trosman, H. (1974). Freud as expert witness: Wagner-Jauregg and the problem of the war neuroses. *Annual of Psychoanalysis, 2,* 3–23.

Gunton, C. (1997). The Trinity, natural theology, and a theology of nature. In K. Vanhoozer (Ed.), *The Trinity in a pluralistic age* (pp. 88–103). Grand Rapids, MI: Wm. B. Eerdmans.

Guntrip, H. (1968). *Schizoid phenomena, object relations and the self.* New York: International Universities Press.

Guthrie, E. (1952). *The psychology of learning.* New York: Harper and Row.

Hadfield, J. A. (1935). Preface. In I. Suttie, *The origins of love and hate* (pp. xlvi–xlviii). London: Free Association Books, 1988.

Hale, N. G. (1971). *James Jackson Putnam and psychoanalysis: Letters between Putnam and Sigmund Freud, Ernest Jones, William James, Sándor Ferenczi, and Morton Prince, 1877–1917.* Cambridge, MA: Harvard University Press.

Haley, J. (1976). *Problem-solving therapy.* San Francisco, CA: Jossey-Bass.

Hall, T., & Brokaw, B. (1995). The relationship of spiritual maturity to level of object relations development and God image. *Pastoral Psychology, 43*(6), 373–391.

Hamburg, S. R. (1985). Leaving the consulting room to provoke enactment in marital therapy. *Journal of Marital and Family Therapy, 11*(2), 187–191.

Hanko, H., Hoeksema, H., & Van Baren, G. (1976). *The five points of Calvinism.* Grandville, MI: Reformed Free Publishing.

Hannay, A. (2001). *Kierkegaard: A biography.* Cambridge, UK: Cambridge University Press.

Harris, W. T. (1895). *Hegel's logic: A book on the genesis of the categories of the mind: A critical exposition.* Chicago: S. C. Griggs and Co.

Hartman, D. (1997). *A living covenant: The innovative spirit in traditional Judaism.* Woodstock, VT: Jewish Lights Publishing.

Hauerwas, S. (2001). *The Hauerwas reader* (J. Berkman & M. Cartwright, Eds.). Durham, NC: Duke University Press.

Haynal, A. (1988). *The technique at issue: Controversies in psychoanalysis from Freud and Ferenczi to Michael Balint* (E. Holder, Trans.). London: Karnac.
Haynal, A. (1992). Introduction. In E. Brabant, E. Falzeder, & E. Giampieri-Deutsch (Eds.), *The correspondence of Sigmund Freud and Sándor Ferenczi: Volume 1, 1908–1914* (pp. xvii–xxxv). Cambridge, MA: Harvard University Press.
Haynal, A. (1997). For a metapsychology of the psychoanalyst: Sándor Ferenczi's quest. *Psychoanalytic Inquiry*, *17*, 437–458.
Haynal, A. (2002). *Disappearing and reviving: Sándor Ferenczi in the history of psychoanalysis*. London: Karnac.
Hazell, J. (1994). *Personal relations therapy: The collected papers of H. J. S. Guntrip*. Northvale, NJ: Jason Aronson.
Hebb, D. (1949). *The organization of behavior*. New York: Wiley.
Hegel, G. (1807/1977). *Phenomenology of spirit* (A. V. Miller, Trans.). London: Oxford University Press.
Hegel, W. F. (1896). Lectures *on the philosophy of religion, together with a work on the proofs of the Existence of God, by Georg Wilhelm Friedrich Hegel* (E. B. Speirs and J. Burdon Sanderson, Trans.). Routledge & Kegan Paul. (Original work published 1895)
Hegel, G. (2006). *Lectures on the philosophy of religion: The lectures of 1827* (P. Hodgson, Ed., R. Brown, P. Hodgson, & J. Stewart, Trans.). Oxford: Oxford University Press.
Heilprin, M. (1861, 11 January). Editorial. *New York Tribune*.
Heschel, A. J. (1959). *Between God and man*. New York: Free Press.
Heschel, S. (1998). *Abraham Geiger and the Jewish Jesus*. Chicago: University of Chicago Press.
Heschel, S. (2006, 18 December). Nativity of the Jews: We came into being with a collective responsibility. Together, we work and wait. *Newsweek*, p. 59.
Himmelfarb, G. (2001). The idea of compassion: The British vs. the French Enlightenment. *The Public Interest*, *145*, 1–12.
Hirsch, I. (1987). Varying modes of analytic participation. *Journal of the American Academy of Psychoanalysis*, *15*, 205–222.
Hitchcock, S. (2005). *Karen Horney, pioneer of feminine psychology*. Philadelphia, PA: Chelsea House Publishers.
Hodgson, P. (2005). *Hegel and Christian theology: A reading of the lectures on the philosophy of religion*. New York: Oxford University Press.
Hoffer, P. (1995). Letter. *International Journal of Psychoanalysis*, *76*, 1046–1047.
Hoffer, W. (1958). Oskar Pfister: 1873–1956. *International Journal of Psychoanalysis*, *39*, 616–617.
Hoffman, I. (1983). The patient as interpreter of the analyst's experience. *Contemporary Psychoanalysis*, *19*, 389–422.
Hoffman, I. (1994). Dialectical thinking and therapeutic action in the psychoanalytic process. *Psychoanalytic Quarterly*, *63*, 187–218.
Hoffman, I. (1998). *Ritual and spontaneity in the psychoanalytic process: A dialectical-constructivist view*. Hillsdale, NJ: The Analytic Press.
Hoffman, L. (2010). Suffering, glory and outcomes in psychotherapy. *Journal of Psychology and Christianity*, *29*, 130–140.
Hoffman, M. (1989). *Enactment in the individual psychotherapies*. Dissertation, Union Institute.

Hoffman, M. (2004). From enemy combatant to strange bedfellow: The role of religious narratives in the work of W. R. D. Fairbairn and D. W. Winnicott. *Psychoanalytic Dialogues*, *14*(6), 769–804.
Hoffman, M. (2006). "Other"-less, "other"-more, "other"-like: Response to discussions. *Psychoanalytic Perspectives*, *4*(1), 83–86.
Hoffman, M. (2008). Fairbairn and Winnicott on my mind: Counterpoints, tension, and oscillations in the clinical setting. *Contemporary Psychoanalysis*, *44*(3), 454–475.
Honneth, A. (1995). *The struggle for recognition*. Cambridge, MA: MIT Press.
Horney, K. (1980). *The adolescent diaries of Karen Horney*. New York: Basic Books.
Horney, K. (1987). *Karen Horney: Final lectures* (D. Ingram, Ed.). New York: Norton.
Howell, E. (2005). *The dissociative mind*. Hillsdale, NJ: The Analytic Press.
Hume, D. (1739). *A treatise of human nature*. Oxford, UK: Clarendon Press.
Jablonka, E., & Lamb, M. J. (2005). *Evolution in four dimensions: Genetic, epigenetic, behavioral, and symbolic variation in the history of life*. Cambridge, MA: MIT Press.
Jablonka, E., & Raz, G. (2009). Transgenerational epigenetic inheritance: Prevalence, mechanisms, and implications for the study of heredity and evolution. *The Quarterly Review of Biology*, *84*(2), 131–176.
Jacobs, J., & Capps, D. (1997). *Religion, society, and psychoanalysis: Readings in contemporary theory*. Boulder, CO: Westview Press.
Jacobs, T. (1986). On countertransference enactments. *Journal of the American Psychoanalytic Association*, *34*, 289–307.
James, M. R. (1921). *The lost apocrypha of the Old Testament: Their titles and fragments*. London: Society for Promoting Christian Knowledge.
James, M. (1979). *The Piggle: An account of the psycho-analytic treatment of a little girl, by D. W. Winnicott*. London: The Hogarth Press, 1978.
Jones, E. (1955). *The life and work of Sigmund Freud*. London: Hogarth Press.
Jones, J. (1991). *Contemporary psychoanalysis and religion: Transference and transcendence*. New Haven, CT: Yale University Press.
Kahr, B. (1996). *D. W. Winnicott: A biographical portrait*. London: Karnac.
Kant, I. (1781/1999). *Critique of pure reason*. Cambridge, UK: Cambridge University Press.
Kapusi K. (2007). *Konyv es Iszap: Ferenczi Sándor gyermekkoráról* (R. Difiore, Trans.). *Muut*.
Kearney, R. (2004). *On Paul Ricoeur: The owl of Minerva*. Burlington, VT: Ashgate.
Kestenberg, J. S. (1976). Regression and reintegration in pregnancy. *Journal of the American Psychoanalytic Association*, 24(Suppl.), 213–250.
Keve, T. (2000). *Triad: The physicists, the analysts, the Kabbalists*. London: Rosenberger & Krausz.
Kierkegaard, S. (1847). *Works of love* (H. Hong & E. Hong, Trans.). New York: Harper Perennial, 1962.
Kierkegaard, S. (1848). *Practice in Christianity* (H. Hong & E. Hong, Trans.). Princeton, NJ: Princeton University Press, 1991.
Kirschner, S. (1996). *The religious and romantic origins of psychoanalysis*. Cambridge, UK: Cambridge University Press.
Kitchin, D., Lewis, J. & Polanyi, K. (Eds.). (1936). *Christianity and the social revolution*. New York: Scribners.

Klein, M. (1957/1975). *Envy and gratitude and other works 1946–1963* (M. Khan, Ed.). London: Hogarth Press.

Kohut, H. (2000). *The analysis of the self: A systematic approach to the psychoanalytic treatment of narcissistic personality disorders*. Madison, CT: International Universities Press.

Kovacs, A. (2006). *The history of the Free Church of Scotland's mission to the Jews in Budapest and its impact on the Reformed Church of Hungary, 1841–1914*. Berlin: Peter Lang.

Kraemer, S. B. (1996). Betwixt the dark and the daylight of maternal subjectivity: Meditations on the threshold. *Psychoanalytic Dialogues*, 6, 765–791.

Kung, H. (1987). *The incarnation of God*. Edinburgh: T. & T. Clark Ltd.

La Cugna, C. (1991). *God for us: The Trinity and Christian life*. San Francisco, CA: Harper.

Lakasing, E. (2005). Michael Balint: An outstanding medical life. *British Journal of General Practice*, *55*(518), 724–725.

Lake, F. (1966). *Clinical theology: A theological and psychiatric basis to clinical pastoral care*. London: Darton, Longman & Todd.

LaMothe, R. (2008). Empire stories: Imperious objects and the necessity of fools. *Psychoanalytic Dialogues*, *18*, 562–585.

Lane, B. (2001). Spirituality as the performance of desire: Calvin on the world as a theatre of God's glory. *Spiritus*, *1*, 1–30.

Lecas, J. C. (2006). Behaviourism and the mechanization of the mind. *C. R. Biologies*, *329*, 386–397.

Lendvai, F. (1997). Religion in Georg Lukács world view. *Trames*, *1*(51), 159–166.

Levenson, E. (1981). Facts or fantasies: On the nature of psychoanalytic data. *Contemporary Psychoanalysis*, *17*, 486–500.

Levi, P. (1993). *Survival in Auschwitz* (S. Woolf, Trans.). New York: Macmillan.

Lichtenberg, J., Lachmann, F., & Fosshage, J. (1992). *Self and motivational systems: Toward a theory of psychoanalytic technique*. Hillsdale, NJ: The Analytic Press.

Lipton, B. (1998). Nature, nurture, and the power of love. *Journal of Prenatal and Perinatal Psychology and Health*, *13*, 3–10.

Loewald, H. W. (1960). On the therapeutic action of psycho-analysis. *International Journal of Psychoanalysis*, *41*, 16–33.

Loewald, H. W. (1962). Internalization, separation, mourning, and the superego. *Psychoanalytic Quarterly*, *31*, 483–504.

Loewald, H. W. (1972). The experience of time. *Psychoanalytic Study of the Child*, *27*, 401–410.

Loewald, H. W. (1988). *Sublimation*. New Haven, CT: Yale University Press.

Lowery, M. (2006). The Trinitarian nature of the transmodern person. In P. Vitz & S. Felch (Eds.), *The self: Beyond the postmodern crisis* (pp. 269–286). Wilmington, DE: ISI Books.

Lukács, G. (1910a). Az utak elváltak. *Nyugat*, *3*, 190–193.

Lukács, G. (1910b). Søren Kierkegaard es Regine Olsen. *Nyugat*, *6*, 378–387.

Lukács, G. (2010). The foundering of form against life: Soren Kierkegaard and Regine Olsen. In *Soul and Form* (pp. 44–58). New York: Columbia University Press.

MacIntyre, A. (1984). *After virtue*. Notre Dame, IN: University of Notre Dame Press.

MacMurray, J. (1936). *The structure of religious experience*. London: Faber.

Macmurray, J. (1961). *Persons in relation.* Atlantic Highlands, NJ: Humanities Press.
Magid, B. (2000). The couch and the cushion: Integrating Zen and psychoanalysis. *Journal of the American Academy of Psychoanalysis, 28*, 513–526.
Makkai, A. (Ed.). (1996). *In quest of the miracle stag: The poetry of Hungary.* Chicago, IL: Atlantis-Centaur, Inc.
Mangis, M. (2007). Kicking the patient: Immediacy in the consulting room. *Journal of Psychology and Theology, 35*(1), 43–51.
Marty, M. (1992). Grace. In D. Musser & J. Price (Eds.), *A new handbook of Christian theologians* (pp. 209–211). Nashville, TN: Abingdon Press.
Mauss, M. (1989). *The gift: The form and reason for exchange in archaic societies.* New York: Norton.
McDargh, J. (1983). *Psychoanalytic object relations theory and the study of religion: On faith and the imaging of God.* Washington, DC: University Press of America.
McLaughlin, J. (1987). The play of transference: Some reflections on enactment in the psychoanalytic situation. *Journal of the American Psychoanalytic Association, 35*, 557–562.
McWilliams, N. (1994). *Psychoanalytic diagnosis: Understanding personality structure in the clinical process.* New York: Guilford Press.
McWilliams, N. (1999). *Psychoanalytic case formulation.* New York: Guilford Press.
McWilliams, N. (2004). *Psychoanalytic psychotherapy: A practitioner's guide.* New York: Guilford Press.
McWilliams, N. (2006). *Psychoanalytic diagnostic manual.* New York: Guilford Press.
McWilliams, N., & Lependorf, S. (1990). Narcissistic pathology of everyday life: The denial of remorse and gratitude. *Contemporary Psychoanalysis, 26*, 430–451.
Meeter, H. H. (1930). *The fundamental principle of Calvinism.* Grand Rapids, MI: Wm B. Eerdmans Publishing Co.
Meissner, W. W. (1984). *Psychoanalysis and religious experience.* New Haven, CT: Yale University Press.
Meissner, W. W. (2009). Toward a neuropsychological reconstruction of projective identification. *Journal of the American Psychoanalytic Association, 57*, 95–129.
Meltzer, D. (1981). Memorial meeting for Dr. Wilfred Bion. *Int. R. Psycho-Anal., 8*, 3–14.
Mendiata, E. (2005). Introduction. Religion as critique. In E. Mendiata (Ed.), *The Frankfurt School on religion.* (pp. 11–17). New York: Routledge.
Meng, H., & Freud, E. (1963). *Psycho-analysis and faith: The letters of Sigmund Freud & Oskar Pfister.* London: Hogarth Press.
Merriam-Webster's dictionary of English usage. (1994). Springfield, MA: Merriam-Webster.
Merriam-Webster's third new international dictionary. (2002). Springfield, MA: Merriam-Webster.
Meserve, H. (1993). Anton Boisen and the cure of souls. *Journal of Religion and Health, 32*(1), 3–8.
Micale, M. (1993). *Beyond the unconscious: Essays of Henri F. Ellenberger in the history of psychiatry.* Princeton, NJ: Princeton University Press.
Miletic, M. (2002). The introduction of a feminine psychology to psychoanalysis: Karen Horney's legacy. *Contemporary Psychoanalysis, 38*, 287–299.

Miller, G. (2008). Scottish psychoanalysis: A rational religion. *Journal of the History of the Behavioral Sciences*, *44*(1), 38–58.
Minuchin, S. (1974). *Families and family therapy*. Cambridge, MA: Harvard University Press.
Mitchell, S. (1988). *Relational concepts in psychoanalysis: An integration*. Cambridge, MA: Harvard University Press.
Mitchell, S. (1995). *Hope and dread in psychoanalysis*. New York: Basic Books.
Mitchell, S. (1997). *Influence and autonomy in psychoanalysis*. Hillsdale, NJ: The Analytic Press.
Molnár, A. (1997). The Protestant ethic in Hungary. *Religion*, *27*, 151–164.
Moltmann, J. (1977). *The Church in the power of the spirit*. Minneapolis, MN: Fortress Press.
Moltmann, J. (1981). *The Trinity and the kingdom of God*. London: SCM Press.
Moltmann, J. (1985). *God in creation*. Minneapolis, MN: Fortress Press.
Moltmann, J. (1990). *The way of Jesus Christ*. Minneapolis, MN: Fortress Press.
Moltmann, J. (1993). *Theology of hope*. Minneapolis, MN: Fortress Press.
Mooney, E. (2010). Erik Erikson: Artist of moral-religious development. In J. Stewart (Ed.), *Kierkegaard and the social sciences*. Surrey, UK: Ashgate.
Moreau-Ricaud, M. (1996). The founding of the Budapest School. In P. Rudnytsky, A. Bókay, & P. Giampieri-Deutsch, Eds. & P. Taylor, Trans.). *Ferenczi's turn in psychoanalysis* (pp. 41–59). New York: New York University Press.
Moreau-Ricaud, M. (2002). Michael Balint: An introduction. *American Journal of Psychoanalysis*, *62*(1), 17–24.
Moreno, J. L. (1953). *Who shall survive?* Beacon, NY: Beacon House.
Nicholas, M. W. (1984). *Change in the context of group therapy*. New York: Brunner/Mazel.
Nordau, M. (1903). Muskeljudentum [Jewry of muscle]. In P. Mendes-Flohr & J. Reinharz (Trans.), *The Jew in the modern world: A documentary history*. New York: Oxford University Press, 1980.
Ogden, T. H. (1986). *The matrix of the mind: Object relations and the psychoanalytic dialogue*. Northvale, NJ: Aronson.
Ogden, T. H. (1994). The analytic third: Working with intersubjective clinical facts. *The International Journal of Psychoanalysis, 75*, 3–19.
Oliver, K. (2001). *Witnessing: Beyond recognition*. Minneapolis, MN: University of Minnesota Press.
Olthuis, J. (2001). *The beautiful risk*. Grand Rapids, MI: Zondervan.
O'Neill, J. (Ed.). (1996). *Hegel's dialectic of desire and recognition*. Albany, NY: SUNY Press.
Oremland, J. (1985). Michelangelo's *ignudi*, hermaphrodism and creativity. *The Psychoanalytic Study of the Child*, *40*, 399–433.
Orfanos, S. (2006). Mythos and logos. *Psychoanalytic Dialogues*, *16*, 481–499.
Oxford English Dictionary (2nd ed.) (1989). Oxford, UK: Oxford University Press.
Paranjpe, A. C. (2000). Review of *Identity's architect: A biography of Erik H. Erikson*. *Canadian Psychology/Psychologie canadienne*, *41*, 288–289.
Paris, B. J. (1994). *Karen Horney: A psychoanalyst's search for self-understanding*. Binghamton, NY: Vail-Ballou Press.
Parker, S. (2008). Winnicott's object relations theory and the work of the Holy Spirit. *Journal of Psychology and Theology*, *36*(4), 285–293.

Parliamentary Archives, National Archives of Hungary (1867–1944). Act of 1867, November 25, 1867.

Parlow, S. (2008). Personal transformation in Karl Rahner's Christianity: Constructed by love. *Psychoanalytic Inquiry*, *28*, 570–579.

Peake, A. S. (1931). *The servant of Yahweh: Three lectures delivered at King's College, London, during 1926, together with the Rylands Lectures on Old Testament and New Testament subjects*. Manchester, England: Manchester University Press.

Perinbanayagam, R. (1985). *Signifying acts: Structure and meaning in everyday life*. Carbondale, IL: Southern Illinois University Press.

Perry, H. (1982). *Psychiatrist of America: The life of Harry Stack Sullivan*. Cambridge, MA: Belknap Press of Harvard University Press.

Petric, R. D. (1987). Group enactment procedures: Theory and application. *Journal for Specialists in Group Work*, *12*(1), 26–30.

Pfister, O. (1917). *The psychoanalytic method* (C. Payne, Trans.). New York: Moffat. (Original work published 1913).

Pfister, O. (1925). *Die Frommigkeit Des Grafen Ludwig Von Zinzendorf (Eine Psycho-Analytische Studie) von Dr. Oskar Pfister*. Leipzig: Franz Deuticke.

Phillips, A. (1988). *Winnicott*. Cambridge, MA: Harvard University Press.

Piaget, J. (1993). Jan Amos Comenius. *Prospects*, *23*(1/2), 173–196.

Piette, M. (1937). *John Wesley in the evolution of Protestantism*. New York: Sheed & Ward.

Pizer, B. (2003). When the crunch is a (k)not: A crimp in relational dialogue. *Psychoanalytic Dialogues*, *13*, 171–192.

Pizer, S. A. (1998). *Building bridges: The negotiation of paradox in psychoanalysis*. Hillsdale, NJ: Analytic Press.

Polanyi, K. (1919). A call to the youth of the Galileo Circle. In the Karl Polanyi Institute, Concordia University, Montreal. Box 1, Hungarian writings, 1919.

Porter, R. (2000). *The creation of the modern world*. New York: W. W. Norton.

Powell, S. (2001). *The Trinity in German thought*. Cambridge, UK: Cambridge University Press.

Pringle-Pattison, A. S. (1920). *The idea of God in the light of recent philosophy*. New York: Oxford University Press.

Putnam, J. (1951). *Addresses on psychoanalysis*. London: Hogarth Press.

Quinn, S. (1987). *A mind of her own*. New York: Summit Books.

Rachman, A. (1997a). *Sándor Ferenczi: The psychotherapist of tenderness and passion*. Northvale, NJ: Jason Aronson.

Rachman, A. (1997b). Sándor Ferenczi and the evolution of a self psychology framework in psychoanalysis. *Progress in Self Psychology*, *13*, 341–365.

Racker, H. (1988). Transference and countertransference. *The International Psycho-Analytical Library*, *73*, 1–196.

Rahner, K. (1967). *Man at play*. New York: Herder and Herder.

Reagan, C. (1996). *Paul Ricoeur: His life and his work*. Chicago, IL: Chicago University Press.

Rector, L. J. (2000). Developmental aspects of the twinship selfobject need and religious experience. *Progress in Self Psychology*, *16*, 257–275.

Reichel, V. G. (1911). *Zinzendorfs Frommigkeit im Lichte der Psychoanalys*. Tubingen: Mohr.

Reik, T. (1924). Some remarks on the study of resistances. *International Journal of Psychoanalysis*, *5*, 141–154.
Reik, T. (1930). Final phases of belief found in religion and in obsessional neurosis. *International Journal of Psychoanalysis*, *11*, 258–291.
Richards, G. (2000). Psychology and the churches in Britain 1919–39: Symptoms of conversion. *History of the Human Sciences*, *13*(57), 57–84.
Rickman, J. (1957). Need for belief in God (1938). *The International Psycho-Analytical Library*, *52*, 384–390.
Rickman, J. (2003). *No ordinary psychoanalyst: The exceptional contributions of John Rickman* (P. King, Ed.). London: Karnac.
Ricoeur, P. (1966). *Freedom and nature: The voluntary and the involuntary* (E. Kohak, Trans.). Evanston, IL: Northwestern University Press.
Ricoeur, P. (1967). *The symbolism of evil*. Boston: Beacon Press.
Ricoeur, P. (1970). *Freud and philosophy: An essay on interpretation*. New Haven, CT: Yale University Press.
Ricoeur, P. (1985). Evil: A challenge to philosophy and theology. *Journal of the American Academy of Religion*, *53*(3), 635–648.
Ricoeur, P. (1986). *Fallible man*. New York: Fordham University Press.
Ricoeur, P. (1995). *Figuring the sacred*. Minneapolis, MN: Fortress.
Ricoeur, P. (2004). *Memory, history, forgetting*. Chicago: University of Chicago Press.
Ricoeur, P. (2005). *The course of recognition*. Cambridge, MA: Harvard University Press.
Rieff, P. (1979). *Freud: The mind of the moralist*. Chicago: University of Chicago Press.
Rizzuto, A. (1979). *The birth of the living God*. Chicago: University of Chicago Press.
Rizzuto, A. (1998). *Why did Freud reject God? A psychodynamic interpretation*. New Haven, CT: Yale University Press.
Roazen, P. (1993). The illusion of a future. *Int. Jour. of Psycho-Anal*, *74*, 559–579.
Rodman, F. R. (2003). *Winnicott: Life and work*. Cambridge, MA: Perseus.
Roth, P., & Lemma, A. (Eds.). (2008). *Envy and gratitude revisited*. London: Karnac.
Rubens, R. (1998). Fairbairn's theory of depression. In N. Skolnick & D. Scharff (Eds.), *Fairbairn, then and now* (pp. 215–234). Hillsdale, NJ: The Analytic Press.
Rubens, R. (2000). Fairbairn's structural theory. In J. Grotstein & D. Rinsley (Eds.), *Fairbairn and the origins of object relations* (pp. 151–173). New York: Other Press.
Rubin, J. (1996). *Psychotherapy and Buddhism: Toward an integration*. New York: Plenum Press.
Rubins, J. (1978). *Karen Horney: Gentle rebel of psychoanalysis*. New York: Dial Press.
Rudnytsky, P. (2002). *Reading psychoanalysis*. Ithaca, NY: Cornell University Press.
Salberg, J. (2007). Hidden in plain sight: Freud's Jewish identity revisited. *Psychoanalytic Dialogues*, *17*(2), 197–217.
Samuels, A. (2001). *Politics on the couch: Citizenship and the internal life*. New York: Other Press.
Sander, L. (2002). Thinking differently: Principles of process in living systems and the specificity of being known. *Psychoanalytic Dialogues*, *12*, 11–42.
Satir, V. (1967). *Conjoint family therapy: A guide to theory and technique*. Palo Alto, California: Science and Behavior Books, Inc.

Sayers, J. (1991). *Mothers of psychoanalysis: Helene Deutsch, Karen Horney, Anna Freud, Melanie Klein*. New York: W. W. Norton.

Schacht, L. (1977). Introduction. In G. Groddeck, *The Meaning of Illness: Selected Psychoanalytic Writings Including His Correspondence With Sigmund Freud. The International Psycho-Analytical Library, 105*, 1–266. London: The Hogarth Press.

Schaffer, R. (1992). *Retelling a life: Narration and dialogue in psychoanalysis*. New York: Basic Books.

Scharff, D., & Birtles, E. F. (Eds.). (1994). *From instinct to self, vol. 1*. Northvale, NJ: Aronson.

Scharff, D., & Scharff, J. (1998). *Object relations individual therapy*. Northvale, NJ: Aronson.

Schecter, D. (1983). Notes on the development of creativity. *Contemporary Psychoanalysis, 19*, 193–199.

Schepeler, E. M. (1993). Jean Piaget's experiences on the couch: Some clues to a mystery. *International Journal of Psychoanalysis, 74*, 255–273.

Schore, A. (2003). *Affect regulation and the repair of the self*. New York: W. W. Norton.

Seeman, H., & Wiener, D. J. (1985). Comparing and using psychodrama with family therapy: Some cautions. *Journal of Group Psychotherapy, Psychodrama, and Sociometry, 37*(4), 143–156.

Seif, N. (1980). *Otto Rank: On human evil*. Unpublished dissertation. Yeshiva University, New York City.

Sekoff, J. (1999). The undead: Necromancy and the inner world. In G. Kohon (Ed.), *The dead mother: The work of Andre Green* (pp. 109-127). London: Routledge.

Shabad, P. (2001). *Despair and the return of hope: Echoes of mourning in psychotherapy*. Lanham, MD: Jason Aronson.

Shapiro, B. (1990). *Divine madness and the absurd paradox: Ibsen's Peer Gynt and the philosophy of Kierkegaard*. New York: Greenwood Press.

Shaw, D. (2003). On the therapeutic action of analytic love. *Contemporary Psychoanalysis, 39*, 251–278.

Silver, A. S. (1993). Countertransference, Ferenczi, and Washington, DC. *Journal of the American Academy of Psychoanalysis, 21*, 637–654.

Silver, A. S. (2003). The psychotherapy of schizophrenia: Its place in the modern world. *Journal of the American Academy of Psychoanalysis, 31*, 325–341.

Simmonds, J. (2006). The oceanic feeling and a sea change: Historical challenges to reductionist attitudes to religion and spirit from within psychoanalysis. *Psychoanalytic Psychology, 23*, 128–142.

Singh, D. (2008). Resurrection as surplus and possibility: Moltmann and Ricoeur. *Scottish Journal of Theology, 61*, 251–269.

Skelton, R. (1983). Jonathan Hanaghan: The founder of psychoanalysis in Ireland. *The Crane Bag, 7*(2), 183–190.

Skolnick, N. (1998). The good, the bad, and the ambivalent: Fairbairn's difficulty locating the good object in the endopsychic structure. In N. Skolnick & D. Scharff (Eds.), *Fairbairn, then and now* (pp. 137–159). Hillsdale, NJ: The Analytic Press.

Skolnick, N., & Scharff, D. (Eds.). (1998). *Fairbairn, then and now*. Hillsdale, NJ: The Analytic Press.

Slochower, J. (1996). *Holding and psychoanalysis: A relational perspective.* Hillsdale, NJ: The Analytic Press.

Smith, J. (1976). *Psychiatry and the humanities, volume I.* New Haven, CT: Yale University Press.

Smith, N. (1998a). The strength of "creative impulse" in the aftermath of trauma: Discussion of "I made a picture of my life—a life from the picture" by Pirkko Siltala (1998). *International Forum of Psychoanalysis*, 7, 159–162.

Smith, N. (1998b). "Orpha reviving": Toward an honorable recognition of Elizabeth Severn. *International Forum of Psychoanalysis*, 7, 241–246.

Smith, N. (2001). Angels in the architecture: Contemporary case of an orphic functioning. *Journal of American Academy of Psychoanalysis*, *29*, 575–583.

Smith, N. (2004). "To return, to eat, to tell the story": Primo Levi's lessons on living and dying in the aftermath of trauma. *International Forum of Psychoanalysis*, *13*, 66–70.

Sorenson, R. L. (2004). *Minding spirituality.* Hillsdale, NJ: The Analytic Press.

Speck, R. V. & Attneave, C. (1972). *Family networks.* New York: Pantheon.

Spero, M. H. (1996). Original sin, the symbolization of desire, and the development of the mind: A psychoanalytic gloss on the Garden of Eden. *Psychoanalysis and Contemporary Thought*, *19*, 499–562.

Stanton, M. (1991). *Sándor Ferenczi: Reconsidering active intervention.* Northvale, NJ: Jason Aronson.

Starr, K. (2008). *Repair of the soul: Metaphors of transformation in Jewish mysticism and psychoanalysis.* New York: Routledge.

Stern, Daniel. (1985). *The interpersonal world of the infant: A view from psychoanalysis and developmental psychology.* New York: Basic Books.

Stern, Donnel. (2003). *Unformulated experience: From dissociation to imagination in psychoanalysis.* Hillsdale, NJ: The Analytic Press.

Stern, Donnel. (2004). The eye sees itself: Dissociation, enactment, and the achievement of conflict. *Contemporary Psychoanalysis*, *40*, 197–237.

Stewart, H., Elder, A., & Gosling, R. (1996). *Michael Balint: Object relations pure and applied.* London: Routledge.

Stolorow, R., & Atwood, G. (1996). The intersubjective perspective. *Psychoanalytic Review*, *83*, 181–194.

Stolorow, R., Brandchaft, B., & Atwood, G. (1987). *Psychoanalytic treatment: An intersubjective approach.* Hillsdale, NJ: The Analytic Press.

St. Patrick. (9th century). St. Patrick's Breastplate. Book of Armagh.

Stratton, S. (2006). Self, attachment, and agency: Love and the Trinitarian concept of personhood. In P. Vitz & S. Felch (Eds.), *The self: Beyond the postmodern crisis* (pp. 247–268). Wilmington, DE: Intercollegiate Studies Institute.

Strawn, B. (2004). Restoring moral affections of heart: How does psychotherapy cure? *Journal of Psychology and Christianity*, *23*(2), 140–148.

Strenger, C. (1989). The classic and the romantic vision in psychoanalysis. *International Journal of Psychoanalysis*, *70*, 593–610.

Strozier, C. (2001). *Heinz Kohut: The making of a psychoanalyst.* New York: Other Press.

Sullivan, A. (2006). My problem with Christianism [Electronic version]. *Time.* Retrieved September 9, 2010, from http://www.time.com/time/magazine/article/0,9171,1191826,00.html.

Summers, F. (2003). The future as intrinsic to the psyche and psychoanalytic therapy. *Contemporary Psychoanalysis, 39*, 135–153.
Sutherland, J. D. (1971). Michael Bálint (1896–1970). *International Journal of Psychoanalysis, 52*, 331–333.
Sutherland, J. D. (1980). The British object relations theorists: Balint, Winnicott, Fairbairn, Guntrip. *Journal of the American Psychoanalytic Association, 28*, 829–860.
Sutherland, J. D. (1989). *Fairbairn's journey into the interior*. London: Free Association Books.
Suttie, I. (1935). *The origins of love and hate*. London: Free Association Books, 1988.
Swerdloff, B. (2002). An interview with Michael Balint. *American Journal of Psychoanalysis, 62*(4), 383–413.
Taylor, C. (2007). *A secular age*. Cambridge, MA: Belknap Press of Harvard University Press.
Terrell, C. J. (2007). A discussion of intentional incarnational integration in relational psychodynamic psychotherapy. *Journal of Psychology and Christianity, 26*, 159–165.
Thompson, C. (1953). Towards a psychology of women. *Pastoral Psychology, 4*(34), 29–38.
Thompson, C. (1959). The unmarried woman. *Pastoral Psychology, 10*(3), 43–45.
Thompson, C. (1988). Sándor Ferenczi, 1873–1933. *Contemporary Psychoanalysis, 24*, 182–195.
Thorndike, E. (1911). *Animal intelligence*. New York: MacMillan.
Tillich, P. (1953). Karen Horney: A funeral address. *Pastoral Psychology, 4*(34), 11–13.
Tonnesmann, M. (1980). Adolescent re-enactment, trauma and reconstruction. *Journal of Child Psychotherapy, 6*, 23–44.
Trevarthen, C. (2009). The intersubjective psychobiology of human meaning: Learning of culture depends on interest for co-operative practical work—and affection for the joyful art of good company. *Psychoanalytic Dialogues, 19*, 507–518.
Trevarthen, C., Aitken, K. J., Vandekerckhove, M., Delafield-Butt, J., & Nagy, E. (2006). Collaborative regulations of vitality in early childhood: Stress in intimate relationships and postnatal psychopathology. In D. Cicchetti & D. J. Cohen (Eds.). *Developmental psychopathology, volume 2, Developmental neuroscience* (pp. 65–126). New York: Wiley.
Ulanov, A. (2001). *Finding space: Winnicott, God, and psychic reality*. Louisville, KY: Westminster John Knox Press.
Van der Kolk, B. A., & Greenberg, M. S. (1987). The psychobiology of the trauma response: Hyperarousal, constriction and addiction to trauma reexposure. In B. A. Van der Kolk (Ed.), *Psychological trauma* (pp. 63–87). Washington, DC: American Psychiatric Press.
Van Lieburg, F., & Lindmark, D. (Eds.). (2008). *Pietism, revivalism, and modernity*, 1650–1850. Newcastle Upon Tyne, UK: Cambridge Scholars Publishing.
Vida, J. (1997). The voice of Ferenczi echoes from the past. *Psychoanalytic Inquiry, 17*, 404–415.
Vitz, P. (1988). *Sigmund Freud's Christian unconscious*. Grand Rapids, MI: Eerdmans Publishing Co.
Vitz, P., & Felch, S. (2006). *The self: Beyond the postmodern crisis*. Wilmington, DE: Intercollegiate Studies Institute.

Wakefield, J. C. (1992). Freud and the intentionality of affect. *Psychoanalytic Psychology*, *9*, 1–23.
Wall, J. (2001). The economy of the gift: Paul Ricoeur's significance for theological ethics. *Journal of Religious Ethics*, *29*(2), 235–260.
Wall, J. (2005). *Moral creativity: Paul Ricoeur and the poetics of possibility*. New York: Oxford University Press.
Waterstradt, R. (2002). Evil—What's the problem? The completeness of the fault in Paul Ricoeur's philosophy of the will. Unpublished symposium presentation, Fordham University.
Watson, R. (2007). Ready or not, here I come: Surrender, recognition, and mutuality in psychotherapy. *Journal of Psychology and Theology*, *35*(1), 65–73.
Werner, L. (2007). *The restless love of thinking*. Helsinki: University of Helsinki Press.
Wesley, J. (1889). *A collection of hymns, for the use of the people called Methodists*. London: Wesleyan Methodist Bookroom.
Westkott, M. (1986). *The feminist legacy of Karen Horney*. New Haven, CT: Yale University Press.
Williams, R. (1997). *Hegel's ethics of recognition*. Berkeley, CA: University of California Press.
Winnicott, C. (Ed.). (1989). D. W. W.: A reflection. In *Psycho-analytic explorations* (pp. 1–18). Cambridge, MA: Harvard University Press.
Winnicott, D. W. (1950). Some thoughts on the meaning of the word "democracy." In C. Winnicott, R. Sheperd, & M. Davis (Eds.), *Home is where we start from: Essays by a psychoanalyst* (pp. 239–259). New York: Norton, 1986.
Winnicott, D. W. (1959). The fate of the transitional object. In C. Winnicott, R. Sheperd, & M. Davis (Eds.), *Psycho-analytic explorations* (pp. 53–58). Cambridge, MA: Harvard University Press, 1989.
Winnicott, D. W. (1960). Theory of parent infant relationship. In *The maturational process and the facilitating environment* (pp. 37–55). London: Hogarth Press, 1965.
Winnicott, D. W. (1962). The theory of the parent-infant relationship—further remarks. *Int. Jour. Of Psycho-Anal.*, *43*, 238–239.
Winnicott, D. W. (1963a). The development of the capacity for concern. In *The maturational process and the facilitating environment* (pp. 73–82). London: Hogarth Press, 1965.
Winnicott, D. W. (1963b). Communicating and not communicating leading to a study of certain opposites. In *The maturational process and the facilitating environment* (pp. 179–192). London: Hogarth Press, 1965.
Winnicott, D. W. (1963c). Morals and education. In *The maturational process and the facilitating environment* (pp. 93–105). London: Hogarth Press, 1965.
Winnicott, D. W. (1964). *The child, the family and the outside world*. London: Penguin Books.
Winnicott, D. W. (1966). The absence of a sense of guilt. In C. Winnicott, R. Shepherd, & M. Davis (Eds.), *Deprivation and delinquency* (pp. 106–112). London: Routledge, 1990.
Winnicott, D. W. (1968). The use of an object and relating through identifications. In C. Winnicott, R. Shepherd, & M. Davis (Eds.), *Psycho-analytic explorations* (pp. 218–227). Cambridge, MA: Harvard University Press, 1989.

Winnicott, D. W. (1971a). Creativity and its origins. In *Playing and reality* (pp. 76–100). New York: Penguin.
Winnicott, D. W. (1971b). *Playing and reality*. London: Tavistock.
Wolf, E. (1978). Review of *Psychiatry and the Humanities: Vol. 1*. New Haven, CT: Yale University Press, 1976.
Wright, R., & Strawn, B. (2010). Grief, hope and prophetic imagination: Psychoanalysis and the Christian tradition in dialogue. *Journal of Psychology and Christianity*, 29(2), 149–157.
Wynkoop, M. B. (1972). *Theology of love: The dynamic of Wesleyanism*. Kansas City, MO: Beacon Hill Press.
Yerushalmi, Y. (1993). *Freud's Moses: Judaism terminable and interminable*. New Haven, CT: Yale University Press.
Yoder, J. (2008). *The Jewish-Christian schism revisited* (M. Cartwright, & P. Ochs, Eds.). Scottdale, PA: Herald Press.
Young-Eisendrath, P., & Muramoto, S, (Eds.). (2002). *Awakening and insight: Zen Buddhism and psychotherapy*. London: Routledge.
Zizek, S., & Milbank, J. (2009). *The monstrosity of Christ*. (C. Davis, Ed.) Cambridge, MA: MIT Press.
Zizioulas, J. (1997). *Being as communion: Studies in personhood and the Church*. Crestwood, NY: St. Vladimir's Seminary Press.
Zsuffa, J. (1987). *Béla Balàzs: The man and the artist*. Berkeley, CA: University of California Press.

Index

G

H

I

S

T

U

W

Y

Z